PENGUIN BOOKS

THE GOOD ROOM

David McWilliams is Ireland's most influential economist, and a columnist for the *Irish Independent* and the *Sunday Business Post*. He is the author of the bestsellers *The Pope's Children*, *The Generation Game* and *Follow the Money*.

www.davidmcwilliams.ie

D0610469

CL 1223224 6

The Good Room

*Why we ended up in a debtors' prison – and
how we can break free*

DAVID MCWILLIAMS

PENGUIN BOOKS

PENGUIN BOOKS

Published by the Penguin Group
Penguin Books Ltd, 80 Strand, London WC2R ORL, England
Penguin Group (USA) Inc., 375 Hudson Street, New York, New York 10014, USA
Penguin Group (Canada), 90 Eglinton Avenue East, Suite 700, Toronto, Ontario, Canada M4P 2Y3
(a division of Pearson Penguin Canada Inc.)
Penguin Ireland, 25 St Stephen's Green, Dublin 2, Ireland (a division of Penguin Books Ltd)
Penguin Group (Australia), 707 Collins Street, Melbourne, Victoria 3008, Australia
(a division of Pearson Australia Group Pty Ltd)
Penguin Books India Pvt Ltd, 11 Community Centre, Panchsheel Park, New Delhi – 110 017, India
Penguin Group (NZ), 67 Apollo Drive, Rosedale, Auckland 0632, New Zealand
(a division of Pearson New Zealand Ltd)
Penguin Books (South Africa) (Pty) Ltd, Block D, Rosebank Office Park,
181 Jan Smuts Avenue, Parktown North, Gauteng 2193, South Africa

Penguin Books Ltd, Registered Offices: 80 Strand, London WC2R ORL, England

www.penguin.com

First published by Penguin Ireland 2012
Published in Penguin Books 2013
001

Copyright © David McWilliams, 2012
All rights reserved

The moral right of the author has been asserted

Typeset by Jouve (UK), Milton Keynes
Printed in Great Britain by Clays Ltd, St Ives plc

Except in the United States of America, this book is sold subject
to the condition that it shall not, by way of trade or otherwise, be lent,
re-sold, hired out, or otherwise circulated without the publisher's
prior consent in any form of binding or cover other than that in
which it is published and without a similar condition including this
condition being imposed on the subsequent purchaser

ISBN: 978-0-241-95620-5

www.greenpenguin.co.uk

MIX
Paper from
responsible sources
FSC   FSC™ C018179
www.fsc.org

Penguin Books is committed to a sustainable
future for our business, our readers and our planet.
This book is made from Forest Stewardship
Council™ certified paper.

ALWAYS LEARNING   **PEARSON**

To Sian, Lucy and Cal

Contents

1. Generation Skype and Hope's Children   1
2. Olivia at Five Weeks   13
3. The Debtors' Prison   25
4. Eleven Weeks   42
5. Contagion   53
6. Fourteen Weeks   67
7. Mario's Magic Money   76
8. Seventeen Weeks   94
9. Let Them Eat Fish   104
10. Twenty Weeks   117
11. The Good Room   122
12. Twenty-four Weeks   131
13. A Long War   141
14. Twenty-seven Weeks   151
15. Meet the Germans   160
16. Twenty-eight Weeks   171
17. The Mortgage Crisis – and What to Do about It   182
18. Thirty Weeks   193
19. What Next?   205
20. Forty Weeks   218

    Notes   229

    Acknowledgements   237

    Index   239

1. Generation Skype and Hope's Children

The footballers of Castlegregory

The drive from Castlegregory, on the Dingle peninsula, to Killarney is a round trip of just over a hundred kilometres. In preparation for the All-Ireland junior club championship of 2010, the Gaelic footballers of Castlegregory trained in Killarney, to suit the lads coming from their universities in Cork and Limerick. The round trips to Killarney from those cities are 170 and 250 kilometres respectively.

When you're winning, the season stretches: each win buys the team a few more weeks. For the full year leading up to the final in Croke Park, Castlegregory trained without a break. No one was complaining. The Dingle peninsula is football country.

Matches in the local West Kerry league toughen everyone up. Castlegregory against the likes of Dingle – these matches regularly pit neighbours and families head to head. Scores are settled, not just counted. Next up is the county league, eleven games between March and October; and – in parallel – the county championship knockout tournament. From the county final in July, training was ratcheted up a notch or seven for the Munster championship – and then on to the Holy Grail, the All-Ireland.

Lives were offered up on the altar of GAA success. There was always an all-day strategy session on Saturday, followed by the game on Sunday. Scouts were sent out across Munster to snoop on the opposition. Sometimes they would venture further afield, to Meath or Galway, to see what the other teams were at; nothing was left to chance.

The man in charge of the players' mental and physical preparation was the manager, Ger O'Callaghan. Ger knew that the body was the simple part. By building up stamina and strength you can manage the physical side. The vomit-inducing runs on the beach with the rain driving in hard from the Atlantic, or up the mountains back towards the Gaeltacht – these were par for the course. The tricky bit, O'Callaghan understood, is the brain. If a man's head isn't right, it can destroy him in a game; and once one man has lost the mental battle, the whole team becomes infected.

The most important thing was the knowledge that success was possible. In 2002 the Gaeltacht Club, from the other side of Mount Brandon, had won the All-Ireland. Why couldn't Castlegregory?

The final was held in Croke Park on Valentine's Day 2010. The Mansells came home from Boston for it, as did the Deans and Spillanes from Australia, and countless others – Fitzgeralds, O'Connors, O'Callaghans, Horgans and Sullivans – from London.

The night before the final, the team bunked down at the Clarion Hotel in Liffey Valley. That night the lads talked about all the battles past and what they had learned from each one. They re-examined the clash with the Claremen of Clooney Quin and then the scare at Glanworth, deep in the good farming land of North Cork, when the wheels nearly came off. They reworked the pivotal moments of their struggle with Mountcollins of West Limerick, and laughed about the huge win over local Kerry rivals Beaufort. Then there was Longwood of Meath in the semis, which could have gone either way right up to the final whistle. Castle' had come through all of these, and the lads were stronger for the experiences.

Father Gene O'Donnell, a Castlegregory man with a parish in America, had come home for the final. On the eve of the showdown with Kiltimagh of Mayo, he took confession. You might as well start the day clean, even if you didn't finish it that way. And on the morning of the game, Father Gene said Mass for the team in the same function room in which they had watched match videos all the previous day. Half-eleven Mass was less about divine intervention than about routine. This is what they did at home on a Sunday and Ger knew that he had to adhere to the familiar rhythm.

During the Creed, Ger O'Callaghan thought to himself: What do we actually believe?

We believe in ourselves, in our parish. We believe in our place. We believe in home. We believe in each other.

This was their chance. By night, they'd be winners or losers. No matter what the outcome, they were doing it for their place, the place that had made them.

At half-time the Mayo men were ahead by two points. With two minutes to go there were still two points in it, and Castle' needed something special. Long free into the box, deft flick, back of the net. Noses in front. Kiltimagh free, last kick of the game, floated high and over. Scores level: twenty minutes of extra time.

All the sweat and pain in those 112 training sessions counted now. Ger knew his boys were harder. They were fitter. They could do it. He looked into their eyes for weakness; there was none. Ger told them to go and do it for the parish.

When the ref blew, the scoreboard told it all: Castlegregory 1–14, Kiltimagh 0–15.

For the people of Castlegregory, nothing – not even the most thrilling victories of the great Kerry teams over the years – could compare to the feeling of winning an All-Ireland club final.

The local Guards escorted them home, sirens going, lights flashing. Five kilometres out from the village, the team were met by the sight of a huge bonfire blazing on the high ground, before the road veered left-wards down to the sea. The place was a mass of green and gold. A tourist might have thought they had brought people in from all over Kerry. But they hadn't. These were their people. Castle' men and women from all over the world changed their annual holidays to be home to celebrate something you can't buy: the local, the rural – home itself.

The village was heaving that night. Ferriter's stayed open until the morning, as did Leonard's and Murray's. They were winners. Castle-gregory, a tiny place in West Kerry wedged between the mountains and the Atlantic, were All-Ireland champions for the first time.

When it all settled down, Ger O'Callaghan (manager, father, electrician, and now local hero) knew he could build on the victory. Most of the team were young. He could mould them, and they could keep on winning.

Two years later

The fire is blazing at the back of Ferriter's. The place smells welcomingly of turf. But there's hardly anyone to welcome. Ger O'Callaghan is sitting at the back, waiting to watch the rugby – Ireland against Wales. The bar is empty except for one farmer up at the counter. The village is silent.

The brilliant 2010 team never progressed. Not because they weren't good enough, but because they disappeared.

Eight of the fifteen players who started the 2010 All-Ireland final left the country over the next two years. Of the twenty-one lads in the panel who were on the pitch in Croke Park that day, twelve are gone. Five are in Australia. Three are in London. The others are scattered all over the place.

The tale of what happened to the 2010 All-Ireland junior champions is the story of a generation of Irish people. They were born during the last great Irish recession of the mid 1980s. They watched Italia '90 as toddlers and just remember Ray Houghton's chip over the Italian keeper at Giants Stadium in '94. They were in primary school when the IRA ceasefire was announced. By the time they were doing the Leaving Cert, the banking bonanza was already in full swing. They left school amidst the credit binge of the mid noughties, when Ireland was hyping itself up to anyone who cared to listen, driven by the 'when I have it I spend it' creed of the finance minister, Charlie McCreevy.

They were Generation Hype; they are now Generation Skype.

They were young enough not to have settled down yet old enough to leave, and they did so in huge numbers.

When Brian O'Driscoll, after Ireland's victory over Australia at the 2011 Rugby World Cup in Auckland, laughed that 'You'd swear we were in Dublin with that crowd,' these were the people he was referring to. Most of the tens of thousands in green packed into Eden Park had not travelled across the world for the match; they were living in New Zealand or Australia. Two of the Castlegregory lads were in the stands that day.

Last year alone 40,000 young Irish people left the country. Another 30,000 foreign residents, mainly East Europeans – the ones who were going to do great things for our gene pool – headed out as well. Over 300,000 people have left Ireland since 2006.

Anyone who has seen sunburned lads in Waterford jerseys and tight little GAA knicks offending the fashion sensibilities of bronzed and plucked Adonises on Bondi Beach will know the score. As has always been the case, when the going gets tough, the Irish get going. The last generation to flee the country kept in touch by 'reversing the charges' from AT&T phone booths all over America; these new exiles Skype home, log on and chat away. But the point is they have gone. They are not here, and the place is different without them. In some places, like Castlegregory, it feels empty.

In 2011 ninety-five out of every hundred people who emigrated were between the ages of nineteen and forty-four. That year saw a 50 per cent rise in the number of young women leaving the country. The first two years of the slump had hit men hardest, because the building sites of Ireland were the ground zero of the crash. We were having a Mancession – a slump affecting men disproportionately – and the pinch was felt most severely in Breakfast Roll Man's pocket. Many of these guys headed straight to Bondi or Clapham Junction in the first wave of emigration. But in the past two years, young women also lost jobs in huge numbers, as the recession broadened out from the construction industry to services – above all retail, sales and marketing. Unemployment amongst young women is now rising faster than amongst young men.

A 2012 *Irish Times*/Ipsos MRBI poll on the education levels of Generation Skype reveals that 69 per cent have at least a primary degree – which makes them our most educated emigrants ever. For a country the size of Ireland, this is a huge talent drain.

In the past five years, Irish unemployment has risen from 3 per cent to 14.9 per cent. Dramatic though they are, these numbers significantly understate the crisis, because they don't take account of those who, like the twelve members of the Castlegregory panel, have removed themselves from the job market by emigrating.

The birthday lottery

One curious thing about Ireland is that the year you were born really matters to your prospects, arguably more than in any other European country. This is because the economy has been so badly mismanaged for so long, looted by one generation at the expense of the next.

Consider those born in the huge baby boom of the late 1970s, the Pope's Children. They were blindsided by the credit binge, mistaking a large overdraft for real prosperity. Many are now the wrong side of thirty – too old and with too many responsibilities just to head away, but far too young to throw in the towel.

They're trapped by the huge mortgages they're struggling to repay, and/or by the negative equity that makes it impossible for them to sell their property. Many have children and subscribe to the enduring Irish notion that, if at all possible, their children should be brought up here, at home.

There are hundreds of thousands of them. They were born in the wrong time. They were teenagers in the 1990s, bought homes in the 2000s, and now find themselves in a debtors' prison.

Their Ireland is suburban, and it is also ridiculously fertile. In the past five years, an average of 73,000 babies have been born each year – the biggest baby boom since the foundation of the state, even bigger than the one that produced the Pope's Children. If you've been knocked off a footpath by an outsized buggy or amazed by the increase in class sizes in primary schools, it's because Ireland is reacting to one of the deepest economic depressions in the history of any country in Europe by having lots and lots of babies. Many of these newborns are the Pope's Children's children.

Ireland is yet again the great outlier in European demographics. If there is one overriding reason why we – the adults of Ireland – need to get our economy going, it is for these children. They are a sign that we have not lost hope; in fact they are the most concrete sign yet that those who have stayed here believe in the future of Ireland. The Pope's Children are now raising Hope's Children.

But if that hope is dashed by bad decision-making in the next few crucial years, it could quickly turn to rage. Very soon these children will be passing through school and into the workforce. With youth unemployment now at 30 per cent, what hope are we offering them with the present policies?

Let's drive out on our boom-era roads to see this trampoline-land, a place of communions, weekend soccer, and flat-packed book-shelves and double beds – a place where negative equity and positive energy collide.

Trackerville

Come with me to Trackerville, a place that knows no county bound-aries. It is a vast swathe of thousands of starter homes that were financed by tracker mortgages, built at the height of the boom, exist-ing in the precarious twilight world between huge loans that can only go up in cost and depleted take-home incomes that can only decline further still as taxes rise and unemployment encroaches.

You may remember an ad, which first appeared on Irish television screens in 2006, in which a bloke on the upper level of a Dublin bus stands up and admits to his fellow passengers, 'I don't know what a tracker mortgage is.' Others on the bus follow suit with confessions of their own ignorance of financial terms and concepts. The magic of the ad was that it captured the confusion of the average punter in an era when everyone was using financial jargon, pretending they knew what it meant but scared stiff to confess that they had no idea what they were talking about.

The supreme and cruel irony was that the ad was actually designed to promote the Financial Regulator as a source of useful information for ordinary citizens. What was not generally understood at the time was that, while the Financial Regulator might have been able to explain what a tracker mortgage was, it had no more ability to regulate the banks than the bewildered lad on the top of the bus.

There is, in fact, nothing particularly complex about tracker mortgages: their interest rates track the European Central Bank rate, and there is a tiny margin, usually 1 per cent, to pay to the bank on top of that. Most of the people who took out such loans probably understood that reasonably well.

Starting in the early 2000s, trackers spread through the country like a virus. As with all pandemics, the rapidity of its transmission through the population was driven by the virulence of the strain, the susceptibility of the host and the conditions in the external environment. The great Irish tracker pandemic was fuelled by people who were desperate to get on the housing 'ladder', for fear that, if they didn't, they would be left behind. The low ECB rate – never more than 4.75 per cent during the bubble years, and as low as 2 per cent for an uninterrupted span of over two years between 2003 and 2005 – and the modest margin added by the banks made the tracker attractive to home-buyers. Bank of Scotland, a new entrant to the Irish market, pioneered the product in 2001, and the other mortgage lenders quickly followed. The margin they charged over and above the cost of borrowing was so small it hardly covered their own costs, let alone the cost of even a tiny rate of default. The banks' margin was actually less than 1 per cent, because banks generally borrowed from the market at a rate slightly higher than the ECB rate.

What most of the people who took trackers probably did not understand was why the banks were so keen to sell these products. The banks jostling for position in an increasingly competitive – and lucrative – Irish lending market decided that they would be willing to accept a small profit or even lose money on the tracker, because selling other products – such as car loans, overdrafts, credit cards or that must-have home-improvement finance deal – to existing mortgage customers was easier than selling them to anybody else. The bankers' trick was to hook you in with a cheap tracker and then sell you an expensive car loan or kitchen-extension loan. This was how they would recoup their costs.

Just five years after Bank of Scotland first introduced tracker mortgages to Ireland, the number of tracker products and tracker-based offshoots in the Irish market stood at 57, compared to just 19 of the traditional standard-variable-rate products. The credit released by the cheap new trackers fed into house prices, driving them ever upwards. This in turn emboldened developers to build yet more houses. We know the result: in a dramatic deviation from what Leaving Cert economics students are taught about supply and demand, both the supply of homes and the price of homes rocketed to unsustainable levels.

The figures for tracker mortgages are startling. There are about 400,000 tracker mortgages in Ireland. Trackers account for close to 60 per cent of the €26 billion in residential loans issued by Permanent TSB. Just over half of AIB's €27 billion mortgage book is accounted for by trackers, as is a quarter of the €16 billion lent by EBS. The prize for King of the Trackers goes to Bank of Ireland: tracker loans make up 62 per cent of its €28 billion mortgage book.

Over half of the outstanding residential-property debt in Ireland consists of trackers; and 85 per cent of those mortgages were lent in the space of just five years, between 2004 and 2008, when they effectively financed the construction of vast numbers of new suburban estates. The tracker mortgage, which did not arrive in the Irish market until 2001, accounted for 43 per cent of mortgages originating in 2004 and 67 per cent of all mortgages originating in 2008. Their share of the market peaked in 2007 at 74 per cent. After this splurge, the total value of tracker mortgages in Ireland is €51 billion. Just to put the size of the €51 billion Irish tracker market into perspective for you: if you were to spend €1 million a day, it would take you 139 years to spend that much money.

Where did all this money come from? It certainly didn't come from the cash deposits of the Irish banks' retail customers. By the time the tracker boom started, the banks were lending out more

money than they were taking in on deposit; by 2006 the ratio was
1.6 to 1. The difference was borrowed from foreign banks.

For the moment Trackerville remains relatively placid, but it is a
ticking time bomb. Having crept upwards in 2006 and 2007, the ECB
interest rate levelled off and then plunged to nearly zero in response
to the crash. So the problem in Trackerville is not that people's
tracker-loan repayments have become higher – they haven't. The
problem is that the denizens of Trackerville bought at the worst possible time and borrowed far too much money in order to do so. That
means negative equity; and, more significantly, in a time of rising
taxes and unemployment, it means people are struggling to make
their payments despite historically low interest rates. What will
happen when interest rates rise, as they eventually will? Trackerville
is going to be the epicentre of a battle between the banks and the
people.

Trackerville is already a huge headache for the banks. They were
happy, during the boom, to accept tiny profit margins on tracker
loans. They were interested in market share, not profit margins.
Now, post-crash, the banks are obsessed with margins as they try to
rebuild their balance sheets. They are also trying to lower their loan-
to-deposit ratios, which means they must offer generous interest rates
to secure deposits. Because they're taking such a beating on trackers –
the banks are bringing in a lower rate of interest on their tracker loans
than they're paying their customers for deposits – they have tried,
without much success, to convince customers to switch to different
types of mortgage.

So, for the moment, trackers might seem a bigger problem for the
banks than for the borrowers. But the Trackerville time bomb is ticking, and the whole country will feel the force of the explosion. The
impact of negative equity and the collapse in employment on Trackerville can be seen in the dramatic change in the type of person who
is in difficulty now, as opposed to 2007. In 2007 only 2 per cent of
clients of the Money Advice and Budgeting Service had a mortgage;
just three years later that figure was 35 per cent. For thousands of
people, the monthly choice is between living properly and paying

back debt. With austerity policies all but guaranteeing that the economic slump will drag on, and with only one way for interest rates to go, things can only get worse in Trackerville.

Predictably irrational

Economics, as taught in our schools and universities, begins with the assumption that we are rational. Nothing could be further from the truth. Humans are possibly the most irrational of animals. We are driven by emotions, exuberances, impulses and frenzies. We fall in love, gamble and even support useless football teams. These irrational, illogical and beautifully human urges dominate our decision-making.

We don't generally learn from mistakes; we think that next time it will be different. Even when faced with overwhelming statistical and analytical evidence, we ignore it. We imagine that the odds that apply to other people do not apply to us; the National Lottery, with its 'It could be you' slogan, trades on this.

But it's not just the average Joseph or Mary on the street who takes irrational risks. Consider those who gamble on horses. The Irish display an amazing weakness for backing an Irish horse even when the form tells them a foreign horse has a better chance of winning. I asked the quants desk at Paddy Power for figures on Irish betting patterns, and the data confirmed what we all probably suspected: that we are deeply irrational. In Paddy Power's shops on the main streets of most Irish towns and cities, the average Irish-trained runner in a race in the UK takes 21 per cent more of the book than an equivalent UK-trained runner. The figures from Paddy Power's online, phone and mobile business – by far the fastest-growing side of the business – are even more remarkable: the average Irish-trained runner, competing in a race in the UK, takes 24 per cent more of the book than an equivalent UK-trained runner.

If the guys who read the form and calculate the odds are so irrationally driven by emotion, what hope is there for the rest of us?

Our irrationality has profound implications for the way economics works. When the economy is thriving, we believe that things will continue to go well and we get overly exuberant. When things are going badly, we become overly pessimistic, overly self-doubting, and gripped by depression, angst and insecurity.

The investors who actually make money are those who sell when everyone else is buying and buy when everyone else is selling. They are the exceptions; the norm is the rest of us. So the exceptional ones behave in the way economists like to think the rest of us do, and the rest of us behave the way economists think is the exception.

Of course, not every economist misunderstands the importance of human irrationality – in Chapter 3 we'll meet some great economists who understood it very well. And we'll try to follow their example by looking at Ireland's current crisis as an economic phenomenon that can be comprehended only in human terms. Economics matters because people matter: people like the emigrants of Castlegregory, or the Pope's Children's children, born into the depths of an epic recession. This book ranges widely through economic ideas and economic history in an attempt to explain how we got into this mess and how we can get out of it; but the question it is always fundamentally asking is: how does this affect ordinary people?

People like Olivia Vickers . . .

2.   Olivia at Five Weeks

The boys were in the usual formation. Half were paying attention, half staring zombie-like, because it was the class before morning break and sugar levels were dropping.

Olivia was distracted. Usually it was easy to manage this bunch of teenagers – deploy a raised eyebrow here, a meaningful frown there, and occasionally raise her voice. The secret to teaching is knowing how to make people listen, and she could do it. Her mother said she was born for the front of the classroom, although Olivia never knew if that was a backhanded compliment.

She wasn't on top of things today. The murmur of conversation was reaching the point where she wouldn't be able to close it down without seeming aggravated. She tried to make a mental list of what needed to be done, but her brain was cotton wool.

The test had been blue. She'd taken it twice, and would have done so again, but there were only two in the pack. It sat in her handbag like an anchor, dragging her down. There was no mistake. She was pregnant. Eight months from now she'd be giving birth to baby number two.

She became aware of silence. The class had noticed she was miles away, and now she could sense some of the troublemakers teetering on the edge, wondering what they could get away with, while the nicer ones had the look of concerned relatives at a hospital bed. They were good lads, these sixth years; even chancers like O'Brien and Hannon were reasonably studious. No arrogant rugger buggers or complete eejits, as in some of the other classes. She was lucky to have them as her form class.

They were loud and lairy like any bunch of teenagers, but the Leaving Cert had concentrated their minds. The exam was still months away, but she could see the change in them, the new focus. They'd need it, with all the rote learning ahead of them.

'Right, then, gentlemen. Let's get down to work.' She looked around for a safe bet.

'Kevin, could you tell the class about how Redmond handled the beginning of the Great War and the suspension of the Third Home Rule Bill in 1914?'

Skinny, pale Kevin Gavigan squinted through the winter sun's glare. He was so fair the sun almost shone through him.

With a bit of luck – Olivia and her students hoped – John Redmond and the Home Rule Party's demise, and the rise of Sinn Féin, would be on the honours paper. They had revised it over and over again – she was betting that the run-up to the anniversary of the Rising would mean examiners were likely to set questions on the pre-Independence decade for the next few years. The perfect Leaving Cert answer – the one that would get most points without giving the marker anything to think about – ticked three or four essential boxes. The examiner was like a Google search algorithm: key words and notions were rewarded. It was history by numbers. Olivia wasn't a fan of the system, but for most of these boys the idea was to notch up the points, and she was paid to help them do that.

Kevin was a good student and a great kid – friendly and clever. He was smaller than the others, and it was easy to feel overprotective towards him, but Olivia was careful to remain even-handed, perhaps even a touch critical. She didn't want to get him into trouble. After all, being teacher's pet at seventeen – irrespective of whether the teacher was halfway popular, as she was – wasn't cool.

The low sun split the class in two, half in brilliant brightness, the other half in shade. A stain of sweat emerged slowly under Kevin's arms. Beside him – as he blinked and sniffed – the light of the sun had precisely the opposite effect on Gary Costigan, who had a deep olive tan. While Kevin's practically translucent skin disappeared in the light, Costigan's shone. His dark hair looked almost blue and he sat back, making himself big, photosynthesizing.

Maybe it was the blue strip on the pregnancy test in her bag, but

Olivia was fascinated by genetics this morning. She looked at the two young men and marvelled at how genes worked. How sometimes they skipped generations and then elbowed their way in when you least expected.

Her own family was the same. She was as Mediterranean as an Irishwoman comes, but her brother Barry was a ringer for Gavigan, red-haired, fair and freckly, like one of those demented redsers on the 11850 ad.

She wondered what the baby inside her would turn out to be like.

She remembered the shock of little Sam coming out with a flaming head of red hair. The ancient midwife, probably as old as the Coombe itself, looked at the two dark-haired parents and almost crossed herself. Some mad part of Olivia wanted to say, 'It's the milkman's,' but she didn't think that would go down so well. After everyone had left, and the ward was quiet, she took his tiny soft body into her arms and snuggled him into her, listening to the sound of his breathing and feeling the warmth of him. Could he really be hers? She was so very glad he was.

Whose genes would dominate this time? What ancestor – perhaps some distant granny in some grainy photo – would make her imprint felt in the complexion of Olivia's new baby?

Kevin Gavigan was still going, breathing asthmatically, and breaking out in a heat rash in late November, God love him.

'The Irish Parliamentary Party got complacent and failed to realize that the country had changed,' he said. 'They didn't seem to understand that there is a limit to people's tolerance of sacrifice, particularly if, in terms of their sons on the Western Front, it was no guarantee of success on the Home Rule question.'

This wasn't exactly how Olivia had framed it. Gavigan was obviously doing his reading and thinking for himself.

'Maybe because Redmond had been leader of the party for so long and spent so much of his career in London, he invested too much in the idea that if he persuaded Irish nationalists to fight for the King, the British would regard this good behaviour favourably and then give us what we wanted.' Kevin was on a roll.

'He thought that being the best boy in the class —'

'Like yourself, Gavigan,' yelled someone.

'Aidan Walsh, I know I didn't just hear you interrupting the class again,' said Olivia, glaring at the culprit. 'Please carry on, Kevin.'

Kevin nodded. 'Anyway, politics doesn't reward nice guys. Lloyd George ignored him at the Treaty of Versailles. There was plenty given to the Czechs and Slovaks, who had fought against the Allies, but nothing in recognition of the Irish soldiers who'd died in their tens of thousands for the Allies.

'But —' Kevin gulped for air, his ideas racing out of his mouth faster than he could breathe, 'we need to see this in the context of revolutionary changes all over Europe, which were happening at the same time.

'I mean, Miss, had you said in 1912 that just ten years later Ireland would be independent of the greatest empire in the world, or Russia would be communist, or the Ottoman Empire would be a republic governed by Young Turks whose first act was to change the alphabet, or that Imperial Germany would have been replaced by the Weimar Republic, people would have told you that you were mad. Yet all these things happened.'

His excitement was wonderful to see. She'd miss Kevin when he graduated.

'Can you imagine: if you had said that after a world war, which seemed remote even in early 1914, Britain would defeat Germany and yet by 1922 have lost more of its landmass than the country it defeated, people would have said, Miss, that you were a half-wit.'

Nervous sniggers from the other students. She smiled and the sniggers relaxed into proper laughter. Hopefully Dick Murphy, the principal, wasn't passing on his rounds.

'Thanks, Kevin. I hope you — and the rest of you — will bear in mind that, while I encourage as much extra reading as possible, you have the Leaving in a few months. Some of the older, more traditional markers just want the textbook answers with as little opinion and digression as possible. I'm glad you're reading widely and thinking for yourselves, but for now, let's stick to the course.'

Olivia had no time for those exam aids like *Get the Points!*, which turned history into a rote list. She hated herself for reining the boys in. She wanted them to be curious, rebellious and iconoclastic. She wanted them to question everything. It was why she went into teaching in the first place.

But that was before her first parent–teacher meeting, which put paid to her personal educational manifesto and any ambitions she might have had of breaking the mould. Olivia was enthusing to a parent about the wonderful dramatic talent of a particular student, when the mother lowered her glasses and snapped: 'If I had wanted Colin Farrell, I'd have sent him to Billie Barry. Why did he only get a B1 in the summer exams?'

The parents had a straightforward deal with the school: they paid fees for access to the professions, not for education. Parents had no interest in anything personal, much less experimental. The purpose of the education system was not to create well-adjusted young adults, she thought; it was to create well-trained robots. The school's job was to replicate the status quo for the next generation. Her school was successful in this regard. It was a conveyor belt to university and then on to professional careers. The parents didn't pay the huge fees for their sons to be different; they paid for them to be the same.

The right school was a one-way corporate bullet train heading straight for A&L Goodbody, the Bar or, for the best and the brightest, medicine. The price of the ticket was points – precious Leaving Cert points. Teenagers' brains were not to be wasted on something as frivolous as analysis.

Jesus, didn't everyone know that?

Why couldn't she just accept it?

She remembered going home in shock after that first parental collision. She'd texted Sean, furious. One parent had actually told her the reason her son was learning Spanish, Olivia's other subject: because it was easier than French. A B1 in Spanish would lever her son into Law at UCD, and after that he would 'never have to speak another line again in his life'. Except to order cocktails on the Costa, Olivia could have added.

The class was getting restless. They'd been sitting long enough, and Gavigan's soliloquy had tipped them over. The clock was counting down and it was obvious she wasn't on the ball today.

'Right, gentlemen. Journals out. I want two pages on the Home Rule Party's decline by this day next week. Show why and how the decisions of John Redmond, in parallel with the changes taking place across Europe, led to a seismic shift in Irish politics.' She reeled the assignment off mechanically. The boys were so pleased the class was winding down there wasn't even the customary 'Aww, Miss . . .'

She had to phone Sean with the good news. He'd be delighted. She was sure he would. He needed something to look forward to.

But, then, maybe he wouldn't, after everything that had happened in the past few months. She was certain he'd find another full-time job. That was always Sean's way.

Her salary and his part-time work covered the mortgage, just. A few grinds a week here and there in the frantic run-up to the Leaving should make up the difference. They'd be OK. It was Olivia's nature to look for the positives, even when they were hard to find. It wasn't a case of being naive – she was realistic about the economy and all that – but if you didn't try to be optimistic for yourself, no one would do it for you.

'I want to see a conclusion based on your personal analysis of the facts, gentlemen. No cribbing from *Get the Points!*' She couldn't resist. Her class would think for themselves at least once before they were all farmed off to grinds.

The bell buzzed as she spoke and twenty-five young men trundled past her mumbling, 'Thanks, Miss Vickers.'

Olivia sat in the empty classroom after the last of these lads had barrelled out the door. She was about five weeks gone. That meant a birth in late July or early August. Five months' maternity leave would bring her to the end of the year. If she'd been permanent staff that would be fine, but she wasn't. Few of the younger teachers were. There was a chance that if she wasn't present and correct at the start of the term, her hours might be cut. There was an outside chance that her contract wouldn't be renewed at all.

Oh, Jesus.

Olivia texted Sean to see where he was and if he was sitting down. No reply. She walked, still dazed, to the staffroom.

The staffroom was stuffy and dusty. The older teachers didn't like open windows, so when the place filled up it was like being trapped in a lift full of tweed, old newspapers and cheese sandwiches.

Olivia sat down beside Barbara Gogan, her closest friend at the school. She was dying to tell someone about the pregnancy test, but Barbara had other things on her mind. They were about to head into yet another 'Democracy in the Staffroom' plenary session ahead of the budget next week.

Dick Murphy, the first lay principal and a master of optics, had introduced 'Democracy in the Staffroom' after the priests finally relinquished control in 2002, in order to show how much had changed and how radical was the school's move to secularism. All teachers would now be consulted on matters of day-to-day school management – in theory.

It was a typically makey-uppy move, Olivia thought; as she knew from some of her older colleagues, teachers had already been running things for a number of years by the time the priests officially withdrew. It was all for show. As her history class could testify, every new regime gains a little bit more legitimacy by undermining the previous one. It was just the way things went. The school was no different.

In reality, it was nothing more than inserting middle-management gobbledygook into the education system, creating more administrative work and more potential for feuding. It was one of those boom-time affectations that allowed teachers, who had seen their status fall relative to that of bank managers, to play dress-up by using the jargon of the Harvard Business School. It meant teachers wasted time sniping amongst themselves instead of preparing to teach.

It also meant any cuts in the Department of Education budget and their knock-on effects were filtered through Avril O'Connor – the head of the French Department and chairperson of 'Democracy in the Staffroom'. Avril and all the members of her committee were ensconced in permanent jobs, and whatever happened they would be safe.

Avril O'Connor sat over her laptop, weighed down under her US weather-girl hairdo, looking up the price of checking golf bags on a Ryanair flight to Carcassonne. She rarely stayed at home during the Christmas holidays. 'With the twins grown up and in Australia, there's no point hanging around, Olivia,' she'd said. 'I Skype them in the morning. More than enough contact. Anyway I don't understand people who have a second home and don't make full use of it. It's wasteful, don't you think?'

Olivia had got used to counting to ten around Avril.

When Olivia listened to the arguments that pitted the public sector against the private sector, which the media seemed to love, she always felt they missed the point. The public sector wasn't one homogeneous bloc, but consisted of many vested interests, many levels and many prospects, often at odds with one another. When it came down to it, the staffroom was split by age. The older teachers, who had been there since the 1970s and 1980s, when Olivia was still in national school, lived locally in solid houses with no mortgages. Quite a few had second homes somewhere down the country or abroad. During the boom their salaries had increased dramatically and they were fully paid-up members of the Croke Park Agreement club. By now they had had all their increments and were permanent and pensionable. If the truth be known, they seemed to be concerned mainly with whether they should retire early and take the lump sum now, or wait – after all, what would they do all day?

It was understandable, Olivia thought. That was how the career had been presented to them. But the younger teachers – struggling to pay their mortgages, trapped by negative equity, uncertain of their employment prospects and pensions – couldn't help but feel resentful. She imagined there was a similar tension between young and old software engineers in tech companies, because the elders had been fortunate enough to pick up shares on the ground floor.

Carmel McGrath, the chemistry teacher, a little bird of a thing in her late fifties, sat perched by the radiator. She was always moaning about everything and anything – including her perennially under-achieving children, who had never moved out and were still mooching around home well into their thirties. She now had company in this: over the past few months at least four other teachers had announced that their children had moved back home, casualties of the recession, clogging up box rooms and annoying everyone in the house.

The most conspicuous new tenant was Damien D'Arcy, son of Vice-Principal Mike D'Arcy. Olivia knew Damien from university, and he had seemed to be destined for great things, but the past four years had seen him crash. First the job went, then his wife and, finally, the house. Now he slept in the same room he had slept in as a ten-year-old, probably under the same duvet. It was grim, and there had already been enough tight months when Olivia and Sean had wondered whether they might have to do the same.

Olivia had heard Carmel trying to reassure Mike D'Arcy. 'Oh, the first year back home is the best,' she said. 'It's only when they get desperate in year two and lose hope altogether in year three that the problems really start. The late-night telly and the stuff they're up to on the internet at all hours of the day or night, God forbid.' Carmel would cross herself, which she liked to do to emphasize important points.

'And then there's the weight. The weight-gain is a terrible sight for any parent. Linked to the state of mind, they say. Just watch them balloon.' Now she would nod sadly and return to her perch, having not just emptied the glass of optimism, but smashed it on the floor.

The principal, Dick Murphy, folded his newspaper and gestured at a heap of beer cans under the rugby posts, left over from Saturday night's disco in the school hall. 'We might have to put an end to this disco carry-on,' he whispered. 'Two more letters from parents, three neighbours complaining and a squad car – it's hardly the image we're trying to present.'

Olivia nodded. Dick wasn't really looking for a response.

He had a lot on his mind. Fees and grants were down, and the collapse in revenue made the bill for the huge boom-time extension unmanageable. The school had played its part in the building craze, just like the parents and teachers, and now they were all caught. Olivia knew that her school was not alone in this. Many of Dublin's fee-paying schools had fallen under the spell of a pushy past pupil who wanted to build a mini-Harvard on the Dodder. They'd plunged themselves headlong into an arms race with other schools to build the biggest gym, the most advanced language lab, the most up-to-date swimming pool, science rooms as advanced as CERN. Before the crash it had been easy to raise the money. On top of the Department of Education's cash, there were charity dos, speaking events, lunches before each rugby international – home and away – and, of course, the annual whip-around from the past pupils' union. But this cash only paid the interest; ultimately the real money came from the bank.

Everything had to be bigger, better, glitzier, showier. This was what the parents demanded, forcing the schools into a beauty contest for their future.

Now fees were drying up. People who had seemed rich were broke. The school's contingency fund to help those who had fallen on hard times was almost empty and would certainly be bare by next September. The rumour was that Dick had signed three dozen 'late-payment reminder' letters this month alone.

There had, for a time, been talk of solidarity amongst teachers – a suggestion that the older ones might retire early to give the younger ones a chance. Many indicated that they might move on as they got closer to sixty, but this mood had quickly evaporated once the back-of-the-envelope calculations were completed. The older teachers were the bed-blockers of the school. If hours were to be cut, it would be the younger teachers who would suffer: they were on contract. Olivia, Barbara and the three lads from the last intake were in limbo. They shared the same long commute, the same negative equity in flimsy 'starter homes' in quickly constructed estates and the same child-care bills. They understood that the more the teachers' unions baulked at cuts in pay or conditions and insisted that the Croke Park Agreement be implemented in full, the more likely it was that they would get their hours reduced. But this was just the start of it.

Primal Scream's 'Loaded' buzzed from Olivia's phone. She stepped outside.

'Hey, babe,' said Sean.

'Hey, sweetheart. Are you sitting down?'

'No. I'm kind of leaning against the fridge. Why?'

'I'm pregnant.' It was one of those words that had weight.

'No way. Really? Are you sure?'

'Yes way. I think so.'

'Oh fuck.'

'What?'

'I mean fucking brilliant,' Sean laughed. 'Awesome. Are you sure you're sure?'

'We'll need to confirm it with Doctor Boyle. I've got an appointment for this afternoon.'

'Oh, wow, babe.'

'Can you check the current account and sort something for dinner? I've got to go.'

'Sure. Love you.'

'Love you too, sweets.'

That wasn't so bad, she thought. Maybe it would all work out.

Later, as she sat on the Dart opposite three boisterous teenagers in baseball caps, she hoped that the financial mess would be over by the time they were looking for jobs. They seemed oblivious to what was happening in the country. But maybe they weren't. Possibly their parents were having the same worries over money, afraid of the next set of bills and wondering when it would all end.

Olivia looked at herself in the reflection of the window of the carriage. The state of her: thirty-two, pregnant, possibly soon to be unemployed, in massive negative equity.

She should be depressed, but she was elated. She felt so excited, so special; something beautiful was forming inside her, something that no one could take away. It would be a little person whom she would love and who would love her back.

Recession or no recession, money or no money, life goes on, beautiful life goes on.

She looked out at the grey, cold sea and craved ice cream.

3. The Debtors' Prison

Turning the corner

How many times over the past four years have we heard an Irish politician or business leader suggest that we are turning the corner? We've lost count. Yet the Department of Finance has downgraded its forecasts for economic growth seven times in the past four years. Every time the economy was supposed to start recovering, it slumped back.

Politicians say that we should be a bit more upbeat and that 'negativity' is hampering recovery. And it's not just politicians. David Beers, chief economist of the ratings agency Standard & Poor's, said in Washington in October 2010 that 'Ireland's competitiveness is improving because the labour market is flexible; they're cutting wages and salaries. So we think that among the peripheral countries it would be the first to begin to recover.' He went on to pat us on the head by praising our fortitude: 'People think that the Irish political establishment may be suffering from exhaustion, reform fatigue. We actually do not detect that.'

Olivier Blanchard, a serious academic economist and now chief economist of the IMF, said in October 2011 that Ireland had 'turned a corner', citing export growth and improving competitiveness.

At least Beers and Blanchard, highly questionable though their assessments were, referred to actual economic phenomena when making their predictions. Too much of the discussion of the economy in this country has been based on the premise that it operates like a large self-help group: that we can collectively emote the economy into growth through the power of positive thinking. We've been here before. During the boom, there were hysterical attacks on anyone seen to be 'talking down' the economy.

Obviously confidence and mood play an enormous role in booms, downturns and recoveries. J. P. Morgan – the American banking titan of the early twentieth century and a man who had seen a number of booms come and go – understood this and caught the essence of the madness of a boom when he noted that 'Nothing so undermines your financial judgement as the sight of your neighbour getting rich.'

We know that the collective mood influences economic behaviour (and we will explore this in detail later in the chapter); but we also know that no amount of talk can derail a genuinely robust economy – or kick-start a fundamentally dysfunctional one. The question we need to answer is: why has it taken Ireland so long to recover, to turn the fabled corner? After all, since the end of the Second World War, most recessions have lasted less than ten months. Why is this one different?

The paradox of thrift and the perversity of austerity

The reason we haven't turned the corner within a 'normal' span of time is because this isn't a 'normal' downturn.

The dynamics of the Irish crash have brought about what John Maynard Keynes termed the 'paradox of thrift'. In the face of high levels of debt and/or falling income – a situation faced by many Irish households and firms – you might rationally decide to improve your own financial position by spending less and saving more. But if large numbers of people and companies make the same decision, the aggregate effect of this thriftiness on the overall economy is destructively deflationary. So, whereas an economist might advise an individual or a firm to cut spending and use the savings to pay down debt, the same economist would recognize that it would be bad news if everyone followed such advice.

The vast majority of Irish people are employed in industries that sell goods and services within Ireland. As the great Anglo-Irish economist and Renaissance man Wynne Godley observed, economies have 'sectoral financial balances' – between, for example, expenditure and income. Your spending is my income (and vice versa); and ultimately our savings depend on our income. Thus, if we all stop spending at the same time, not only do we reduce demand and activity in the economy, we end up reducing the general level of savings.

The premise governing current Irish government policy, and the European Fiscal Compact, is that we must balance our books as quickly as possible. In itself, this sounds perfectly reasonable. But if we all seek to balance our books at the same time, by reducing spending and increasing savings, we are cannibalizing our income, and our position will remain unimproved. The result is what the economist Richard Koo calls a 'balance-sheet recession': a slump that persists, despite low interest rates, because companies and individuals are trying to repair their balance sheets by paying off debt.

Once we appreciate this dynamic, we can see that if the private sector starts to save in order to fix its balance sheet, it is up to the government to spend in order to keep demand and incomes reasonably buoyant. The worst thing a government can do for the economy is to stop spending at a time when the private sector is not spending. But this is exactly what our government is doing; it is compelled to do so by the terms of the Troika bailout, and it will be compelled to carry on doing so by the European Fiscal Compact.

In November 2010 the Troika gave the Irish state specific targets as a condition of receiving the bailout loan: these mainly involved slashing spending. The government of the time enthusiastically endorsed the Troika's view and appealed to our sense of good housekeeping; and the present government has stuck to the same line.

But if we return to the notion that your spending is my income, it's not hard to see where this leads. The state is the single biggest source of demand in the economy. If it stops spending just when the private sector has stopped spending, the economy seizes up. Due to the EU-wide embrace of austerity, as enshrined in the Fiscal Compact, this phenomenon is playing out all over the Continent. And, although austerity is aimed at appeasing the financial markets, the reality is that it keeps us stuck in a cycle of rolling financial crises. By cutting off any hope of a return to growth, this policy undermines the original objective of achieving good housekeeping.

On the general point of principle, the Troika and the Irish government are right: it is prudent for the state to balance the books over time. But it does not make sense to undertake a massive programme of cuts just when the private sector is deleveraging. What we are seeing in Ireland, and in other countries that have adopted austerity, is the destruction that results when the state acts in a pro-cyclical, rather than an anti-cyclical, way. All over peripheral Europe, GDP is falling, unemployment is rising, and asset prices are plummeting.

Bizarrely, we are still following to the letter the economic policies of former finance minister Charlie McCreevy, as captured in his immortal remark, 'When I have it I spend it, and when I don't I don't.' This is a recipe for disaster, because it amplifies the booms and busts. As Keynes showed, the time for government austerity is when the economy is booming, and the time for government spending is when the economy is faltering. The present policy, adopted not just here but across the EU, is precisely the opposite.

Debt and classical economics

Let's look at another piece of the present jigsaw, one that adds to our understanding of why this recession is still going on.

Most recessions are shallow and short, because normally the average person or the average company does not enter the recession with a crushing burden of debt.

Without debt, classical economic theory – based on the central notion that when the price of something goes down, the demand will eventually react by going up – corresponds pretty accurately to reality. In classical economics, unemployment is always temporary: it's the result of wages being too high. When wages fall, employers take more people on. Eventually people go back to work, but at lower wages.

At the trough of a recession, wages fall, because there are so many people on the dole. Interest rates also fall, because nobody is borrowing. The demand for credit collapses.

In the traditionally accepted view of the economy, the central bank's role is to kick-start the motor when private-sector demand slumps. It notices that the banks that used to borrow from the central bank every day are now depositing money at the central bank. There is no demand for credit.

When there is no demand, cut the price: that's what classical economics tells us to do, and this is what central banks traditionally do. The central bank makes more and more credit available at lower and lower rates of interest. It encourages the commercial banks to pass on this new, cheaper credit. The price of credit – i.e. the rate of interest – falls, and the availability of credit rises. Banks begin to offer all sorts of deals to people prepared to borrow and invest.

Over time, as the interest rate falls, people who have savings decide now is the time to invest in expanding their businesses, taking on workers at lower wage levels. In short, they see the recession as an opportunity. They remember how much things cost in the good times and see the current prices as bargain-basement.

Since huge amounts of credit are available, the banks are happy to lend. People start borrowing and spending again, and the price of stuff in the shops stops falling. People regain confidence, because they see friends and neighbours who had lost their jobs getting taken on. This makes them think that prices have stopped falling and will go up. If they can 'lock in' the cheaper prices today, they will be getting a great deal. They bring forward spending on big-ticket items such as cars, washing machines and houses.

This is what has been happening in Germany, despite the weakness of the global economy over the past few years. The various reductions in interest rates worked in the way that classical economics would lead us to expect. The economy roared ahead, unemployment hit a 35-year low and house prices in Germany's major cities skyrocketed. The banks were lending, and the country was still attracting immigrants looking for work.

Why have we not seen the same things happening in Ireland, or in Spain for that matter? The crucial difference is debt. German individuals and firms did not indulge in the borrowing frenzy of the credit boom in the way that individuals and firms in Ireland and elsewhere did.

Credit availability affects the way people behave, and by extension the way the economy behaves. Think about house prices in Ireland from 1997 to 2007. As the prices kept going up, demand didn't go down, in the way predicted by classical economics – in fact, the complete opposite occurred. Why?

In the mania stage of the boom, when people saw prices soar, they thought, 'If I don't buy now, I'll be shut out of the market.' Thus every time they opened the *Irish Times* property section and saw what was happening to prices, they panicked. If they didn't act now, they reckoned, the price would be higher next week. And it was the banks' continued provision of easy credit that made the cycle possible.

So why didn't the huge increase in demand for credit push up the price of credit, as we would normally expect? Because our interest rates are determined by the eurozone as a whole, of which the Irish economy, even at its boomiest, never constituted more than a tiny fraction. Interest rates were falling to suit conditions in the eurozone as a whole, and the biggest eurozone economy was Germany's.

Thus, when the demand for credit was going through the roof in Ireland, the interest rates on offer to punters were going through the floor. And not only did the price of credit fall, but availability exploded, with banks falling over each other to lend.

After a few years of this, the economy became saturated with debt, asset prices became artificially inflated, and investors increasingly did silly things in search of returns. As John Stuart Mill observed with regard to the railway bubble of the 1840s, 'Panics do not destroy capital; they merely reveal the extent to which it has been previously destroyed by its betrayal into hopelessly unproductive works.' The consequences of too much debt become clear only after the economic crisis has begun. The epiphany, when it comes, is always too late.

As we have seen, in classical economics there is an assumption that in a recession, if interest rates fall enough, people will start to borrow again and the banks will lend again. But what happens if, no matter how low interest rates go, credit doesn't start to flow?

Keynes referred to this as a liquidity trap. Banks have too much bad debt on their books and don't want to resume lending; and the private sector is too indebted and doesn't want to borrow, no matter how low the interest rate. Once an economy has fallen into a liquidity trap, Keynes said, lowering interest rates becomes as useful as 'pushing on a string'. This dynamic has played out in Europe over recent years: interest rates have dropped to nearly zero, but there has been no accompanying flow of credit.

Another piece of this unpleasant jigsaw is what the great American economist of the 1930s, Irving Fisher, described as 'debt-deflation'. This describes the situation that the US found itself in at the depths of the Great Depression, when both asset prices and incomes were falling. People who had to pay back huge debts found it difficult to do so, because, while their incomes were falling in tandem with the contraction of the economy, their debts were fixed. As they tried to pay back what they owed, they took money out of the economy; and as the paradox of thrift took hold, their incomes fell yet further. Sound familiar?

Two sages of the crash

During the course of this book we are going to take a look at the works of two great economists who recognized the importance of the human propensity to panic, to indulge in herd behaviour and to believe our own propaganda: Charles Kindleberger and Hyman Minsky.

Both Minsky and Kindleberger, working separately but aware of each other's efforts, outlined the stages of a credit boom, where investors go from optimism and euphoria to depression and panic – a journey that leads to the destruction of wealth.

They understood human nature; and, even though they never set foot in Ireland, they would have immediately understood why Irish gamblers back Irish horses. Because we are herd animals, we are basically pro-cyclic – that is, we tend to act in ways that reinforce whatever economic trend prevails at a given time. As Kindleberger put it, 'Each of the participants in the market changes his or her own views at the same time and moves as a herd.' In other words, most people are what is known in the financial markets as 'momentum investors', who follow the crowd, buoyed up by the excitement of it all, rather than 'value investors', who constantly ask themselves whether prices are reflecting real value or something else. The predominance of momentum investors has the effect of amplifying the high and low points of cycles.

It is this sort of behaviour that can lead to bubbles and also push the economy off kilter for long periods. As Minsky put it, 'In a world with capitalist finance it is simply not true that the pursuit by each unit of its own self-interest will lead an economy to equilibrium. The self-interest of banks, levered investors, and investment producers can lead the economy to inflationary expansion and unemployment-creating contractions.'

I have been a fan of Kindleberger since reading *Manias, Panics and Crashes*, his work on speculative bubbles and crashes. The book was originally published in 1978; I picked up a copy in Barnes & Noble in New York in 1998 and couldn't put it down. In 2003 I wanted to interview Kindleberger for a radio programme I was presenting. In late June of that year, I obtained and dialled his home number in Boston. A very elderly gentleman answered and said that he would have no problem about being interviewed; he was watching events in Ireland with interest. We scheduled the interview for the following week. I phoned as arranged, only to be told by a voice at the other end of the line that Kindleberger had passed away the day before. He was ninety-three.

Charles Kindleberger was a member of what the Americans call the Greatest Generation – the ones who lived through the Depression, fought the Second World War and shaped the post-war peace.

As chief of the Division for German and Austrian Economic Affairs, head of the committee that prepared cost estimates for the Marshall Plan, and a key adviser on German reparations, Kindleberger had been at the heart of American policy towards Germany. He knew that imposing reparations on the Germans, as had been done after the First World War, would destabilize the country and lead to further problems. 'We'd stay up all night, night after night,' he later recalled. 'The first work ever done that I know about in economics on computers used the Pentagon's computers at night for the Marshall Plan. I had a tremendous sense of gratification from working so hard on it.' Later, at MIT, he taught some of the great economists of our time, such as the future Nobel Prize-winner Paul Krugman.

Kindleberger rejected two ideas widely held in economics: that financial markets are efficient, and that people are rational. 'Positive feedback develops, as new investment leads to increases in income that stimulate further investment and further income increases,' he wrote. 'When the number of firms and households indulging in these practices grows large, bringing in segments of the population that are normally aloof from such ventures, speculation for profit leads away from normal, rational behavior.' In *Manias, Panics and Crashes*, he quoted Isaac Newton: 'I can calculate the motions of the heavenly bodies but not the madness of crowds.'

According to Kindleberger, there are three factors common to all crashes, and these explain why some economies don't right themselves quickly. First, he noted that financial panics can go on for a long time. This certainly rings true with us in Ireland, five years on from the turn of the housing market, which led to the bank guarantee, the surrender of economic sovereignty to the Troika and a deep recession that shows no sign of ending any time soon.

Kindleberger's second observation was on the nature of contagion: that a big panic can be sparked by a relatively trivial event. He pointed out that the great currency crash of the early 1930s had as its trigger not the stock-market crash of 1929, but the failure of a bank in Austria, Creditanstalt, in May 1931. This bank failure caused people to panic in neighbouring Germany: they sold marks for gold. A series of events was then triggered, with the result that, in the space of a few months, both Germany and the UK had left the Gold Standard. We can see this phenomenon in our present crisis, whereby the failure of the banking sector in one small country (Ireland), or chicanery in the public accounts of another small country (Greece), can threaten the health of the global economy.

The third concept that Kindleberger stressed is the absolute need for a leading power to seize control of events in a financial crash. A hegemon must take ownership of the crisis, show leadership and reassure the little guys that someone is in control. If this doesn't happen, crises will tip economies into depression. Kindleberger cited the squabbles between the various central banks in 1931, with no one taking control, as an example of what happens in the absence of a hegemon. Today in the eurozone, the natural leader, Germany, is reluctant to assume this role, and the ECB is unable to do so because of Germany's reluctance. This absence of political, financial and economic leadership is making a difficult situation almost impossible, as capital ebbs out of the countries of the European periphery.

The second economist whose thinking on crashes will be a touchstone in this book is Hyman Minsky, a contemporary of Kindleberger, who, like him, developed ideas about how the world works that were largely ignored during his lifetime but that look remarkably perceptive now. My thinking on the importance of Minsky was shaped during the 1990s, when I worked as an economist with Paul McCulley, who was the chief economist at UBS.

As a mentor and a boss, McCulley constantly stressed to us younger economists the importance of Minsky when attempting to understand financial markets. He coined the phrase 'Minsky moment' to describe the panic selling of assets during the Russian crisis in 1998. In later years, when he was the managing director of PIMCO – the world's largest bond fund – McCulley's analysis and the Minsky framework came to figure more and more in contemporary thinking about how panics in financial markets materialize.

Looking at the Great Depression of the 1930s, Minsky observed how the financial system can go from rude health to fragility very quickly. The five sequential stages of a credit crisis, as schematized by Minsky, are displacement, boom, euphoria, profit-taking and panic.

At the beginning, displacement occurs – a financial event that changes people's behaviour. In Ireland's case, the displacement event was joining the euro, which led to a dramatic fall in the rate of interest. When interest rates fall sharply, we tend to borrow, and in Ireland ordinary people mainly borrow to buy houses. This caused house prices to rise quickly, creating a property boom – corresponding to the second stage in the Minsky model. The momentum drove more and more people into the market.

Around 2004, with the economy growing healthily and property prices continuing to soar, Ireland entered what Minsky called the euphoria phase. The banks fell over themselves to lend to anyone who turned up. This is when cheap tracker mortgages took off, when developers were getting all the money they wanted, and when the Irish banks were borrowing hand over fist from foreign banks to fund their lending at home.

When the market is at its most euphoric, some players – displaying unusual rationality – start to sell, taking profits. But the herd never does. As Minsky wrote about human nature in a boom, 'Success breeds a disregard of the possibility of failure.' The profit-taking phase happened in Ireland in 2007 – but relatively few Irish investors actually participated in it.

Finally, as property prices began to slip and the credit crunch kicked in, the foreign banks that had lent to Irish banks suddenly panicked and withdrew their money from Ireland. Very late in the day, they recognized that prices were ludicrously high and investment yields dangerously low. And when the foreign banks withdrew, the entire credit edifice collapsed.

If you look in detail at Minsky's or Kindleberger's thinking, it becomes apparent that debt build-up combined with old-fashioned human nature fuels humanity's pathological optimism – and we end up believing our own propaganda and talking up our own book.

The three types of borrowers

Looking at the Great Depression, Minsky identified three types of borrowers who obtain financing in the boom and then get into trouble when values plummet in the bust.

The first kind are what he called 'hedge borrowers'. These people can finance the interest and capital payments of loans out of their income. The second are 'speculative borrowers' – those who can cover the interest payments on their borrowing, but who need to roll over the principal. The final type are the 'Ponzi borrowers'. This is the guy who borrows even though he can't afford to make the payments; only the rising value of the asset makes his investment viable, at least temporarily. In a deal like this, money doesn't actually change hands: the Ponzi borrower borrows on paper and sells on paper, and if the market goes up quickly enough he can make a tidy killing. Once the market stops going up, he is goosed.

When the bubble goes pop, the falling value of the asset means that the Ponzi borrower goes bust first – but it doesn't stop there. The generalized fall in asset values affects the speculative borrower too, because the bank will allow him to roll over the principal only so long as the asset has value; if that value falls, the bank puts the brakes on.

Finally, as the withdrawal of credit causes the economy to seize up, everyone's income falls. This affects even the hedge borrower's creditworthiness. Remember, he could finance both the capital and the interest out of his income, but when all incomes fall, so does his, making it difficult for him to meet his payments.

Even though Minsky was writing about the US in the 1920s, in the run-up to the Great Crash, the types he identified can be seen in the financial waste land that is post-crash Ireland.

Here, the Ponzi borrowers are the property developers and investors, who, with the connivance of the banks, took on levels of debt that never had a hope of being sustainable once the market inevitably turned.

The Irish equivalent of Minsky's 'speculative borrowers' are those who took interest-only mortgages. This became very common in Ireland during the boom.

Finally, there are the 'hedge borrowers' – people who were able to afford capital and interest payments on their mortgages at the time, because their incomes covered the payments. But we all know that no one can say with any real confidence that they'll be able to afford their mortgage ten or twenty or thirty years down the road. And, whereas in most places at most times banks build this uncertainty into lending decisions, with the effect that most people in most places at most times have been able to pay their mortgages, the Irish banks during the boom abdicated from this role and lent recklessly. Ordinary people with robust incomes, living in entirely unremarkable homes, were left with no savings at the end of the month – sometimes because of imprudent consumption, but often because their mortgages were just too bloody big.

One way to visualize what happens in a time of deleveraging, in the aftermath of a Minsky cycle, is to imagine a three-storey apartment block that is hit by a tsunami. The people on the ground floor – the Ponzi borrowers – are flooded first. Then, as the water rises, the speculative borrowers on the second floor are hit. The fate of the hedge borrowers on the third floor really depends on where the rising water stops. If it stops at the second floor, they will be OK. But if it doesn't, they'll drown too.

All this would be difficult enough without the rest of the world also being on the brink – but it is.

The outside world

We are in the middle of a massive crisis in the eurozone, resulting from excessive borrowing by what is called 'the periphery' – Ireland and the Mediterranean countries – and excessive lending by 'the core', i.e. Germany. This stems from the hard truth that European monetary union didn't make Greeks any more German, nor did it make Germans any more Spanish. Instead, we all behaved as expected. Idiosyncratic human nature, as observed for centuries, was victorious once more. The Germans saved; the Irish spent everything they could lay their hands on. The Dutch saved; the Spanish spent. The Greeks pretended all was fine; the French pretended they were rich Germans. Ultimately, all pretences were exposed.

The German banks lent loads; then, when it became clear that some of this lending had not been very wise, they panicked and went looking for their money. Given that the banks most exposed to the European debt mountain are German and French, the governments of Germany and France have been insistent that no country should be allowed to default. No surprise there.

But the financial markets are one step ahead of the politicians. The markets understand that a country simply can't pay its debts once the debt-to-GNP ratio becomes too high. There are various ways of calculating a country's debt-to-GNP ratio, but, however you measure it, Ireland has more debt than it can reasonably be expected to service.

In response to a parliamentary question in September 2011, Minister for Finance Michael Noonan put total Irish debt at 494 per cent of GNP. The breakdown of this enormous figure was as follows: government debt at 137 per cent of GNP; household debt at 147 per cent of GNP; and corporate debt at 210 per cent of GNP. In 2012 a McKinsey study on global indebtedness put Ireland's debt-to-GDP figure at an even higher level: 650 per cent. Just take a breath and hold on to something if you have to.

Taking the minister's figures, a back-of-the-envelope calculation shows that the economy would have to grow five times faster than the prevailing rate of interest just to keep the debt-to-GNP ratio stable, to say nothing of reducing it. There is no version of reality yet discovered or imagined in which that is going to happen.

The Irish government has always claimed it could repay all its creditors. In 2010, ignoring our government's optimism (or bravado), the markets scoffed and capital fled the country. It is very important to grasp exactly why the markets gave up on us. The reason lenders ran scared of Ireland, pushing our borrowing costs up and causing us to accept an onerous bailout from the Troika, was not because we threatened not to pay our debts; it was because we boasted that we could pay all of them.

So now we have the spectacle of Ireland borrowing more from the Troika, adding yet more debt to a balance sheet that was carrying too much debt to begin with. And all the while the economy continues to weaken. Someone very clever, I am not sure whether it was Albert Einstein or Roy Keane, once said that the definition of insanity is doing the same thing over and over and expecting a different result. That is what we are doing.

At the peak of the boom the German banks were owed €127 billion by Irish banks. This exposure to Ireland might have been manageable, but when you factor in Germany's exposure to the rest of the periphery, Angela Merkel's government would have had to write a truly enormous cheque to make the problem go away. Moreover, a default or a bank failure in Ireland might have triggered a domino effect all around Europe. Some Irish bank could have been the Creditanstalt of the twenty-first century. Ireland, in the autumn of 2010, was the canary in the coalmine.

Having guaranteed the dizzyingly large liabilities of its banks in 2008, in order to prevent a bank run, the Irish government could have allowed the guarantee to lapse in September 2010, after it emerged that the banks had presented a misleading picture of the scale of their potential losses; but the government never showed any inclination to do this, and in 2010 it was instructed by the ECB to ensure that the holders of the nationalized bank debt, and other sovereign debt, were repaid. It was understood that the ECB would close its discount window to Irish banks if its orders were not complied with. So the purpose of the Troika's loan to Ireland was to facilitate the repayment of debt to other countries' banks and bondholders. The same has held true for the subsequent bailouts of Portugal, Greece and Spain. All of these bailouts were nothing more than parachutes for the banks and other creditors who had lent money unwisely in the great euro-credit binge.

The dirty little secret that nobody wants to acknowledge is that all the bailouts of the periphery have been nothing more than the transfer of more and more private debt to ordinary people who had nothing to do with the debt in the first place. We are seeing the gradual socialization of private debt all over Europe, whereby the wealth of the rich is protected at the expense of everyone else.

When the EU starts to do that sort of thing, it loses political legitimacy. The strength of the EU has always been that it moves gradually in a direction determined by collective decision-making. Are we now going down a strange road leading to the destruction of the countries of the EU by the European elite in order to save the common currency?

When you take a bit of Keynes, add a pinch of Minsky and Kindleberger, and spice the dish up with Fisher, you get a clear picture of a situation in which an economy can't right itself on its own. In the light of this, the eurozone-wide policy of repaying private creditors and cutting government spending threatens to create an enduring depression, 1930s style.

From spending to saving

One useful way of representing what is happening to Ireland is via the savings ratio. The savings ratio measures the level of our net spending relative to our income.

In 2006, when Ireland was just beginning to feel the first tremors of the coming crash, net household savings were at minus 9 per cent. In other words, we were spending 109 per cent of our income.

Between 2006 and 2009, when people stopped borrowing, the banks stopped lending and people started to try to pay back debt, we went from being net borrowers to net savers, putting away 5 per cent of income – a swing of 14 percentage points.

Much the same thing is happening in private companies. Accountants come in and cut back everywhere. People lose their jobs. The paradox of thrift is working its way through the corporate sector.

What looks good for one company's balance sheet means depression in the aggregate. This is a time when companies are rewarded by the markets not for vision but for the speed at which they pay down debt. The overall private-sector savings rate increased by over 21 per cent between 2006 and 2009, as households and companies paid down debt and saved.

The banks don't want to lend because their books are riddled with bad loans. The traditional mechanism for getting out of a recession – the lowering of interest rates by the central bank – is useless, because of the liquidity trap.

So the failure of Ireland to recover, or turn the corner, should not come as any surprise at all. What is happening is precisely what traditional economic theory tells you to expect. Keynes, Kindleberger, Minsky, Fisher, Krugman – these are all mainstream economists. Some, such as Krugman, could be described as being on the left, others on the right (Fisher, for example, was described by Milton Friedman, a hero of the right wing, as the 'greatest economist the United States ever produced'). And Keynes is Keynes.

Something very odd has happened in Ireland and in Europe in the past few years. Mainstream economic thought has been labelled as radical, and the truly radical has been rebranded as mainstream, to suit the ambitions of the European political elite and the short-term interests of the banking system. It is as if the lunatics – or, at the very least, some really weird people – have taken over the asylum.

4. Eleven Weeks

Olivia bolted up in the bed. She'd noticed that her dreams were moving into psychedelic territory, but this one – of herself and Sean Gallagher going to his debs in the back seat of her mother's old green Daihatsu Charade – was beyond weird. She groped frantically across the bed for her own Sean. He was there, breathing heavily, sleepily, a little pungently. Onions with a faint hint of Toffee Crisp and Heineken. Her sense of smell had gone berserk. Having the olfactory reach of a bloodhound had proved particularly unpleasant in the classroom, filled as it was with adolescent males.

The laptop was still in the bed, under the covers.

Olivia couldn't believe that some woman actually let the whole birth thing be filmed. She couldn't imagine anything worse. Some fool – her husband with a mobile phone halfway up her – waiting for the magical moment as she roared trying to push a child out of her, all under the flattering rays of fluorescent lights. If Sean wanted a photo of her grimacing and gurning, squealing and contorting, she would be happy to oblige the next time she was hammered at a party. But the birth palaver, what were they thinking?

This was the last time she was going to type 'baby' into Google. It wasn't as though she hadn't already had one. She'd started by looking for cute, fluffy Babygros and ended up in a YouTube hell of childbirth videos, being horrified by something called breast tails, which she could fully expect to protrude out of her underarms in a few months' time.

Shit – it was Thursday. She always forgot green-bin day, but then so did the rest of the estate, apart from the English couple in No. 86. Her Thursday timetable was all over the place, starting with a sixth-year double-history class at nine and then nothing until third year at two. Usually she marked papers in the staffroom, planned football and swimming lifts for Sam, and figured out what to get in Tesco for the weekend. Sometimes she engaged in a bit of turbo-charged multi-tasking that might see her ending up anywhere from the Spar to the chiropodist.

This Thursday, though, she didn't have the energy to do anything. School had just started back after the Christmas break. She had forgotten what it was like in the first trimester and just how tired she could get. To stay awake in class she drank enough water to fill half of Lough Neagh – the pressure on her bladder kept her from falling asleep. It was uncomfortable but it worked. The boys were beginning to knuckle down for the long run-in to the Leaving Cert.

The language teachers were huddled in the corner, and she knew they were gossiping about her.

'We were just remarking how lovely your hair is looking these days, Liv,' cooed Avril O'Connor.

It was true – she was like a walking L'Oréal ad since the little test had gone blue. Her bra was on the loosest clasp, she was sweating unpleasantly, and she wanted to puke constantly. But her hair looked sensational.

'Thanks, Avril.'

She was out the door before the staffroom Gestapo could interrogate her further.

Thursday was her day for the car, because Sam had to be picked up in Bray after Cubs. She drove towards town in a daze, working through a packet of ginger snaps. Her kitchen had become a shrine to ginger – real ginger ale, ginger tea, ginger sweets, anything ginger to quell the sickness. Olivia was busy winning the prize for most ginger biscuits in any human's mouth at one time.

On the radio, certain heads were discussing politics and economics and the proposed new Treaty with Europe that no one really seemed to have the foggiest about.

Her phone rang.

She rarely took calls while driving now, after having had a brush with a cop on a bicycle a few months back. She'd actually thought the bizarre little man on a bike was on an English stag night, and she'd driven off. Irish cops on bicycles in Westmoreland Street? Really? By the time she'd reached Parnell Square, two squad cars were getting all *Law & Order* on her, demanding that she 'get out of the car'. She couldn't help herself – she laughed at them. But the €200 fine and the two penalty points taught her never to smirk at a cop on a bike again.

'If we vote no, we will begin the unravelling of the political architecture that we have been constructing since 1973,' someone opined on the radio.

She glanced down at the phone. It was only Barry. OK, chance it.

'The Four Courts? . . . I can't, I'm between periods at work . . . Who, little Shane Whelan? In trouble? What sort of trouble? . . . How much? . . . OK, Barry, I don't feel too well. I have to be gone by one o'clock, OK? Right?'

She rubbed her tummy. She couldn't feel anything yet, not even the tiniest bump. She wanted to see it growing, the little arms and legs, the alien-looking head, all being nourished by her, sustained by her, Olivia Vickers, and her mountain of ginger biscuits.

Olivia hadn't intended to linger. Barry had just asked her to drop him in to the Four Courts – he was there to support his friend Shane, who was in arrears on his mortgage and being sued by the lender – but she lucked into a good parking place, and curiosity got the better of her.

She and her brother watched Court 17 fill up quickly. Underneath his court gown, the young barrister representing the lender looked more like a Brown Thomas personal shopper than a courtroom operator. His immaculately groomed hair was as yet unruffled by the court wig neatly placed on the desk in front of him.

The barrister bowed to the judge unselfconsciously, just as he might tie his shoelaces. Shane sat up front, looking like a twelve-year-old in front of the headmaster. Arrayed along the back wall was a crowd of what Olivia took to be other defendants, each wearing a defeated expression. Not knowing where to look or what to do with their hands, they adopted the international body language of the powerless: head down, eyes clamped on their shoes.

Olivia nudged Barry. 'Shane looks miserable,' she whispered. 'How's he been?'

'Not great,' Barry replied. 'He's had a really rough year.'

'At least it's all out in the open now,' she said. 'He'll get closure.'

'Closure my hole,' Barry said.

They were directly behind the bank's barrister, who was wiping his seat with what looked like a monogrammed handkerchief.

'What happened?'

'Do you remember his sister Trish?'

'The one married to the tool who was always playing away even when she was up the duff?'

'Yep. Well, she divorced him.'

'Good for her.'

'Not that simple. You remember she had that small nail-bar type of place off George's Street.'

'Yeah, it was doing well, wasn't it? Giving all the young ones Rihanna's nails?'

'Apart from a big €25,000 VAT bill that Trish had run up over the previous two-odd years, and guess what?'

'Oh, shit.'

'Here's where Shane gets involved. It's now early 2007. Remember the year we all went to Ibiza and got mullered for a fortnight?'

She remembered it well, the clubbing and the nonsense. The early mornings, the beautiful dawns and the beautiful people, all loved up. Long time ago now, just before she got pregnant with Sam, before they bought the house.

'So,' continued Barry, 'he had bought his gaff and was motoring, job going well – the radio station was doing OK and the marketing department was meeting its targets. He was a good bet and a soft touch, if you ask me.'

'Oh, no – don't tell me.'

'Of course, he doesn't have €25k in the back pocket. So, fecking eejit remortgages his gaff and gives the €25,000 to Trish so she can pay off the tax man. Even back then the normal banks weren't going to give a guy a loan to pay off his sister's tax bill. Do you remember all the ads for easy money a few years back – the ones that said things like "no questions asked"?'

'Yeah.'

'Well, these were the fellas behind them. They targeted people, mainly small-business guys with cash-flow or tax problems. Called the loans "self-cert": they asked you how much you earned and you gave them the figure that would allow them to give you the loan. So the sister's in the middle of a messy divorce, which means she can't take out the loan herself. She needs cash to keep the business open. Shane steps in. All he had to do was put his house down as collateral. He gets the new lads to pay off AIB – the original lender. They then throw in €25,000 on top and he's in the hole to these guys for the guts of 300 big ones.

'Of course they told him not to worry about the rates: he could always refinance with one of the normal banks in a few years, and the higher rates would come down, and as house prices were rising there'd be no problem, sure it was only 300 grand. They were all at this game.'

'Did he talk to you about it?'

'He didn't. He thought things were always going to be grand. Job was going well. Repayments easy to make, or at least not killing him. After his own parents separated, Shane wanted to be the big man of the house and help his sister. So he did the right thing. Or tried to, at least.'

Olivia looked over at Shane, who didn't seem to have a barrister. He hadn't a hope in this bear pit.

'Then what happens? It's 2008 and the whole fuckin' thing crashes. Property advertising stops. The station's revenue collapses, because it all comes from ads for flats, houses, Woodies and Harvey Norman, and all that jazz. Shane is turfed out because the station doesn't need marketing graduates talking about strategy; it needs salesmen, proper revenue generators. So Muggins is out on his ear – and suddenly he can't make his repayments and he has these fuckers coming after him.'

The barrister glanced over at them.

'Tenner his nipples are pierced,' Barry whispered. 'Twenty says he's got a Prince Albert too.'

Olivia stifled a laugh, and almost choked. 'Shut up, sicko,' she whispered back. 'Listen to herself.'

The judge, a small, sparrow-like woman, adjusted her glasses, then spoke, signalling that proceedings had started. The stenographers typed. Tap tap tap.

The lender's barrister was first on his feet, rocking back and forth like a Yeshiva student. His voice was much deeper than she had expected. He presented his case in the slow cadences of a Ballygowan advert.

Olivia was fond of Shane – had been ever since he'd invited her to his debs when she was in university. She couldn't bring herself to say no, even though she was three years older. He was a classic eighteen-year-old: tongue-tied and nervous, and he got too drunk too fast. But he was sweet and polite and didn't try it on, even though it was clear that was all he wanted. If he'd been a couple of years older things might have been different.

But the real reason she was curious about his case was because she mightn't be a million miles away from this place herself in a few months' time. She'd been looking at the calendar. The baby was due in early August, and her maternity leave would take them up to December. Fine if she was permanent, but a part-timer had no guarantee that the job was going to be there when she got back.

Maybe Sean would find something – but if he didn't, and if her hours were cut just when the new baby was eating into their weekly budget, it might not be possible to keep up the mortgage payments.

The case before the judge was pretty straightforward. Shane Whelan had lost his job and said he didn't have the money to service his debts. The finance company wanted either to be repaid or to get Shane's house.

The barrister cleared his throat and dropped a disdainful glance towards the stalls before assembling the case against Shane. He was suggesting that Shane was richer than he was letting on. The evidence consisted of a number of small, unaccounted-for lodgements. A Taoiseach might have said he won the money on the horses, but, unlike Bertie Ahern, Shane had made the rookie mistake of having a bank account – so everything was there in black and white.

The barrister announced that on six occasions over the past year, amounts between €160 and €200 were lodged into Shane's account, over and above his dole income. These sums and their provenance were shrouded in mystery, he said.

To Olivia, it sounded more like an old-fashioned Irish nixer than an out-take from the Enron trial. She couldn't see the point of the barrister's line of questioning. Would the discovery of an extra grand over the course of a year really change the fact that Shane couldn't pay his mortgage? Apart from showing that the guy was still trying to work, what was the big deal? Even with a nixer or seven, Shane still couldn't afford to pay his loans. Couldn't the lender see that? What world did they all live in?

Barry leaned over, sensing what was on his sister's mind.

'They weren't regulated, did you know that, Liv? These mortgage outfits. You know in Ireland you need a licence to have a dog or a telly, but you can lend hundreds of millions against houses in this country and you need no permission from anyone at all.'

She looked across at Shane, sitting red-faced in his Marks & Spencer suit. He was some distance from the sweet and enthusiastic young man who'd talked her ear off about his big plans for the future barely ten years ago. The natives of the court spoke over his head, playing out their own game – he was just another body occupying the seat between now and lunch.

The stenographers continued tap, tap, tapping. Listening to the arcane lexicon of the barrister and the judge, Barry remembered how it felt to be so confused that you wanted to scream. He knew what it was like to sit in helpless frustration, like Shane was doing.

'C'mon, Barry, it's not hard.' Miss Ridge was kind, but Barry could hear irritation in her voice. 'This is the easy one. Look at it harder. Tell me what it says.'

You don't understand. I just can't see it.

He didn't know why he was so dumb.

The little boy looked down at the page again.

```
        eon,' sai    sy. 'W              r     eqon'h
'Com         dBet    ehav  di cku  I    d o n. W     avet
                     eto    pth sqo c                 o
```

Miss Ridge pointed down at the page. 'Come on, Barry,' she said quietly. 'This is the easy stuff.'

He blinked, terrified he would lose his place. Losing that foothold would be the worst thing that could happen. Everyone would know.

'Try harder: you can do it, Barry.'

You have no idea how hard I am trying. But the letters are jumping.

It didn't matter that he was concentrating so hard he felt his head might blow apart from the strain.

He opened his mouth and took a chance: 'Come and speeding.'

The laughter erupted before he'd finished.

'Barry, we did this page yesterday. It's simple.'

The more she said it was simple, the more frustrated Barry became. He was locked in. Words and letters were sneaky things that moved and danced and played tricks on him.

He concentrated. His finger was on the word 'popcorn'. He knew that was the word because they had read it yesterday and he had memorized every line, every word, so he could just sing out his memory and pretend like in Mass.

Then he looked down at the book, ready to pretend to read, the way he always did, but something happened. He got stuck. He forgot the word. He saw 'doqc or n'.

He pressed down on the page, trying to smooth out the letters. But when he took away his hands, they crashed back over the paper like waves.

Why does it look like this?

Miss Ridge gave up. 'OK. Let's move on. Shane, please take up where Maurice left off.' She turned away.

Shane Whelan's confident voice trilled: 'OK, Miss. From popcorn in the last sentence, or the next one?'

'Just start from the top of the page.'

Barry sat, head down and ashamed, as his friend Shane Whelan, the decoder in chief, read with such ease.

'Come on, Betsy. We have to pick up the popcorn, we don't have to . . .'

Today, in Court 17, the roles had been reversed: Barry was free and Shane was trapped. Olivia, sitting beside her brother, was lost in her hormonal thoughts. The next seven months, her little sister Vivienne's wedding in six weeks' time, the baby, maternity pay for part-time teachers and whether the school would take her back – all of it was coming at her.

Beside her, Barry knew why Shane had got into this mess, but he still couldn't understand why someone as smart as Shane didn't see the risks of being over-borrowed, even in 2007.

It was clear to Barry that Shane and the other borrowers being hauled to court for mortgage arrears really hadn't had a clue about numbers and money. He didn't buy the 'we were all hoodwinked' line. But he could also see that when a debt can't be paid, it won't be paid, and the only people making money here were the lads in the wigs.

Shane, Mister 450 points in his Leaving Cert, had been swept along, just like so many others. They'd all believed that houses prices couldn't fall, that they'd never lose their jobs. With all his brains and his business degree, Shane still wasn't able to see that if things turned down, all that credit was only a fast route to bankruptcy. Or he understood it in the abstract, but simply never imagined it could ever happen to him.

Sometimes Barry wondered what they actually taught them in university. They apparently didn't tell them about risk. Shane was just a decent skin, a product of the system, like so many others. He had the respectability of a university degree, he believed in the system, he never fathomed that the whole edifice could come crashing down. He was a believer.

Barry, in contrast, was instinctively sceptical. He knew how to lay off risk; how to see when prices were just wrong. All the way through secondary school he'd made good money buying and selling bicycles through eBay. The great thing about the internet was that nobody cared what age you were; if you could do the deal, you did. He'd seen all the fads coming, from hardtail mountain bikes to fluorescent fixies, and he'd had the know-how to turn old ruins from the skip and Garda auctions into real money. He'd learned to sell when others were buying and to buy when others were selling.

When he set up Mobtronix, aimed at providing fleets of company mobiles the same way as, in the old days, distributors provided fleets of company cars, he'd been the only one to see that helping companies save money on mobiles would be big business.

When he'd flogged the company, everyone had thought he was mad. Olivia remembered his response to their father: 'The easiest thing, Dad, is the buy. The hardest is the sell.'

Back in school, when he'd been isolated and picked on for not being able to read, he became a keen observer of the frailties and the neediness of crowds. He witnessed the emergence of bullies and their sycophantic cheerleaders. He learned to walk alone.

He might be dyslexic, but people like Shane were dyslexic in a different way. They were financially dyslexic, and that was dangerous. These poor financial dyslexics – to him, they were the ones with special needs.

The case was deferred, pending a further-information request from the barrister, who seemed convinced that Shane had a Swiss bank account stashed away. Olivia could almost hear the ringing of tills as the conveyor belt moved on to the next defendant in line.

Barry got up to leave, but Olivia lingered – something about the next defendant intrigued her. She looked calm, not pale and frantic like Shane; not intimidated by her surroundings, but detached, like a ghost.

The young woman stood up in the witness box.

'Please repeat your name for the courts.'

She reeled it off in a dry monotone.

'You have no money, is this correct?'

'Yes, we've lost everything.'

'But why do you insist on trying to stay in your present house?'

'Because' – she looked around –'we have nowhere else to go.'

'Judge, might I interject there. We believe that the defendant is not telling the full truth.'

The woman must have been in her late twenties, early thirties max. She was pretty in a drained-out way.

'Discovery has thrown up evidence that there is another source of income but we can't quite get a satisfactory answer as to where exactly it is coming from,' droned the barrister. 'My client believes this income is substantial.'

The woman looked down at her feet, not wanting to catch anyone's eye. She shook a bit, but then regained her composure. She swallowed and gripped her arms. At least she had turned up, not like most people, who had simply given up and were now ignoring court summonses. She wasn't afraid of people like this.

The woman passed a note to the registrar, who scuttled past her and handed it to the judge, who held her head in her hands as she took in the details.

The judge asked the barrister to approach.

'I'm satisfied that I know where the money is coming from,' she said. 'I believe that, given the circumstances, we should adjourn for six months. In this time, maybe the defendant and the bank might be able to come to an arrangement.'

Olivia looked down at the defaulter. The woman was looking directly up at the judge. They were sharing something, some secret. In an instant, Olivia realized what it was. Her stomach sank. She knew why nothing ever changed, why it had all happened before and why it would all happen again. Sooner or later, some women are forced to sell the only thing they have left to sell.

The woman held the judge's gaze. They looked into each other's lives for an instant.

Neither blinked.

5.   Contagion

Bob Marley's toe

Thirty-one years ago, Bob Marley ascended to the great Rasta cook-out in the sky. I remember the day he played Dalymount Park in the summer of 1980. I was too young to go to the gig, but I vividly recall the smell of ganja on the 7A bus that afternoon, as half of the 'Noggin skinned up on their way into town to pay homage to the great man.

Dalymount was the last outdoor concert Marley ever played. He died less than a year later. The cancer, which had originated in a melanoma found under his toenail, spread rapidly. His doctors had recommended that he get the toe amputated. Marley refused, on the grounds that Jah stipulated that humans shouldn't permit their own flesh to be cut. The amputation would also have affected his ability to play football and dance. Marley's life might have been saved had his toe been amputated.

Watching the twists and turns on Europe's road to financial calamity, I'm reminded of Bob Marley's cancerous toe.

Financial market contagion, like cancer, spreads if you don't deal with it early and decisively. And, like many infectious diseases, financial epidemics become resistant to treatment very quickly. This is the lesson of the past four years in Europe. It is also the story of the Asian crisis of 1997 and the Latin American debt crises of previous decades. In Europe's case, the crisis was initially financial, located in bond markets and over-exposed peripheral banks, but it rapidly infected economies and businesses' expectations of the future. As the economies faltered and growth evaporated, along with credit, the crisis exploded, becoming a full-blown political calamity, with governments socializing private debt and imposing punishing austerity.

But financial crises are not new; nor are the remedies. Indeed, looking out beyond this European crisis, the pattern from boom to crisis, from calamity to recovery, has been played out again and again in other parts of the world.

The great Asian crisis of 1997 should have been a warning sign for Europe, but it wasn't heeded. Last year at Kilkenomics, the economics conference in Kilkenny, I interviewed Professor Jeffrey Sachs about the similarities between the two crises. Sachs, who at twenty-eight became the youngest ever tenured professor at Harvard, has been at the forefront of macroeconomic thought for thirty years. In 1998 he was one of the first to see that the initial response to the Asian crisis by the IMF was making things worse. If we look back at 1997, we can see that the EU is making similar mistakes right now.

Have we learned nothing?

Contagion in action

On Halloween night 1997 – seventeen years after the Bob Marley gig – I walked into the foyer of the Grand Hyatt in Hong Kong to meet a man who was worried about his investments in Eastern Europe. At the time, I worked for the French bank BNP in the emerging-markets field. We were there for the annual IMF shindig hosted in Hong Kong, months before the handover to China.

The crisis in the economies of South-East Asia – the so-called Asian Tigers – was raging. Indonesia and Malaysia had succumbed to mass selling of assets. Day by day, the panic spread all over the region. As so often happens, greed had been followed by fear.

One of the remarkable aspects of the Asian crisis was that it was almost totally unexpected. Up until the moment things turned sour, the Asian Tigers were the subjects of glowing reports.

It's often remarked that the best time to sell is when the *Financial Times* or the *Economist* gives a country an effusive thumbs-up. By the time foreign journalists get wind of the story, the shark has been jumped and the financial opportunity is gone. The worlds of finance and financial reporting are as subject to fads and changing trends as the catwalk.

Boom-time reporting often strays into bizarre cultural commentary. Where money goes, embarrassing op-ed pieces follow. When Iceland boomed, books were written suggesting a DNA link between the marauding Vikings and their descendants, the Icelandic speculators who raided foreign countries to buy trophy assets in the mid 2000s.

Up until the eve of the 1997 crash, newspaper articles were offering all sorts of cultural reasons for the extraordinary boom in Asia of the preceding five years. In the heady effervescence of the boom, it didn't really matter whether the stories contradicted each other. One day, the Asian boom was attributed to the connectedness of close-knit families. The next day it was Asian single-mindedness. The growth rates were put down to the Asian capacity to invest wisely – or to the Asian capacity to save prudently. In some reports, the dynamism of the Tigers was the result of Asian willingness to work hard. In others, it was attributed to the importance of Buddhism in Asian culture. You might remember that when Ireland was the apple of the market's eye, the same carry-on could be seen here. The Irish miracle was the result of a random bag of USPs and clichés: the Irish character, our ability to get on with people, the corporate-tax rate, our heritage in building things, the unique Irish model of banking.

The cultural theories of the Asian Tiger miracle overlooked the real economic and financial factors that caused the boom and the crisis. In the autumn of 1997 much of the analysis focused on why a modest currency devaluation in Thailand – a relatively small country in the grand scheme of things – managed to set off a chain of events that resulted in the explosion of the Asian Tiger myth. The same question could be asked of Greece or, indeed, Ireland with regard to the euro-debt crisis. Why did woeful governance in one small country – Greece – or out-of-control lending in another small country – Ireland – end up with a run on Spanish banks and Italian government bonds, threatening the entire eurozone?

For a number of years in the 1990s, something interesting was going on in Asia in terms of growth, productivity and profitability – as was the case in Ireland between 1994 and 2000. When productivity – output per worker – rises, many very beneficial things follow. All wealthy countries have highly productive workers at their core.

In the Asian Tigers, big increases in productivity in the first part of the 1990s coincided with the opening up of much of the world to trade under the various GATT agreements. The combination of low wages and high productivity meant the return on a dollar invested in Thailand was substantially higher than the return on a dollar invested in California.

Between 1990 and 1996, capital inflows into Thailand amounted to 10 per cent of GDP each year. The vast majority came from private banks and corporations borrowing privately. This inflow of cash created a self-reinforcing dynamic called the 'money multiplier'. As demand and wages rise, we have more money in our back pockets, but we also have more money on deposit. Banks can use this newly deposited money to make further loans. Companies post record profits.

In a country with its own currency, the inflow of cash poses a dilemma for the authorities. A Thai finance company or bank borrows cash cheaply in dollars. It uses these dollars to buy local currency, because local people want to borrow in local currency. So the demand for the local currency goes up. Therefore, the price of the local currency rises against the dollar.

If the authorities want the local currency to stay at the same value – because they want exports to remain competitive – they must actively sell the local currency into the local market and buy dollars. Two things happen: the local money supply expands and the country's foreign reserves expand.

This goes on for a while, but as inflation rises in the local economy, local companies become less competitive in the world market. It becomes easier to make money in the local market, by speculating on local assets such as property or shares, rather than competing in the export market.

Gradually the local economy begins to take over from the export economy. In Asia this manifested itself in a current-account deficit as imports were sucked in. For all the Asian Tigers, export growth of 24.8 per cent in 1995 fell to just 7.2 per cent in 1996. (A similar pattern can be seen in Italy, Greece, Spain and Portugal in the 2003–7 period.)

All over Asia, but particularly in Thailand, a property bubble developed as finance companies invested some of their surplus capital in local property. The price of land was rising, and the banks were tricked into ploughing more money into this asset. As they leveraged up, the price kept rising, attracting more players. Thus they entered the boom phase.

Next, the rating agencies and the investment banks wrote flattering pieces about the new Tiger economies – even though the period of true vitality was over and a decadent phase had begun. More money flowed in, attracted by the elixir of high return. The banks began to fight with each other over market share, lending hand over fist.

But what of actual productivity, the development that really started this whole process in the first place? By this point productivity was going the wrong way, very fast. It was falling because more and more workers were being sucked into construction and domestic services at higher wages. (Think about the building sites, retail and restaurants of Ireland in the boom. Where were the new immigrants who had been attracted by the high wages in the local economy? They were behind the hot-food counter in Spar.) Less surplus capital was being invested in productive plants and machinery.

This profoundly negative shift got lost in the excitement of the boom.

In this type of credit cycle, the misallocation of investment becomes self-perpetuating. People are never aware of this. No one rings a bell to signal that the economy is turning.

In countries like Thailand in 1995/6, growth rates were still high, but more and more capital and workers were necessary to generate them, because investment was falling. All the while the export boom, which had initiated the miracle in the first place, was withering away.

Imports were coming in, but countries needed to borrow money to pay for them. Up until the last minute, there seemed to be an insatiable appetite on the part of the Western financial system to lend to the Asian Tigers.

I was in Hong Kong as part of the emerging-markets team of a French bank that was using the deposits of the average Jean-Claude and Claudine to lend cash to an Asian finance firm, which was in turn lending to Thais, Malays and Koreans. This is the same dynamic that we saw in Europe during the 2000s, when the average Günter was effectively lending to Paddy, Stavros, Pablo and Giuseppe.

By 1996 cracks were beginning to appear in Asia. Malaysia's current-account deficit jumped by 8 per cent of GDP, Thailand's by 5 per cent and Korea's by 6 per cent. But still no one shouted halt. Still the money flowed. In Asia, up until the eve of the crisis, the IMF, rating agencies, the World Bank and the major investment banks were all predicting a modest slowdown, to be followed by an upward-growth trajectory.

In Thailand, some investors started to worry and were keen to take money out of the country in the form of dollars. Initially their central bank had loads of foreign reserves, so when the demand for dollars from these investors came through, the central bank simply bought the local currency from them.

Thailand's difficulties were complicated by a property bubble. As we saw in Ireland, when there is a massive bubble in assets, more and more money needs to come in at the bottom to sustain it. Once there was a doubt over the availability of credit, the bubble burst. A large Thai developer, Somprasong Land, missed a repayment on its foreign debt, signalling to everyone that there was a big problem in the land market in Thailand. In Korea at about the same time, early 1997, Hambo Steel collapsed, with $6 billion of debts.

The Minsky cycle began to play itself out and investors raced for the door. The Bank of Thailand lent $8 billion to distressed lenders in the first four months of 1997. But they were already well into a run on their currency. Investors were demanding dollars, not Thai bahts. If the Bank of Thailand wanted to keep its currency pegged with the dollar, it had to give these investors dollars in return for local currency. But although it could print local currency, at this point it had a limited supply of US dollars in its reserves. Investors knew that when it ran out of dollars, the baht would have to be devalued. So everyone, locals and foreigners alike, tried to get out of Thai currency and into dollars, causing a stampede that overwhelmed the central bank. (The same sort of thing occurred in Ireland, Britain, Sweden and Finland in the early 1990s. I remember, as an employee of the Irish central bank during the closing months of 1992, watching our foreign reserves dwindle as money flooded out of the country, leading to the eventual devaluation of January 1993.)

Both Thailand and Korea, driven somewhat by prestige concerns but also by the justified fear that companies and banks that had borrowed in dollars would go bust, tried at all costs to defend their currencies. This involved increasing interest rates and cutting government spending. When things are normal, increasing interest rates might coax investors into keeping their money in the local currency because of the greater return. But in a panic, when companies are going to the wall, the tighter monetary policy and credit conditions become, the more panicked investors become.

That's the thing about panics. As Paul Krugman has observed, the very act of panicking makes the panic itself legitimate. Keynes captured this idea when he observed that 'Markets can remain irrational longer than you can remain solvent.'

In July 1997 the Thai government let one of its big financial companies, Finance One, go bust. Then it let the currency float.

Observers who had seen similar currency crises – in Mexico in 1994, in the UK in 1992, in Scandinavia in 1992 and in Ireland in 1993 – expected the Thai currency to fall in value, after which things would stabilize.

But that was a mistake. The initial devaluation didn't stabilize things. In fact the devaluations in Thailand and Korea – two very different economies – sparked the most virulent bout of financial contagion the world had seen in many years.

Why?

A virulent disease

By the time I touched down in Hong Kong in October 1997, the Asian crisis had reached the full-panic stage. The news was dominated by the anti-Semitic attack launched by the prime minister of Malaysia on the hedge-fund manager George Soros following the collapse of the Malaysian currency. Mahathir Mohamad named Soros as the instigator of the run on the Malaysian ringgit and declared him to be both a 'moron' and a 'menace to Malaysia'. He then upped the ante by stating, 'It is a Jew who triggered the currency plunge.'

Many Korean corporations by this time had gone bust and defaulted, and the strongest currency in the region – the Hong Kong dollar – was under sustained selling pressure. The fickle international press herd had swung from adoration to finger-pointing. The air was thick with talk of Asian corruption; the honest, straight, hardworking Asians of January 1997 had morphed into dodgy and duplicitous 'crony capitalists' by November 1997. The speed and ease of doing business that had been a unique selling proposition was now symptomatic of duplicity.

I pulled up a chair in the enormous foyer of the Grand Hyatt overlooking the harbour. There was a good view of the Star ferry as it shuttled thousands of workers to and from Kowloon. The investor I was meeting explained that he was busy selling his assets in Russia and Eastern Europe because of the events in Asia. This puzzled me. I'd thought Russia did little trade with the Asian Tigers. Why would the crisis in Asia affect it?

The answer lay in the dynamics of financial globalization, which I, an economist in a global bank, had not yet fully grasped.

Many investment banks have proprietary trading desks. These desks use bank depositors' money to gamble on the markets. Their objective is to dramatically increase the return on the bank's money. In order to have some level of security, each bank sets a limit on the trading desk: the amount of the bank's capital that can be put at risk. The bank I was working for, BNP, was using French deposits to speculate in Asia and Russia. Many traders believe themselves to be infallible, view such limits as a nuisance that restricts their genius and become adept at finding ways to circumvent them. Trading desks can also leverage the bank's reputation to get additional credit facilities from other banks.

The trader using other banks' money in this way will normally be required to lodge a deposit of perhaps 10 per cent of the value of the investment with the bank from which he's borrowing. This deposit is known as the 'margin'. So let's say the bank lends him €1,000: this gives him €900 of a stock, over which the bank has a charge; and he deposits €100 at the bank. As long as the end-day position equals the €1,000 lent, everything is fine.

What happens if the value of the stock falls to €800? This triggers a margin call: the margin between the value of the shares and the value of the loan has grown, and the trader now has to make up the difference by adding another €100 in cash to the €100 already on deposit.

The trader now probably has to sell something in his portfolio to get the cash to pay the margin call. This, in microcosm, is contagion: it illustrates the way a crisis in one market can provoke selling in another, perhaps entirely unconnected, market. One trader selling one asset to make one margin call is no big deal; but when a crisis causes heavy falls in asset prices in a certain area, and when the markets are dominated by heavily leveraged traders operating in a wide range of sectors, it's not hard to see how a panic in Thailand can spread across Asia and thence to faraway places like Russia.

This is what causes small crises to blow up into much bigger ones – and it is why the financial world has become less stable in the era of globalization and easy credit. When asset prices are rising, everything is fine. But when asset prices are falling, everyone suddenly needs cash to pay for the margin calls coming at them from all angles. Banks find themselves forced into the interbank market by the need to borrow from each other, in the hope of shoring up their balance sheets. If central banks don't step in and inject liquidity, a short-term cash-flow problem rapidly becomes a credit crunch.

In the Hong Kong foyer that day, the trader's position had nothing to do with economics, trade, investment, the stuff you learn in textbooks. The arithmetic of the trader's position was simple: he had just lost money in Indonesia, so he had to raise it elsewhere to cover his losses. Paul McCulley hadn't yet coined the phrase, but this was a classic 'Minsky moment' – the moment when investors must sell assets to cover their obligations – and it was being played out here in the vertiginous lobby of the Grand Hyatt in Hong Kong.

Because the financial world had lumped huge and disparate parts of the planet into the 'emerging-markets' asset class, it was highly likely that an emerging-markets trader would have both Russian and Indonesian assets on his books. Faced with a margin call on Indonesian assets, he would sell Russian assets to raise the needed cash.

Indirectly, the Asian crisis would prove to be a significant cause of Russia's sovereign default in 1998, which in turn brought down one of the US's top hedge funds, Long-Term Capital Management (which had on its board two Nobel Prize-winning economists).

The power, complexity and interconnectedness of the financial markets has grown dramatically since the Asian crisis. For this very reason, we need real political leadership to protect us against the dangers unfettered markets pose to all of us. But can we count on getting it? Asia's crisis has taught us about the limitations of global technocrats and politicians, who can seem impotent in the face of such markets.

The cavalry to the rescue?

It was ironic that the IMF should have been hosting parties in Asia in the autumn of 1997, because the remedy they were pushing for crisis-struck countries in Asia had, by that time, already made things much worse. As many of the elements of the IMF's strategy for Asia are now being implemented in Europe, its failure should be a warning to us.

One of the most significant lessons of the Great Depression is that when an economy is in a tailspin, official actors must step in to control the situation, boosting demand and offering leadership. The IMF, however, tends to offer austerity as the one-size-fits-all solution to crises.

In the four months after the devaluation of the Thai currency, Thailand, Korea, Indonesia, Malaysia and the Philippines all experienced mass contagion and capital flight. Banks went bust, credit disappeared, inflation spiked, and they were on the brink of default. Unemployment skyrocketed, and there were no reserves left with which to defend their currencies, which by then had fallen dramatically.

The contagion, initially fuelled by traders, began to infect everyone. This is what economists call a negative-feedback loop. The banks stop lending because they have no money and have to repay what they borrowed in the boom. This lack of credit affects confidence, which in turn causes investors to move their money out of the country and to seek the safe haven of the dollar. Once that money leaves, the currency falls further – which brings large corporations and large banks closer to default and bankruptcy, because they can't pay their foreign loans.

In 1997 a number of Asian banks and corporations defaulted. Their governments responded by increasing spending. This, together with falling revenues, created growing budget deficits. The IMF stepped in to try to stop all this by lending to these countries – but, in return for its official loans, it imposed various conditions. There was very little difference between the conditions imposed on each country, despite the fact that the economy of each country was different. The IMF's main objectives were to prevent sovereign default, limit the currency falls, prevent the national budget from exploding and bring down inflation.

So what did it do?

For some reason, the IMF put government budgets at the core of its strategy, even though – as would be the case in Ireland, Spain and Italy – budget deficits had played no part in causing Asia's problems. By forcing the recipients of loans to raise taxes and cut expenditure at a time when they were caught in a vicious liquidity trap, the IMF made the recession worse.

In an effort to stabilize the exchange rates, it also stipulated that the countries must have high interest-rate targets. When things are going well, offering a higher interest rate attracts capital, but when everyone is nervous, higher interest rates slow down the economy even more, guaranteeing that people and corporations with large loans will default. Thus, rather than attracting money, it increases outflows.

The IMF also stipulated that countries must close down banks immediately. On paper this looks like the right thing to do, but if you see banks closing and you're not sure about your own bank, it prompts a 'Who's next?' panic. People reacted to bank closures by withdrawing their money from all of the banks.

All told, the IMF's reaction to the crisis in Asia made things much worse. Sound familiar?

What was driving the IMF in its misguided response to the Asian crisis, and what drives the EU in its equally misguided response to the euro crisis? When you strip everything back, it seems the main imperative is to keep the markets on-side. Ultimately, the IMF wanted financial markets to be doing the lending to the states or banks or corporations in trouble, and it saw its own intervention as a bridge to re-establishing that link. The EU's attitude today is much the same. This is absolutely fine, as far as it goes; but what it over-looks is that the financial markets are always thinking about tomorrow, not yesterday. Markets are more interested in measures that will ensure future growth than they are in measures to rectify past mistakes. Of course no one wants to lose, but losses are part of the game. You take them and you move on. Restoring market confidence is all about making sure the country has a chance to grow in the future. If the remedies proposed make the patient weaker, the markets will not be encouraged. Turning a country into a debt-servicing agency won't inspire confidence; it will repel investors.

This is exactly what happened in Asia. When it became apparent that the IMF's reaction had been excessive, fiscal targets were relaxed.

Guess what happened? Lending started again, because growth, rather than a debt-servicing agenda, was back on the table.

Who's in charge?

I learned one other lesson that night in Hong Kong: just how out of touch politicians can be, and how little influence they have, when they are caught in the middle of global financial panic.

The worried investor and I went for a drink a little later with a friend who worked for British American Tobacco, along with colleagues from the board of BAT. One of them was the ebullient, cigar-puffing Ken Clarke, who after eighteen years in various Tory cabinets had just been rendered a backbencher by the general election victory of New Labour.

Clarke is a hoot. That night he painted a most extraordinary picture of just how clueless politicians can be in the middle of a financial crisis.

He told us that at 4 p.m. on the afternoon of Black Wednesday – 16 September 1992, the day Britain was forced out of the European Exchange Rate Mechanism – the so-called 'War Cabinet' was huddled around a transistor radio in the kitchen of No. 10 Downing Street. Clarke, who was then home secretary, Trade Secretary Michael Heseltine, Chancellor Norman Lamont and Prime Minister John Major were desperately trying to find out what was happening to sterling – the currency of which they were supposedly the masters.

In Europe today we see disturbingly similar scenes. When we witness European political leaders at press conferences in Brussels pretending they are in control, it is worth remembering the chaos that Clarke described. In Europe, as we shall see, the contagion is now mutating almost by the week, from country to country, from asset to asset. The response of policy-makers is almost wholly reactive.

Things were rather different in Asia in the wake of the 1997 shock.

The IMF abandoned much of its original blueprint, and by early 1998 governments were allowing currencies to find their own levels and companies to default. Central banks injected as much currency as necessary. This, added to the import-price increases, generated inflation – which was just what the Asian Tigers needed. In short, inflationary policies gradually rectified the deflationary impact of the Great Asian Crisis. By 1999 all the Asian Tigers were growing strongly again. By the early 2000s the crisis was part of a collective memory, something that had been experienced but that had had no long-term adverse impact on the growth rate or the prosperity of the afflicted countries.

Devaluations, looser fiscal policies, lower interest rates and less stringent credit guidelines – traditional economic remedies – facilitated the recovery of the Asian Tigers. Europe is not following suit. Currency devaluation, of course, is not possible for the countries in the eurozone. The normal economic safety-valve open to the Asian Tigers in the 1990s (or Iceland in 2008, or indeed the USA in 2010) is not available to us. And in the areas where Europe could emulate the Asian playbook, it is choosing not to.

All the while, the elites of Ireland cling to the dream that things will get better without having to resort to any of the remedies that have made things get better in other times and places, suggesting to most sober people that they are smoking something much stronger than the Bob Marley fans on the 7A thirty-one years ago.

6.   Fourteen Weeks

Olivia stared at the elasticized pants in disgust. The change was becoming visible now. In a few weeks' time, she knew, she'd be tipping over into a Teletubby land of acne, sweats and a sore back.

Vivienne's wedding couldn't come soon enough. Soon she'd be lurching around with all the grace of a hippo. Sean said she'd never looked better. It must be the cleavage. Even her feet were expanding.

She tried her jeans once more, a rubber band threaded through the buttonhole – there was no way the button was going in. They were still too tight. Shit. She tried a skirt, unzipping it at the back. Did her pants show? This would do for a week or two more, hopefully. She needed a big shirt over it, something that hung down a bit. That was it for anything tucked in for at least a year. The yoga was helping, but the problem with the second pregnancy, she saw now, was that everything gave way that bit quicker. She was also dreadfully weepy – anything could set her off.

The boys in class were razor-sharp – they'd suss before anyone.

She was getting cranky. She hated the way Sean – like all men she knew – never put things back in the right place. Why couldn't they stick to a simple routine and finish things properly?

Yes, thanks for filling it but, no, love, the dishwasher won't turn on by itself.

Nor does the tap wash the dishes miraculously; it's a sink, not a skip for dirty cups.

The reason we have to get bread, darling, is not because I like being in Tesco at eleven o'clock on a school night, shuffling between the aisles with all the other Tesco ghouls like extras from the 'Thriller' video. It's because we have a five-year-old son who needs his packed lunch tomorrow.

She was getting grumpy as well as cranky, but she couldn't

help herself – everything was coming in on top of her at the same time.

The letter from the bank was in one hand; with the other, she called up the calculator on her phone. She'd just made the Dart at Greystones after the daily dash from their estate outside Rathnew. Sean had had to stop earlier to get a tenner's worth of petrol in Ashford; it would barely get him home. Most mornings he drove her to the Dart. Neither spoke. Money was always on their minds. The bad news on the radio was relentless.

He had never actually bought a tenner's worth of petrol before, but it was the end of the month and things were tight. The price of petrol had been rising, and she minded. A few years ago her world view had been so different. At the beginning of the invasion of Iraq, in 2003, Sean and herself, still in university, had marched to the Dáil from the Garden of Remembrance in protest. Now when she heard of massacres in Syria or something awful in Libya, she worried not about the children in those countries, but about the impact on the price of petrol and the gas bill. She didn't really care whether it was a bloody democracy or whether women could vote; she just wanted the price of filling up their seven-year-old Honda Accord to stop rising.

As the Dart sped past Shankill, she thought about the day they'd moved into the rather preposterous-sounding Hilton Park Estate. Sean had said they'd only be there for a while, until they got a bit more money together and could move up the ladder.

Rathnew was a far cry from Anseo on Camden Street or the little flat they'd shared on Heytesbury Street, but it was their springboard. They'd be back in Dublin in no time. Quite how they'd managed to believe that, Olivia couldn't figure out. It was like a group acid trip: everyone had dropped at the same time, everyone was coming up and no one was allowed to wreck the buzz. They were tripping on property and the idea that it would make them richer. Now, too late, she was starting to understand how dumb the whole idea of the 'ladder' had been.

Not long after they bought, the newest houses in their estate stopped selling and the final phase was never built. She knew Sean would go mad there all day on his own. She could see the fear in his face as she left every morning while he looked forward to a day of job applications to schools that never answered and driving across the city to cover classes for other teachers.

Mum and Dad had been determined that they should 'get on the ladder'. Sean's parents kept insisting that they buy as quickly as they could. House prices would never depreciate – it was all they heard from everyone. Their friends warned that if they left it too long, they wouldn't get within three counties of Dublin. They'd had a baby on the way and needed security. Rathnew was further out than either of them would have liked, but it looked like an OK development, and in any case it was the best they could afford. She'd allowed herself to believe – like everyone else – that it would be a stepping-stone, not a millstone.

She remembered the Sunday dinner in 2006, shortly after she'd discovered that she was pregnant with Sam. Both sets of parents lectured her and Sean about how they'd never seen houses fall in value; nor had their own parents.

They laughed when they reminisced about their early-1970s mortgages, which they thought they'd never be able to pay, and which now seemed so minuscule. They were sure that in twenty years' time Olivia and Sean would also see that today's house prices weren't really that high; it just looks that way when you're young.

Olivia's mum went on her standard riff about renting being dead money. 'How do you think landlords are so rich?' she asked rhetorically.

When it came down to it, they were looking seriously at two estates. One was in Ashbourne, Co. Meath, where a house would cost them €335,000. If they spent €15,000 more, they could get a house in a new development in Rathnew, Co. Wicklow. Both sets of parents agitated for Wicklow. Olivia and Sean, both of whom wanted to be back in Dublin 8 as quickly as possible, had no intention staying long term in Wicklow, and were nervous about getting too stretched.

They also reminded the parents that they had a life to lead over and above being mortgage payers.

'Never mind life,' scoffed Mary Doyle, Sean's mother. 'When the little one arrives, you'll be hard pressed remembering what this life thing was all about. Do you remember, Donal, the two of us sitting in the dark the night we moved in to No. 48? Not a stick, bar a kettle and the *leaba* and your mother's drop-leaf table from the good room. How we prised it from her, I don't know. But sure it hadn't seen any use locked up in there for twenty years. Nice piece, though – solid mahogany, she used to say.' She was on a roll.

'Listen,' she said, nodding to Dermot Vickers, 'Wicklow always beats Meath in the capital-appreciation stakes, wouldn't you agree.' It wasn't a question; it was a statement of fact – and Dermot was only supposed to nod back in agreement, as he did without hesitation.

'Sure the Dart's right beside you,' she added, in the direction of Sean and Olivia.

'It's fifteen miles away, Mum – be realistic.'

'Get in now,' insisted Donal Doyle – not a man given to impulse. He had done his homework. 'The way things are going, prices will be up close to 400 before the end of the year and then where will we all be?'

This was exactly what was terrifying Olivia. Prices were going up so quickly. If they'd bought last year, they'd have saved €70,000 at least. Every price move was more and more debt for them. But, like Sean, she couldn't really get her head around the numbers. They had a combined income of €58,000. House prices were going up by more than that every year. €350,000 was six times their combined income. Sean had read somewhere that the banks wouldn't, or weren't allowed to, give you more than three or maybe four times your income. But Sean had just been told that the bank – the one where Vivienne, her younger sister, worked – could 'stretch' towards €350,000.

In the end, the two sets of parents, keen that Olivia and Sean should move quickly and grab the Wicklow address, contributed a €25,000 'makeweight' towards the deposit. That settled it.

Together with the €10,000 they put up from their savings, the parents' contribution qualified them for a 90 per cent mortgage worth €350,000, with the interest rate fixed for six years. Olivia had wondered whether they should take out one of those tracker things, but Sean's dad convinced them that the banks were forever trying to sucker people into 'all classes of highfalutin gimmicks', and that trackers must be one of them. And anyway, anyone who said he could tell you where interest rates were going was 'talking through his bonnet'. He urged them to take out what he called 'an honest to God mortgage'. So they did.

The broker gave them a few options, but, even though variable or interest-only were cheaper, Olivia and Sean agreed with Sean's dad: it was safer to know what you had to pay every month – for the first six years, anyway. Olivia assumed by the time the variable rate kicked in she and Sean would be earning more and maybe interest rates would be lower, who could tell?

They only wanted their own little place. The three of them – Olivia, Sean and the baby who'd be there later that year – wrapped up together, safe and secure. It wasn't because of greed that Olivia and Sean ended up in negative equity and with a mortgage they could barely pay; it was because of love. Love, the one emotion you can't fight or rationalize. It was for the love of her child and the love of her husband and the love of her new family.

And now it was so hard to hold it all together. So hard.

The rain was making the glass fog up so that she couldn't see Dalkey Island as the packed Dart swept past Whiterock. The milk-fed St Andrew's pupils sat on the ground, laughing, hockey bags damp around them.

She looked again at the bank's letter. The six years had passed so quickly.

Dear Mr and Mrs S. Doyle

Christ, how did she ever end up being Mrs Doyle? She hated it and never used it, but she was married to Sean Doyle. If another drunk fool at a wedding said to her, 'Ah go on, go on, go on, you will, you will, you will,' she'd throttle them.

The Bank would like to inform you that your mortgage, on No. 228 Hilton Park, Rathnew, Co. Wicklow, taken out in January 2006, is due to switch from a fixed rate of interest to a variable rate, as stipulated in the contract signed by you on 27 February 2006. The change will commence on 1 March 2012.

The day they signed, Sean had just been made 'Director of Studies' at the TEFL school. It sounded better than it was, but it meant a small pay rise. That's what happened to people with Master's degrees in English literature: they ended up teaching foreigners about the pluperfect tense.

But, although Sean moaned about his station, it wasn't too bad and the future looked bright. He would move on in time, but for now, with the boom, he was in the right place. Ireland had attracted huge numbers of immigrants, many of whom needed to improve their English, which had created a new market in language schools. Ireland's entry requirements were much less draconian than the UK's, and armies of students poured in, working during the day and taking classes in the evenings. Schools were popping up all over the place, but Sean's school had been around for a long time; they figured that even if the supposed downturn happened, it would survive.

But things didn't work out that way. As the recession wore on, many of the immigrants left – and soon Sean's school was surviving mainly on Brazilian students in the evenings and the summer boost from Spanish teenagers. The 'Director of Studies' post was eliminated and he started working twelve-hour days to cover for the now greatly reduced staff. On the upside, the extra hours meant Sean's income remained close to what it had been.

In January 2011 someone in the Department of Justice and Equality decided that Ireland was far too lax with these foreign students and changed the rules. Now all the Brazilians had to study during the day. That was the death knell. Ireland's attractiveness to Brazilians was largely based on two things: our proximity to the Continent and the availability of part-time work. Without the latter, the place suddenly didn't seem so appealing.

One of Sean's friends, who taught at another language school, woke one morning to a text message telling her that the company where she'd worked for four years had closed. Her outstanding salary would remain just that – outstanding.

Sean told his employers about it. They said things weren't that bad, and besides, they'd never do something like that to him. And they didn't. He was given two weeks' notice, and he even got most of his final pay cheque.

Your current monthly payment, fixed at an interest rate of 4.92 per cent, is €1,675.62.

As of next week, the mortgage will revert to the current variable interest rate of 5.19 per cent. The monthly payments for the next 24 years at this rate will be €1,727.75 per month.

Olivia got out the calculator on her phone and punched in 1,727.75 minus 1,675.62: a difference of €52.13 per month.

She typed 12 × 1,675.62 × 6. Jesus, she had already paid €120,644.64. She typed in 1,727.75 × 12 × 24.

The cross-looking man beside her with a copy of the *Irish Times* sighed as Olivia burst out laughing. Assuming an unchanging interest rate, she and Sean would be paying the bank €497,592 over the next twenty-four years, on top of the €120,644.64 already gone: well over €600,000 for a house now worth €150,000 max. So this is what they meant by compound interest. The history teacher in her understood why the Romans had banned it.

By now, Olivia was laughing to herself, half shocked, half mortified, but fully aware that someone was taking the piss. She looked around the packed Dart at all these mortgage payers, all the young men and women who usually got on with her at Greystones, some of them having already driven a long distance to get to the bloody beginning of the Dart Line. The same faces every day, most of them sitting in the same seats. There are thousands of us in the same boat, she thought, and we don't even know it because we haven't bothered to do the sums.

Looking around the Dart, she felt like screaming.

Sean was taking in €720 a month after tax, after scraping together fifteen hours a week standing in for someone at a TEFL school. The job could be gone next week. She was earning just over two grand a month, but who knew how long her job would be there.

She jotted down their outgoings. Even with her doing extra grinds and classes, and even if Sean got more work, they would still be running a deficit of over €400 a month. What little savings they had left wouldn't last long.

But even if they did chop every ounce of fat off their budget, there was still no scope for error. What if someone got sick? €60 for a doctor's visit – never mind the cost of medicine. She had been putting off the dentist for a good while now, and she'd have to put it off some more. The NCT was due in a few months. They wouldn't have the money to book the test, let alone any repairs that needed doing.

And what happened when Sam started school properly, or when the baby did? What about holidays, schoolbooks, Santa Claus? Jesus, what kind of future were they giving their kids?

There was no space at all. She folded up the letter and her scrawled budget and put them away.

She stared at the newspaper, which the cross man now held aloft in self-defence, shutting out the sight of the plain people of Ireland all around him on the train.

Olivia focused on the headline on the business page: COULD ECB RATE GO EVEN LOWER?

She leaned closer, so that she could make out the body of the article. *With interest rates already at a historic low, the ECB has indicated that it might move lower still, pushing its key lending rate below 1 per cent for the first time ever.*

Olivia was puzzled. How could interest rates be at 1 per cent and yet the new variable rate she would be paying was 5.19 per cent? How the hell could that happen? And why, if the ECB rate was at an historic low, was her mortgage about to get more expensive?

Surely there must be some mistake. The letter from the bank couldn't be right. After all, the variable thingy was supposed to mean that you paid less when interest rates went down.

Someone must have made an error, pressed the wrong button.

She'd get to the bottom of this – ring the bank and get them to rectify their mistake.

She rubbed her tummy as she looked out at the morning swimmers, dipping their toes, moving like frozen pelicans into the icy water at Seapoint. Why do they do it?

'Don't worry, baby,' she whispered. 'Mummy will sort this out. Don't worry, Mummy will make sure everything will work out fine. Mummy will look after all of us.'

7. Mario's Magic Money

The bond illusion

Maybe it was Clint Eastwood's rousing 'Halftime in America' Super Bowl address a week or two earlier, or perhaps he'd had a double espresso on the plane. Either way, Enda Kenny was fired up when he arrived in New York on a cold February day in 2012.

The previous October, at the Global Irish Economic Forum in Dublin Castle, Bill Clinton had announced his willingness to host an event bringing together the great and the good of American business to listen to the Taoiseach giving an 'elevator pitch' on behalf of Ireland. The ex-president delivered on his word twelve weeks later. Given that Ireland's stated recovery strategy was broadly based on the twin pillars of exports by multinationals and 'getting back into the markets' (i.e., borrowing money from lenders around the world), February's event at New York University was a significant date in Kenny's calendar.

Clinton did his homespun, optimistic, apple-pie routine, telling the Irish delegation that everyone loved them and our nation shouldn't be so hard on itself. He wasn't lying: everyone still loves us. If we could buy our way out of the recession with goodwill, our problems would be over.

Enda pulled the David-versus-Goliath 'great little nation getting back up again' card out of his back pocket. Flanked by the paternal Clinton, he spoke enthusiastically about the falling interest rate on Irish bonds. Since the eruption of the sovereign-debt crisis in Europe, bonds had become the international litmus test for determining whether a country sinks or swims. The bond market is the emperor at the Coliseum; the country is the gladiator who, after pushing himself to the limit, waits with fierce hope for the emperor's verdict. Clinton's own mercurial adviser, James Carville, the man who came up with the brilliant 'It's the economy, stupid' slogan, famously said that if he could be reincarnated, he would want to 'come back as the bond market'. By this he meant the markets were so powerful that their reaction alone could sink political initiatives; having worked at the right hand of a president, he was all too aware of their power. By the end of his presidential term, Clinton had a balanced budget and a roaring economy and was the toast of the bond market. But in the early days, when the markets had mistrusted the 'tax-and-spend' ambitions of this upstart Democratic president, things had been very different.

So Clinton would have understood Enda Kenny's worries about the bond market. But, unlike Kenny, Clinton had never had to run a country that had lost its ability to borrow money through normal commercial channels. This was Ireland's experience in the run-up to the Troika bailout in November 2010. Ireland was now on the Troika's life-support machine, but the bond market still monitored progress. Eventually, if it wanted to reclaim its economic sovereignty, the Irish state would need to borrow long term on the international markets again.

Our economic sovereignty is tied up with how the bond markets see us. If yields fall in the secondary market for Irish bonds – where they are bought and sold at prices that may differ dramatically from the original sum borrowed by the Irish state – it means investors are buying; they are feeling a bit more optimistic about the likelihood of the bonds being repaid, and, by extension, it *could* be taken to mean that those investors expect the Irish economy to recover. But it could also mean something else. There are many factors influencing Irish bond yields – particularly in the middle of a debt crisis – but sometimes we can't see beyond the parochial.

A fall in yields in early 2012 was widely reported as a sign that the markets thought the economy was improving. In the weeks before the Taoiseach's trip to New York, we were led to believe that the Bond Emperor had given Ireland the thumbs-up. Bond prices rose as the interest rate fell. Enda declared this was a sign the rest of the world was becoming more confident about Ireland's prospects.

On 17 February 2012, the last day of Enda Kenny's three-day visit to New York, the *Irish Times* published an opinion article whose author observed, 'Ireland's fundamental backdrop has provided a solid underpinning for the improvement in bond market sentiment . . . providing grounds for optimism that a corner is finally being turned, however slowly.' At the bottom of the article, the author was described as 'global strategist at Davy' – a firm of stockbrokers. The views of stockbrokers are often sought by newspapers, TV and radio, but rarely do their comments come with the caveat that when the Irish state sells bonds, the Irish stockbroking community profits.

Irish stockbrokers apply for, pay for and are granted a licence to be first seller in the primary market for government bonds. The more bonds the Irish government issues, the more money primary dealers in Irish government bonds make. Put bluntly: the deeper into debt we go, the richer they get. Unfortunately, this conflict of interest is rarely pointed out to radio listeners or TV viewers, where the opinions of stockbroker economists and strategists are often taken to be objective. The truth is, they are no more objective about the market for sovereign bonds than an estate agent is about the housing market.

On the face of it, the logic of the stockbroker and others at the time purveyed seems clear enough. The bond market is supposed to tell us how likely it is that a country will pay its debts back in the future. And a country's ability to pay back its debts is usually closely tied to the state of the national economy.

But there was a problem. The data on the economy – the real statistics of employment, emigration, loan arrears and so on – hadn't improved at all in the period that had seen the Irish bond yields fall. Unemployment, which had trebled since 2008, was continuing to rise. Emigration was relentless, while mortgage lending had reached an all-time low; fewer Irish home loans were given out in 2011 than in 1972. House prices were falling at the fastest rate in the past three years, tax revenue was behind target, and the construction and industrial sectors were extremely weak. National income figures in the first three months of 2012 show that the economy continued to contract. And in Trackerville, the number of people in financial difficulty continued to increase. We were not turning any corners: all the economic indicators were pointing downwards.

Seen from a local perspective, there was precious little evidence to back up what was happening in the bond market. Unless of course, the bond investors understood that Ireland was a country run by people who were prepared to turn its economy into a large debt-servicing agency – no matter how weak the domestic economy became – and who were also intent on outsourcing the responsibility for building a globally competitive manufacturing base to foreigners.

So who was buying Irish government bonds, and what was influencing them?

To answer this question, we need to look towards Frankfurt, where the European Central Bank, long stifled by a limited mandate and unimaginative leadership, was starting to get creative.

The Central Banker's dilemma

The same week Enda Kenny met Bill Clinton in New York, Mario Draghi was celebrating his first hundred days in Frankfurt as governor of the European Central Bank. ECB governors aren't normally the type to pop the champagne so early, but Draghi was a break from the past, a sign that things were being shaken up a bit. After all, when the pope is a German and the head of the European Central Bank an Italian, you know things aren't quite what they used to be.

One of the decisions Draghi took during those hundred days is the key to understanding the Irish bond-yield puzzle; but before we look at that, let's look at the drama that made the bulk of the headlines during the same period: the crisis in Greece. While Enda Kenny was schmoozing the Americans, Draghi was preparing to address the ECB's top brass, as his phone constantly beeped with updates from the ongoing drama in Greece.

The Greek state had run out of money. Despite having been

granted two emergency loans from the Troika – €110 billion in May 2010 and €130 billion in October 2011 – it faced a default by early March 2012 and would need a massive loan to stave off the first sovereign default by a Western nation for fifty years. In return for the bailout, the Greek government would have to make more cuts. But the Greek economy had already contracted by 28 per cent since the crisis began. Over 100,000 Greek companies had gone out of business since 2009. Citizens were protesting on the streets. Austerity heaped upon austerity might have been what Greece needed to qualify for new loans, but was hardly the most reassuring policy if you wanted to ensure those loans would be paid back.

Greece had seen its debts rise substantially over the previous decade as investors from elsewhere in the eurozone mistook the absence of exchange-rate risk for the absence of any sort of risk. The promise of the euro was that all countries would become more German as a result of sharing one currency. But it didn't happen. Peripheral Europe remained, and remains, firmly un-Germanic. Indeed, it could be argued that the countries used German money and the promise of it to reinforce their own un-Germanness. They wanted a German lifestyle but didn't want to pay for it, so they took it on credit. When the Germans – and others – came looking for their money, it was all gone.

When a country is in straits as dire as Greece's, it has no choice but to default. Most creditors accepted this. The question was not whether Greece would default, but how the default would play out.

In February, Evangelos Venizelos, the Greek finance minister, was in Brussels begging his EU partners for more time in which to sell greater austerity to the Greek people. Greece had already slashed its primary budget deficit – that is, the deficit before you take into account interest payments on outstanding debt – from 10.6 per cent of GDP in 2009 to 2.3 per cent of GDP by late 2011. But the Germans and the other creditor nations wanted more, and they were running out of patience.

The man sitting opposite Venizelos at any number of meetings around this time was Ollie Rehn, the EU's commissioner for economic and monetary affairs and the euro. Rehn himself had been in a position not wholly unlike that which the Greeks now found themselves in. He was a member of the Finnish cabinet back in 1992, when Finland was facing the meltdown of its banks and the prospect of a long recession. After contemplating the austerity route, the government decided instead to burn its foreign bondholders with a surprise 40 per cent devaluation of the Finnish markka against the German mark – contrary to previous promises that it would not do so.

The underlying cause of the Finnish banking crisis was excessive property lending; the trigger was the collapse of the Soviet Union, an important market for Finland. Like Thailand in 1997, the Finnish government decided it had to let its currency fall in order to generate export growth. The devaluation meant that, although Finland repaid its markka-denominated loans at face value, the money repaid was worth considerably less than the money lent.

Finland did what most countries do when in a crisis: it acted to protect its own citizens, even though this meant burning foreign investors. So Rehn knew first-hand that it was possible for a respectable country to renege on its promises in order to return to prosperity, as Finland had. But Venizelos was in a much tougher position than that of his Finnish counterpart in 1992. Greece couldn't do what Finland had done, because it was part of a currency union.

The timing of this latest crescendo in the Greek crisis was driven by the repayment schedule on pre-existing loans. Greece, already massively in debt, was borrowing from tomorrow to pay for yesterday. Today wasn't even going to get a look-in.

Of course, with debt running at over 160 per cent of GDP, Greece was already in way over its head. Common sense will tell you the only way to fix a debt-ridden balance sheet is less debt, not more. But fixing their balance sheet was a distant goal. The Greek government was firefighting, doing whatever was necessary from day to day to meet obligations as they fell due.

Had Greece been a business, it would have declared itself bankrupt. Under the principle of co-responsibility, bankruptcy involves a cost both to the insolvent borrower – whose scope for business activity will be curtailed for a time and who will need to meet conditions before borrowing again – and to the disappointed creditors, who will not get all of their money back. The truth implicitly recognized by co-responsibility is that a loan is never a sure thing.

It is not common for countries effectively to declare themselves bankrupt, but it is not unheard of. Iceland more or less did it in 2008: the creditors were told they simply wouldn't be getting paid in full, and any repayment would take time. The Icelandic government tightened its belt, and allowed the national currency to fall dramatically in value. Not only has the economy revived but Iceland was borrowing on international markets again by 2011 and the value of the currency has rallied. Simply put, the markets have no memory. They move on. This is why they were prepared to lend to a country that only two years earlier had been a pariah.

Under capitalism, this is a legitimate way for a country or a company to right itself if it has a massive debt overhang. In Irish business we call it putting the company into administration; in America, it's called Chapter 11. However, within the eurozone this automatic righting process has been disabled, because of hyper-interconnectedness. There is a fear that if one country – or even one bank – in the eurozone defaults, it will set off a catastrophic chain reaction.

Greece did not declare itself bankrupt and default unilaterally on its loans, in part because the government wished to remain in the euro. Given its euro membership, it could not take the Finnish route and devalue. But default was inevitable. The only question was whether it would default within the euro, or finally conclude that the conditions imposed by euro membership were too onerous, and default outside of it.

In early March, in an agreement brokered by the EU, Greece defaulted on a tranche of €206 billion of government debt. It did not walk away from the full €206 billion. Instead, it issued new bonds to the value of €107 billion. Greece's creditors wrote off the other €99 billion. Ultimately, the default brought total Greek sovereign debt down to €240 billion, or 117 per cent of GDP.

It is interesting to recall how much rubbish was spouted just before the biggest sovereign default in financial history. Right up to the last minute, the ECB, the EU, various governments and the IMF all denied that a Greek default was possible or acceptable. Then the EU brokered the biggest sovereign default in history. Why? Because of the danger that Greece, exhausted by austerity and political unrest, would default anyway, on its own terms. Without a prearranged agreement, the moment Greece defaulted the price of their bonds would fall towards zero, as had been the case in Russia in 1998 and Argentina in 2001–2. This would show up on the balance sheets of the banks that owned Greek bonds and had to 'mark to market' these assets every day: that is, declare their value based on the current market price. Thus, if Greece hadn't hammered out a deal, the price of Greek bonds would have plummeted and banks would have had to take large losses. The EU feared, further, that such a default would be seen as giving other countries permission to default; the global knock-on effects of a disorderly Greek default, it was widely predicted, would be greater than those of the failure of Lehman Brothers. The Greeks had a choice; the EU did not.

For many in the financial markets, accustomed to seeing companies go bankrupt in difficult times, the problem of February and March 2012 was not 'Will Greece default?' It was 'What if Greece isn't allowed to default enough?' If the default did not resolve the country's debt crisis, there could well be another crisis not far down the road. However, the deal had to address a number of separate concerns. First, the amount of debt Greece needed to write off to improve its overall position had to be assessed. The default would have to be substantial enough to make a difference. The reason countries default is so that they can maintain current expenditure or demand out of their current tax revenues. If you want to maintain spending on hospitals or schools, your choice is between using your tax revenue to pay your debts or using it to pay your doctors. If the debt payments were still overwhelming after the default, there would be little point in defaulting. In such a case, you would suffer all the opprobrium of being a defaulter, while not being able to retain enough revenue for current spending – which would be politically unpalatable. It would also force the economy to contract further, because the money generated would still be going straight into the pockets of foreign creditors.

With regard to Greece, this concern had to be weighed up against the amount of money that the EU was prepared to come up with. There was, and is, a limit to how much citizens of the richer European countries will stump up. At the end of the day it is not only a question of economics but also of politics.

A separate concern was that any Greek deal had to address the extent of losses that banks could shoulder, given that their balance sheets were already fragile.

Finally, there was the not insignificant problem of the relative debt levels of the rest of the periphery. Italy's debt ratio was already 120 per cent of its national income – a bit higher than that of Greece post-bailout.

The challenges facing Draghi would have been difficult for any central banker. But the peculiarities of the ECB itself made his position even trickier.

The ECB is a strange hybrid. It is the central bank for a currency group comprising twelve independent countries, each with a different economy, a different set of politics and different views about what the role of a central bank should be. Traditionally, the job of a central bank in a crisis is to provide enough liquidity to get the system going again. This is, for example, why the US Federal Reserve was set up in 1913. Before then, successive banking crises in the US had to be solved by private banks coming together to bail out the private bank that had got into difficulty. Pre-1913, the legendary banker J. P. Morgan would have a whip-round amongst the big banks to provide a bailout fund for any insolvent banks.

A central bank is the lender of last resort; it lends to banks no one else would touch. In reality, although no one says so openly, this means that central banks are set up to be defaulted upon. And because it prints the money, it can't actually go bust itself.

One normal function of a central bank is to buy up government debt – in other words, to lend money to the government. Central banks tend to be careful about this type of financing, because if a government feels that it can just turn up at the discount window with lots of IOUs, getting real cash in return, two things are liable to happen. First, if the government over-borrows, there will be too much cash chasing too few goods. This will lead to inflation: as the value of cash falls, the price of goods rises and the rate of inflation takes off. Unions will then see that the price of things is rising and will move to get bigger wage increases. A wage/price inflation spiral could materialize, triggered by the government's initial over-borrowing.

The second potential problem is that the value of the country's currency will fall against those of its competitors, because the central bank is expanding the money supply too aggressively. Once this happens, the price of imports rises and the rate of inflation rises even more. The central bank can curb the enthusiasm of the government by raising interest rates, as demanded by inflation, the supply of bonds or exchange-rate targets. But this will put it on a political collision course with its own government.

My former employer, the Central Bank of Ireland, bought significant amounts of Irish government debt in the 1980s. This prevented Irish bond interest rates from rising as they otherwise would have, given the chaos in the public finances, and arguably encouraged the governments of the 1980s to drive up the debt ratio during that decade. In Latin America in the 1970s, governments spent and spent, forcing the central banks to print money; the result was wild inflation. Crucially, this was the type of policy that led to Germany's hyper-inflation in the early 1920s.

These episodes of extreme economic mismanagement are not the norm. But, because of this folk memory of inflation from the period of economic chaos in the early 1920s, and because that chaos is seen as having created fertile ground for the rise of the Nazis, the Germans insisted when they gave up the mark that the ECB would be explicitly debarred from buying up government stock. This makes it different from the Bank of England, the Fed, the Bank of Japan and other central banks across the world that lend money directly to governments at the discount window.

At this stage it is important to understand why the central banks are prepared to open the discount window to the banks in a crisis like the one we are experiencing.

We are suffering from a liquidity trap – the nexus where Keynes meets Kindleberger and Minsky. In a liquidity trap, banks don't lend and people don't borrow, so traditional monetary policy – for example, the lowering of interest rates to stimulate demand – doesn't work. The banks cease to function as the link between the central bank and the local economy.

In these extreme cases, the central bank must turn to unorthodox policies and increase its direct lending to the government. As a result, the Bank of England bought 42 per cent of new issuances of UK debt in 2011 and now owns 30 per cent of total gilt stock, compared to zero in 2008. The Fed in 2011 owned 11.3 per cent of all US Treasury stock, while at the end of 2010 the Bank of Japan had an 8 per cent share of its sovereign's stock.

If Draghi had had the powers of the boss of the Bank of England or the Fed, he would have followed the example of the other central banks and lent money to the Greek government. But the rules of the ECB made this impossible, and even as the crisis deepened, threatening the very existence of the euro, the Germans maintained their opposition to any deviation from this rule.

In this impossible situation, the creditor nations and the ECB felt they were the hostages in a kidnap drama, with Greece as the kidnapper. The Greeks knew that the possibility of pulling out of the euro gave them a powerful weapon. If they left – the nuclear option – the whole system might unravel. Both the EU and the ECB were terrified. Should Greece default chaotically, the fragile banks would take too much of a hit. But should Greece pull out of the euro and institute a new drachma, all hell would break loose, toppling banks across the European periphery. People in those countries would take their deposits out of their local banks because they'd rightly fear their own country would follow the Greek example.

As an economist, Mario Draghi knew a Greek default was inevitable. But he had to manage it as best he could. He had observed the inactivity of his predecessor, Jean-Claude Trichet, throughout 2011. He had seen the European banking system seize up in autumn 2011, when banks stopped lending to each other. So, barely a few weeks into the job, he knew he had to act decisively. He also knew that any meaningful action would put him on a collision course with the Germans, at the top of the European central-banking universe. But it was a fight he knew he had to take on.

Greece was the most urgent of Draghi's worries, but by no means the biggest. A Greek bailout would buy a bit of time; but Draghi's deeper fear – from day one of his tenure – was that bigger eurozone states would become insolvent as their bond yields rose. He had already seen sovereign-debt markets shut to three eurozone members: Ireland, Greece and Portugal. In the case of each country, markets had gone from mild concern to full-blown crisis in a matter of weeks. The lessons of contagion in Asia were not lost on Draghi. Default by Greece would be manageable; default by Italy or Spain would not be.

Italy and Spain were giants. There wasn't then – and still isn't – enough public money to fund them. Draghi needed to do a deal to coax fleeing private investors back into the market for Italian and Spanish debt.

Looking into 2012, he saw that Italy and Spain had to roll over close to €400 billion of debt. In the normal course of events – and all the more so in a debt crisis – governments will refinance borrowings as repayments fall due. But when the cost of borrowing starts to rise it gets harder and harder for a government to roll over debt. It faces a painful choice between a rising debt-to-GDP ratio and politically unpalatable spending cuts or tax increases.

Imagine what was going on in Draghi's head as he sat looking out from the thirtieth floor of the ECB's Eurotower in Frankfurt on his first days in the job, fielding calls from cautious Germans and anxious Spaniards while watching Europe's bond markets turn red on his Bloomberg screen as Italian and Spanish bonds were dumped. The share prices of banks all around Europe were plummeting. He could see, via the ECB's internal accounting mechanism, that there was massive capital flight from Spain. That chilled him.

If lots of money is leaving banks in Spain, the Spanish central bank has to replace that money with new money. So it goes to the ECB and gets new euros. In return it will have a debt at the ECB's account. In contrast, if Germany is experiencing inflows – Spanish money looking for a safer home – the Bundesbank will have to take this surplus money out of the German money supply – which it does by depositing the money at the ECB and getting a corresponding credit in its ECB account.

Draghi looked at the explosion of the Bundesbank's credits at the ECB and saw that they corresponded exactly with the debits in the accounts of the central banks of the peripheral countries. He was seeing a massive flight of money from the periphery to the core.

As a former governor of the Italian central bank, Draghi was well aware of his own country's predicament. With Italian bond yields moving towards 7 per cent, an added problem presented itself. Certain types of risk-averse investors – pension funds for example – have rules that govern whether or not they can hold a particular asset; once bond yields go beyond a certain threshold, or once the credit rating of the bond is downgraded beneath a certain level, they are required to sell. Such sell-offs drive the price down even more. In time, the selling becomes uncontrollable.

Draghi, looking out over the River Main, knew that Spanish and Italian bond yields were moving into the danger zone, and that only the ECB's muscle could prevent Spain and Italy from being locked out of the markets in this way; he also knew that flexing that muscle would drive him into a head-on confrontation with Germany.

Cash for trash

Draghi also appreciated that any parachute he came up with would need the full backing of the financial markets – the very players that had caused so much of the instability in the first place. His next move had to be one that would lead the European bond market from panic to stability.

European countries that had been running deficits for years needed to understand that busts could happen in Europe. They thought they would never need to reassess the mantra that governments can't go bust – that only happened to Latin American countries.

Draghi wasn't so sure. He was Italian, after all. Having spent much of his career at the top of Italian institutions he knew that sometimes pragmatism trumps rulebook certainty. More critically, he had served in the officer class in Goldman Sachs. He was as attuned to the concerns of the fat cats in Wall Street and the City of London as he was to those of EU apparatchiks.

Draghi couldn't buy government bonds himself, but he had to find a mechanism to increase demand for them, in order to bring down yields and ease the balance-sheet squeeze on the banks. He also had to inject enough cash into the banking system to ensure that the banks were strong enough to withstand another Greek grenade – which was sure to be thrown sooner or later. This would both arm banks and disarm the Greeks. Draghi couldn't tolerate the creditworthiness of other European countries, including his own Italy, being undermined by events in Athens.

But the basic problem remained. The financial markets were right to be worried about the fundamental dynamics at the heart of Europe: too much debt, too little growth and no political leadership.

The scheme Draghi dreamed up was ingenious. He would lend to the banks of Europe – and then persuade them to buy government bonds with the money. But the scheme overlooked the fact that the balance sheets of many of the banks in question were littered with assets of dubious quality: loans that might or might not be repaid. It was these assets that the banks would be putting up as collateral for the ECB loans.

In lending at keen rates to banks with poor collateral, for the purpose of getting them to purchase eurozone government debt, Draghi created the largest cash-for-trash scheme the world had ever seen.

The ECB already had a modest 'Long-Term Refinancing Operation', or LTRO, in place: a scheme for refinancing bank debt for periods longer than the standard biweekly or monthly maturation. Shortly after taking office, Draghi launched an LTRO that was much bigger, and had a longer maturity, than had previously been available. Through his LTRO offerings in December 2011 and February 2012, the ECB injected over €1 trillion into the European banking system; the loans were repayable after three years at an interest rate of just 1 per cent.

By offering cash to banks at 1 per cent for three years, Draghi was saying – to the Germans as much as to anyone else – that he didn't care about what happened to inflation over that period: his objective was to get money circulating to prevent the crisis spiralling out of control.

Looking at how the cash-for-trash scheme functions will show why Irish bond yields were falling in February 2012, even though Ireland's economy wasn't turning the corner at all.

Here's how it works. A bank – let's call it AIB – rolls up at the ECB's discount window. It presents a bunch of loans it made to Irish people to improve their homes during the boom. Everyone knows not all of these loans will be repaid, but the ECB overlooks this small problem and lends AIB cash at the super-keen rate of 1 per cent for three years.

AIB is not obliged to do anything in particular with this money, but what Draghi and everyone else understand is that the easiest thing for the bank to do is to lend it on to European governments at rates dramatically higher than 1 per cent. This is called a carry trade.

Under Draghi's scheme, banks in countries such as Spain, Italy, Portugal and Ireland were getting money for 1 per cent at a time when they could lend it on to their own national governments at dramatically higher interest rates. It therefore had the effect of getting cash into the hands of governments (something he could not do directly), fuelling demand for European sovereign debt on the secondary markets (where yields were getting dangerously high) *and* rebuilding the balance sheets of the hundreds of European banks that had availed of the scheme.

In the first two months of Mario's LTRO, Spanish banks' ownership of domestic government debt increased by 26 per cent, Italy's by 31 per cent, Ireland's by 21 per cent and Portugal's by 15 per cent. Meanwhile, German and French banks decreased their holdings of PIIGS debt substantially. National banks have now become more significant owners of their own national bonds. This obviously flies in the face of the aim of a monetary union, which was that national bonds of various member countries would be held by investors from various eurozone countries.

Critics point to this 'domestication' of European bond markets as additional evidence for their claim that the ECB is creating another massive bubble by accepting trashy collateral to create 'funny money'. These critics believe that there is no problem with government bonds going to 7 per cent or higher because it just reflects the fundamentals: European countries are badly run and need to be purged, and higher yields reflect real value. According to this analysis, Draghi's effort to push down the yields with new money is creating a bubble, because it pushes bond prices way up above their fundamental value – to which they must crash back eventually.

But creating liquidity at a time of credit crisis is what central banks do. The huge injection of liquidity and the agreed nature of the Greek default in March meant Draghi prevented contagion – temporarily at least. Because each time there is an official injection of money, less and less time is bought with more and more money. Mario's magic money bought time and stability, but it was rented, not earned. Throughout the summer of 2012, the eurozone-debt crisis became more acute, not less. As growth fell away, it became obvious that Italy and Spain might not be able to pay their way.

Far from kicking the can down the road – an image frequently deployed to describe what happens with each bailout and intervention – a better analogy for what is going on in Europe is rolling a snowball down a hill. The problem gathers momentum, gets bigger and bigger, and ultimately smashes when it hits a rock-hard immovable object. In this case, the immovable object is German public opinion, which is not about to assume responsibility for the debts of the rest without significant guarantees.

But by moving so decisively, Draghi indicated he is prepared to use the ECB for the whole of Europe, not just for Germany. By March it was evident he was on a collision course with the German element in the ECB and with Angela Merkel.

This was reinforced in June. On the night when Italy lined out against Germany in Warsaw, the Germans were hot favourites, only to be mugged by a clever, muscular Italian team. On that same night, Italy lined out against Germany at the European summit. Draghi knew this was his chance to play his trump card against the Germans.

The Italian threat to the Germans was: if you do nothing, Spain will fall to the bond market, followed by Italy. Then you will have to deal with a full-scale catastrophe. Spain had already lined up for a bank bailout, but had been bullied by Germany two weeks previously into taking all the bank liabilities on to the state's balance sheet. The Italians wouldn't let that happen again. With one of their own at the top of the ECB, they had one finger on the printing press.

They ganged up on Germany. And Germany, having appeared unassailable a few weeks before, realized a trap had been sprung. It backed down, allowing European funds to be directly injected into banks for the very first time.

This was the initial battle in what could be a long war between Germany and the rest of Europe. The scrap was always on the cards, but the rolling financial crises of the spring and summer of 2012 brought things to a head. By July, Germany was isolated and Draghi had engineered a situation whereby the German government was pitted not against the rest of Europe but against its own people.

This suited the Irish, who used the cover of the skilful Latin negotiators to get a 'me too' deal on bank debt – in principle. In practice, the terms of this deal will be down to our negotiators. As has been the case all along in the European club, the strength of the Irish position is mainly dependent on the misery of others.

And then, in early September, Draghi unveiled a new plan that drove a coach and several wild horses through German monetary orthodoxy. The ECB announced that it would now buy the bonds of peripheral countries in unlimited quantities.

It is a high-risk strategy, but one that Draghi was prepared to take, given the likely alternative of Spanish and Italian defaults. The move left the Bundesbank completely isolated in Europe. For many Germans it was tantamount to monetizing government debt, which, they remembered, was ultimately how the 1920s Reichsbank had stoked up hyper-inflation.

In less than a year, Mario Draghi has changed the face of European financial politics to such an extent that now the Germans face the prospect of plundering their own savings to bail out the Latins.

The battle for Europe has become a battle for the hearts and minds of Germans.

8.   Seventeen Weeks

Vivienne's stomach rumbled and she pushed her way into the bathroom. Mum had changed this room many times over the years, but as she sat on the loo, looking at the mirror emblazoned with the Irish Mist logo that her dad had triumphantly brought home from a pub quiz years ago, she reflected that it still needed some tweaking.

Jesus, she thought, I slept in my bloody mascara. Why couldn't I have gone to bed earlier?

Olivia was normally the one up till all hours, but she'd quit early on. Not the bride-to-be, though – oh, no, she had to sit there knocking back the wine with Claire, the other bridesmaid, who was back from London for the wedding.

She hadn't had a ridiculous amount. It was that sodding Dukan Diet she'd followed to fit into the size 8 Vera Wang hanging on her door. She hadn't eaten properly for a month and her body couldn't take the alcohol. This was all the fault of Kate Middleton and her bony British arse.

She shuffled downstairs. The Solpadeine took the edge off the pain, but things were far from shipshape. Someone was loudly trying to unlock the door. In the kitchen, Barry was whistling the theme song to *Doctor Who*, not very well.

He probably hadn't even been to bed.

'How's the form, Snow White? Rough night?'

'Feck off, Dopey.' She leaned unsteadily against the door. 'Make us a tea, would you?'

'There's a pot made,' he said, pointing at the table. She poured a cup and sat at the table, willing her head to stop thumping.

'You know, you can still pull out,' he said.

She gave him a look. 'The way I feel right now, I just might. What are you doing up so early?'

'Dad,' he said. 'The old man wants a hand with the speech.'

'And he asked you? Jesus wept.'

'Seriously. He wants me to dig deep and deliver some comedy gems. He can never remember anything. I was thinking of putting in the time you got caught by Sister Assumpta dipping tampons into a pint glass.'

'Barry, don't mess around with me today.'

'Or maybe an A to Z of all the lads you've rode.'

'Barry! Fuck. Off. I'm in bits. Jesus.' Vivienne surprised herself; she was on the edge of tears, just like at her communion when Barry blasted his new football at her. Barry's face right now was a ringer for his four-year-old self.

'Sorry – I was only kidding.' Barry peered at her, making sure bygones were bygones. 'Anyway, what kind of tart is the mother-in-law? I'd say we'll click tonight,' he winked.

'I hope you're not acting the maggot, Barry,' Mr Vickers's voice boomed. 'How are you feeling, darling? You look immaculate.'

She smiled as he hugged her. Dad always said she was immaculate. It was his thing.

Hours later, she said a silent prayer of thanks to the gods of pharmaceuticals as she walked up the aisle.

Vivienne wanted everything to slow down, so she could experience things properly, but the day was whooshing past like a bullet. It was a shame about the rain; that was what a red sky meant, she'd remembered too late; but the photos would be fine. John Paul had organized an expensive photographer and she was sure it would work out.

Still, the view towards the Sugarloaf was obscured by fog. If you knew what to look for, you might spot Lugnaquilla, but that was about it. To everyone else, the world beyond the windows was hidden behind a curtain of grey. If the clouds were anything to go by, the bar would soon smell of wet school gabardine.

The crowd bailed out of the church in double-quick time, eager to get the first official drink of the day. So many people had come back from abroad that it was a reunion as much as a wedding.

Vivienne surveyed her guests. The Devlins were back from Sydney, full of Aussie optimism and more than a few pies, by the looks of things. Billy Flanagan had flown from Canada with an exotic French-speaking girlfriend. He was chuffed; the smugness radiated off him. About twenty or so were home from London, all ready for the usual nonsense. Everyone was flying, catching up, looking back and looking forward.

She could see Barry in the middle of it all, buying rounds, while the rest of the family chased around the place after him so he could be in the photographs. At this rate they'd have to Photoshop his Facebook profile into the album.

It was beginning to dawn on Finola Noble – John Paul's doting mother – that this was not exactly the wedding she would have chosen for her beloved only son. It was a far cry from the marquee they'd organized for Natalie's big day a few years back. As far as she was concerned, you could keep your hotels: real class was an exclusive and private marquee in the back garden.

Finola was the sort of person poker players dream of. Every flash of anger, envy, fear and happiness was telegraphed to the world. Right now, her face was shooting an impending loss of patience into the wedding photographer's lens.

The two families stood in the cutting wind, waiting for a break in the clouds. The photographer was sure they were due some moments of sunshine very soon, he said. Everyone stood in a line – Barry and Dermot did the lanky man's stoop. Pascal looked like he had been squeezed into his suit. Olivia and Natalie were both in worlds of their own, while the two matriarchs were doing a reasonable impression of people enjoying themselves. Vivienne herself stood arm in arm with John Paul, staring steely-eyed into the future.

'This is it, guys – smile!' said the photographer.

Click.

★

Dermot Vickers didn't feel the best. He wasn't used to speaking in public. His mouth was dry; he didn't even want wine. He wanted to get the speeches over before dinner, but it was Viv's day. Finola, the groom's mum, talked at him for an hour over the meal. He didn't understand half of what she was saying, and reckoned the woman thought he was a bit simple by the end of it.

He heard the clink of metal on glass. Could you not give us time to digest, he thought, eyeballing John Paul's best man.

Dermot stood up. Be confident, you big eejit. It's Viv's day. In fairness, you're paying for it. He took a huge gulp of water and found some sort of voice.

'My Lords, Ladies and Gentlemen: how's she cutting? D'ya like the hotel? Glad you do, because yez own it now.'

A roar went up.

Later, when the music was in full swing, and everyone was either hanging out of the bar or each other, Olivia found herself alone with the father of the groom, Pascal Noble, at the head table.

'Did your father go there?' he asked, when Olivia's school came up.

'God, no,' she said. 'He was with the Christian Brothers.'

'Yes,' said Pascal Noble. 'We did worry about the best place for John Paul. In the end we went with the Jesuits.'

'Sure we all make mistakes,' Olivia said, smiling. Then quickly, 'He didn't turn out so bad,' when Pascal's eyes narrowed. 'The Jesuit schools do have a great reputation. Still, I think it's more to do with the teachers than whatever religious order is behind the school, don't you?'

'Well, obviously teachers are important. No one's saying otherwise, my dear,' he said, patting Olivia's arm. 'But tradition counts for a lot. Making the right connections and being in the right place are essential. At the end of the day, you can't buy that sort of thing. I have been thinking about tradition a lot recently.'

Pascal leaned across the table, making a show of whispering. 'In my opinion, we lost too much when we let go of the lessons of the past.'

'I'm sorry,' Olivia said, 'I don't follow. Like what?'

'So many things,' Pascal said, clearly irked by Olivia's slow uptake. 'The banks, for one.' Olivia sighed inwardly. It was an Irish wedding. Inevitably, someone would start the economy rant. Olivia just wished it wasn't the father of the groom, and that she didn't have to hear it.

'The banks? Sorry, I thought we were talking about the Jesuits,' she said.

'It all comes down to the same thing. If the reins of the banks hadn't been handed to blow-ins and upstarts, we'd never have got into this mess. It's like everything else in this country,' Pascal continued, warming to his theme, 'we've thrown the baby out with the bathwater.'

'In fairness, I don't think "upstarts" are to blame for the entire recession,' Olivia said. 'Plenty of people lined their pockets during the boom, and they weren't all johnny-come-latelys.'

Pascal snorted. 'That may well be, but all of the worst offenders – the Anglo gang, the Quinn lot, Ahern and his cronies, all of them in the racing tent – had one thing in common.' He paused for effect. 'Class. They didn't have any.'

'I don't follow,' Olivia said.

'Pedigree, a set of values, tradition.' It was clear Pascal was used to talking to an audience that nodded, not one that replied. 'The sort of thing you should learn in a proper school. They didn't have the background, so they didn't know what to do with all that money.' He swigged from his glass of Rioja.

It was time to bring the conversation back to earth before the old guy made an eejit of himself, Olivia thought.

'The wedding ceremony was wonderful, wasn't it? The priest was very good.'

'Yes,' Pascal said, thrown off a bit. 'He's a family friend.'

They sat in silence for a moment. Where was Sean, Olivia wondered. Had he gone to James's Gate for his pint?

Pascal shifted tack. 'How are your students finding the Leaving Cert?'

Now Olivia was taken off guard. 'Grand – you know. A little

nervous, but that's always the way. The Leaving Cert is such a big thing for them. To be honest, I think they'd be in better shape if there hadn't been so many cutbacks.'

'What do you mean?'

'You see all this money sent out of the country to pay off bond-holders,' Olivia said, 'then you have to tell parents we can't offer their child the support they need because our Learning Support teacher is being made redundant.'

'Perhaps the teachers should be taking a pay cut.'

Olivia tried to keep a lid on her irritation. 'It's not as simple as that. Either way, the amount of money saved by pulling extra language resources or cutting teaching staff is a drop in the ocean. The problem is bad now, but it's going to be horrific in the future. The education my kids will get, or Viv and JP's children – if they have some – is going to be a shadow of what it was or should be.' I should stop now, before things get out of hand, she thought. 'It doesn't matter whether it's provided by the Jesuits or the Moonies. The problems are much bigger.'

Pascal looked affronted. 'With respect, we must pay our debts, no matter how they were incurred. Of course it would be great to provide for everyone. I agree that the government could stand up to the Germans more, but if there's no money, then there's nothing we can do.' His tone implied he had struck the killer blow.

Olivia's back hurt and her glass of water was empty. Everyone else was dancing away; she had no escape from this windbag. Where the hell was her husband?

Screw this anyway, she thought. 'We do have a choice,' she said. 'We don't have to pay. We could tell the bondholders to get stuffed.'

'Oh for goodness' sake,' Pascal said. 'You're in a dreamworld. What do you think would happen if we shirked our responsibilities?'

'Nothing. Nothing would happen,' she said, raising her voice to be heard over 'Eye of the Tiger'. 'We can't pay what we don't have. It's basic capitalism – the bondholders know they don't have a leg to stand on. I don't care what anyone *thinks*: this is about survival.'

★

Pascal stared at Vivienne's sister. He had lost a lot of money on AIB shares, but you wouldn't catch him moaning about being hard done by. Their pension manager had told them banks were safe, so it was a shock, but these things happen. He wasn't about to air his dirty laundry in public. So what if bondholders of the same banks got rescued? Better to be down a few bob than a public embarrassment. 'At the end of the day, my dear,' he said, capping the subject, 'you simply don't welch on your debts. What would happen to our reputation otherwise?'

Deep down he was still the same lad who had escaped rural Carlow and worked his backside off until he reached the top of the heap. He was never going to reveal his hand to some lefty public servant.

He didn't understand why the Anglo guys weren't behind bars, but he was unwilling to be angry in public. Never make a show, his mam always said. Don't stand out, play the game, and you'll move up.

Vivienne's sister was a pampered child. She hadn't lived life as he had. In a way, he envied the freedom of this family, but it wasn't surprising that Olivia couldn't understand that one simply did not walk away from one's obligations. They were lucky – they'd obviously never had it tough. None of them knew what it was to have to take disappointment on the chin.

He would give her an insight, he decided. 'Survival is not just about money. We must be able to look the world in the face. If we don't pay our bills, who will ever do business with us? What would the rest of the world think of us, if we behaved like the bloody Greeks?'

Olivia was sick of the whole conversation. But she couldn't leave it. 'I'm no expert, but the only thing we can say about the last decade is that all the experts were full of shit. First the boom would never end, then house prices would never fall, then the IMF were never going to come in, then we had our final bank bailout, then another, and on and on. The only thing we can be sure about is that money is still going to be around and life will go on. Look at this wedding.'

She half hoped this would be the end of it. She'd ask him up to dance – it might defuse things. Then she could get home and out of this bloody costume.

But he was a dog with a rack of lamb.

'Serious countries pay their debts,' Pascal replied.

'We're not a serious country, though, are we?' Forget the bloody dance, she thought. 'Serious countries don't bail out the banks instead of people. Serious countries don't have the IMF running them, do they?'

Olivia could feel eyes turning towards them. The last thing she wanted was a scene. Just let it go, she thought.

Pascal hadn't noticed, or didn't care. 'We need our banks,' he said, his voice becoming louder and more strident. 'We can't move forward without financing.'

Pascal knew he was repeating a catchphrase. He knew he'd been taken for a ride, but he stuck to the line. 'Buy on dips,' the man had said, and so Pascal had bought AIB at €11 on the way down. The shares were now at 11 cents. Nobody knew this, not even Finola. Certainly not the children. It was his own cross to bear, and he was man enough to do so.

The more he lost, the more he defended the status quo. Everything was bound up in it. If only people would take their medicine, things would be back to normal in a few years.

'They're not OUR banks, though, are they?' Olivia was definitely losing her cool. 'My child is my child, but Bank of Ireland is no more my bank than the ESB is my electricity company. We get to choose, that's the whole point. If I don't like the deal, I can go elsewhere. If the banks screw up, it's their problem, not mine. They take their losses, risk and reward. That's the free market.

'Anyway,' she said, hoping to put a stop to this pointless argument before it got out of hand, 'whatever about all this, I'm sorry. You don't seem to like them either. All I'm saying is: I don't see why we should pay for the gambling debts of crooks.'

'I don't either. But that doesn't mean we welch on our debts.' Pascal would not stand back from this point. It was the cornerstone of everything for him.

Olivia was incredibly frustrated. 'So what's the argument about, then?'

'People in glass houses, Olivia. We can't all be permanently employed in cushy state jobs.'

I don't have a permanent job, Olivia wanted to say, and I'll probably never get one, but Pascal didn't let her get a word in edgeways.

'We need to trim the fat out of this country. We can't afford the welfare system. Those spongers get nearly €200 a week into their hands and all their rent paid. What incentive do they have to do anything except have more children?'

That was it. Olivia couldn't let that kind of bigotry pass. 'So now it's pregnant women who are the problem, is that it?'

'I didn't say that. I merely pointed out that a lot of money is paid out to things that can't be good for the country.'

'Oh, right, I'm sorry – I don't know what I was thinking.' She snarled: 'We should crack down on all those pesky young mothers. We don't want to encourage that carry-on. How about we sterilize them?'

Olivia became acutely aware that people were watching them. She turned. Vivienne stood, feet away, clenching John Paul's arm. He looked furious. Mum's hand was over her mouth, Barry was texting and Dad just sat, a defeated look in his eyes.

Pascal's face went white, as he realized that he was at the centre of a holy show.

'The thing is, *Pascal*,' she said slowly, 'there weren't any single mothers from Tallaght on the Bank of Ireland board. Only respectable people made the grade. People like you.'

She had no idea how far from the grade he was. But he knew and it hurt.

The table fell silent as Pascal Noble got up and strode out of the function room.

Vivienne stood with her mouth open, watching her mother-in-law and her husband chase after her father-in-law. She couldn't take it in. 'Are you happy now, Countess fucking Markievicz?' she asked.

Olivia was ashen. 'I'm sorry,' she said.

Patricia Vickers moved towards her two daughters – too little, too late.

'Viv. Let's calm down now, girls. Olivia, apologize. It's been an emotional day and everyone's had a few, let's make up now, sweets.'

Olivia was so tired, so stressed. She hadn't meant to hurt anyone. He'd started the argument. But the damage was done.

'I'm sorry, Viv. I really am. Sean, take me home. It's not good for the baby.'

'The what?' said Patricia.

'You heard me the first time.'

9. Let Them Eat Fish

The case of Iceland

On a beautiful clear spring day in March 2009, I flew to Iceland. The Icelanders had just told their bondholders where to get off. The 'serious' media and the Irish establishment were suggesting Iceland was a basket case.

The language deployed against Iceland was strikingly vehement. Our own finance minister described the oldest democracy in the world, with an elected parliament since the eleventh century, as 'a hedge fund with 300,000 farmers'.

The crisis that befell Iceland was broadly similar to Ireland's, leading to the widely bandied quip in 2008 that the difference between Ireland and Iceland was 'one letter and six months'. Maybe it was this comparison that led Irish politicians to stress that Ireland was no Iceland when the crisis hit.

Iceland's banks decided to use domestic deposits and, after that, foreign loans to back a small number of local oligarchs in their international investments.

These oligarchs bought all sorts of trophies. A good example was Björgólfur Guðmundsson's acquisition of West Ham Football Club in November 2006 for £75 million, 'plus an agreement to take on the club's £22.5 million debt', according to the *Guardian*. Guðmundsson was a colourful ex-con who had made his money in the gangster-land that was Russia in the 1990s. His wife used to be married to George Lincoln Rockwell, the founder of the American Nazi Party.

The chairman of the club, Eggert Magnússon, predicted West Ham would be in the Champions League in five years' time; but, while the Icelanders splashed the cash, it wasn't clear that they were signing the right players. According to Jason Burt in the *Daily Tele-graph*, 'There was something worrying during a transfer window in which West Ham had splashed out £7.5 million for Craig Bellamy, £6 million for Kieron Dyer and £7 million for Scott Parker, among others, and put them all on contracts worth more than £50,000 a week and capped it by placing Freddie Ljungberg, who cost £3 million and was the ultimate vanity purchase, on a deal worth £85,000 a week.'

The deal to buy West Ham was financed by the Icelandic investment bank Straumur. To fund big international deals like this and others, the Icelandic banks needed an exchange rate that was stable, so that they could borrow in foreign currencies, convert this money into Icelandic króna and then lend it out to local bigwigs if they wanted to buy something in Iceland. If they wanted to finance something abroad, they just had to borrow in the relevant foreign currency.

The Icelandic banks borrowed the foreign currency and lent it to the oligarchs, who then used it to pay for the trophies – which meant that the Icelandic bank had a liability in the foreign currency. If the króna were to fall against the foreign currency at some time in the future, the Icelandic bank would have a problem, unless it could off-load the trophy quickly. But quick offloading at a profit in a crisis doesn't happen.

The Icelandic banks needed to keep borrowing in order to feed the appetite of the oligarchs, who in turn provided the arrangement fees and the interest payments necessary to keep the Icelandic bankers in fancy dinners. So Iceland had to offer an interest rate to the foreign lenders that was above what they could get if they lent elsewhere. As long as the interest differential between Iceland and the rest of the world was positive and the exchange rate stayed stable, the Icelandic banks could raise plenty of money. If you think you have read this story before, well, you have – in its essence, Iceland was a colder version of Thailand in 1997, or indeed a version of what was happening in Ireland as the Irish banks borrowed abroad to lend to Irish developers to build the estates of Trackerville.

Emboldened by the thought that the króna would remain strong, the banks also coaxed locals into borrowing in foreign currency to take advantage of the fact that foreign rates were much lower than local interest rates.

But why were local interest rates so high? Because the Icelandic central bank had to finance a huge current-account deficit, itself the result of all this borrowing abroad. In 2007, the year before the crisis hit, the current-account deficit was 15.8 per cent of GDP.

Just to give you an idea of how monstrous the Icelandic banking system was becoming, total banking-sector assets – that is all the stuff they bought with all this lending – grew from 96 per cent of GDP in 2000 to almost 900 per cent by the second quarter of 2007.

Iceland was a monumental accident waiting to happen. Eventually, as investors started to worry about Icelandic banks' capacity to keep the entire scheme going, they pulled money out of the country. The central bank, hoping to keep the exchange rate stable, had to match this selling of króna by buying króna with its foreign reserves. But as in Thailand, the central bank only had a fixed amount of foreign currency. Initially, it raised interest rates to attract more foreign money; but, as we saw in Asia, raising interest rates at a time when people want to take their money out simply exacerbates the sense of panic.

By summer 2008, with global asset prices falling, a full-scale run on the króna was developing, as it became apparent just how much money the Icelandic banks had borrowed. When asset prices started to fall, Iceland's banks had far more debt than they could afford to service and the state was too small to entertain paying these debts just to keep the banking system solvent.

The country was on its own.

In a sense the very size of the problem and the fact that Iceland had no access to other sources of money – such as ECB loans, which were available to Ireland – meant it had only one choice. It waved its Nordic fingers at its creditors, abandoned efforts to keep the value of its currency stable and waited for Armageddon. In the absence of a state bailout, the banks quickly defaulted on their international obligations.

During the bubble period, Icelandic banks had applied for and received licences to take in ordinary deposits on the main streets of the UK and Holland. They offered slightly higher interest rates than the regular British and Dutch banks. When the banks in Iceland got into trouble, depositors in both countries panicked and queued up to get their money back, but there was none. The Dutch and British governments moved swiftly to compensate their local depositors and were intent on giving the Icelanders the bill. But the Icelandic president used his constitutional powers to prevent the Icelandic government from paying this money, because he felt that the Icelandic people shouldn't be lumbered with the bill for the Icelandic banks. A referendum on the issue was won comfortably and the upshot was that Iceland would pay a greatly reduced sum to the governments of the UK and the Netherlands.

By March of 2009, when I visited Reykjavik, all the major commercial banks had been put into administration, and the creditors had lost their money. The króna, which had been trading at 90 to the euro in early 2008, fell to 340 to the euro in October 2008. As the plane passed the Hebrides and pressed on across the North Atlantic, the question I wanted an answer to was: is there life after debt?

The money? It's all gone

Starting with the taxi drivers, the waiters and the barmen, I took an unscientific straw-poll, which suggested that even by spring 2009, in the immediate aftermath of the disaster, many normal Icelanders had come to terms with what had happened. They were not happy by any means; they raged against the local bigwigs and politicians who had caused the mess or turned a blind eye to it; but they were moving on as best they could.

Sitting in my hotel foyer, watching well-dressed young men and women, the sort of characters I remembered from my investment-banking days, it became apparent that the only people in Iceland who looked really worried were English. The City bankers pacing the foyer of the Hilton in Reykjavik were desperately looking for their money, a sea of repo men in Prada and Gucci. So wrapped up were they in their confidential missions that when I leaned over at break-fast and asked one of them what he was up to, he responded like an actor in a bad spy movie. Like his many colleagues, he wasn't at lib-erty to say who he was, what company he was from, or why he was there.

They were about as skilled at being undercover as Inspector Clouseau.

The new reality for the average Icelander was a currency that had been devalued by 50 per cent, no credit, and shops and cafés closing all around. But, even so, as the finance minister told me in a docu-mentary I made for ABC in Australia, the big things in life were going on 'as if nothing had happened'. The schools and hospitals were open, the bus system functioned, and people were getting up and going to work. Unemployment was rising, but it never rose above 9 per cent.

I asked the finance minister how the country's foreign creditors were going to get paid. He looked at me blankly, squinted and stated the obvious with the tone of someone who's said the same thing every day for months: 'We have no money, it's all gone.'

He paused and looked out at the ocean, past the little house made famous in 1986, when the Soviet Union and the USA, under Gor-bachev and Reagan, had begun the process of ending the Cold War and chosen Reykjavik as the neutral location where they would hold the summit. Scanning the icy waters below the snow-topped moun-tains that act as a natural barrier for Reykjavik Harbour against the roaring Atlantic, he looked back to me and shrugged.

'We can give them fish if they want.'

He wasn't trying to be funny. He knew there was no point in pre-tending that the money was there. There was no point in trying to borrow yet more money to pay back what had already been borrowed. If he lumbered the people with the debts of the past, it would impoverish them for generations. So he did the only thing possible: he told the foreign creditors where to go.

Later, I talked to a taxi driver who told me that his mortgage was in Japanese yen. He had been convinced by one of the Icelandic banks to borrow in yen at 2 per cent, as opposed to borrowing in króna at 10 per cent. The appeal of the lower interest rate was clear, but it exposed him to a massive exchange-rate risk: if the króna ever devalued against the yen, the real value of his debt would grow. The banks told him it wasn't remotely possible. But it happened.

He was left owing huge amounts of yen, with only his devalued króna wages to pay for them. He owed some bank in Japan a fortune. Things seemed bleak. But then he had a realization.

He shrugged his shoulders as we drove through the lunar landscape that constitutes much of Iceland and said, 'Tokyo is very far away – they will hardly come all the way here to get me.'

He laughed at the ludicrousness of it all – a former Icelandic trawlerman, now taxi driver, owing money to a Japanese bank for a house on a small island in the North Atlantic, five and a half thousand miles away from the Land of the Rising Sun.

Iceland v orthodoxy

According to the orthodoxy that currently prevails in Europe, there can be no quick way out of the debt spiral following years of a credit-driven boom. The conventional wisdom is that a country – particularly a small country like Iceland – that presides over a fall in its exchange rate will not get any competitive gain, because of the inflation that results from more expensive imports. Equally, the orthodox view is that a country that fails to cover the debts of its banking system will get punished by being locked out of the debt market for a long period.

Fortunately for the people of Iceland, the current European orthodoxy is wrong. Iceland refused to play the game of socialism for the rich and capitalism for the poor. Instead, the Icelanders let the normal rules of capitalism be applied across the board, so that the people and institutions that lent to Icelandic banks and reaped huge premiums in the good times took their fair share of the losses when the tide turned.

The Icelandic economy recovered quickly – in dramatic contrast to the similarly debt-blighted eurozone economies. Unemployment stopped rising in 2010 and has been falling back since. Emigration – although it soared dramatically in 2008 and 2009, particularly as Polish workers employed in the boom went home – did not become a fixture of Icelandic life. Having spiked to 18 per cent in 2008, Icelandic interest rates fell sharply to as low as 4.25 per cent, and are now edging up as the economy recovers. And in 2011 foreign investors returned to lend money to the Icelandic government in a successful bond issue.

In short, the Icelandic approach worked and the economy has grown in the past two years, just fourteen months after the biggest banking crash, relative to GDP, seen anywhere in the world, ever. Meanwhile, four years after the onset of the crisis, the euro governments are still struggling with debt and their economies remain stuck, with an ever-growing human cost in unemployment and rising poverty.

The Free World, tied up in knots

My taxi man with the yen mortgage dropped me off, chuckling at the bizarreness of it all, at the house where Gorbachev and Reagan had sat down to dismantle the superpowers' atomic arsenals in 1986. Just to the left of the house was the enormous new steel-and-chrome headquarters of Kaupthing Bank, one of the three big banks that nearly broke Iceland.

In one sense, much of the dramatic change that has happened worldwide in banking, currencies and financial markets in the past twenty years can be traced back to this little innocuous square in Reykjavik.

The 1986 superpower summit signalled the beginning of the end of the Soviet Union. It crumbled with remarkable speed – and when it crumbled, there was no counter-balance to the ideology of the man who sat opposite Gorbachev in Reykjavik that day: Ronald Reagan. And nowhere was Reagan's ideology of free and unfettered markets, led by a vanguard of speculative capital, embraced more thoroughly than right here on this small island in the North Atlantic.

But the end of the Soviet Union didn't just spell the beginning of an era of free capital movements, unregulated banks and the proliferation of hedge and investment funds playing the markets with impunity. It also led directly to European Monetary Union.

The crumbling of the USSR cleared the pathway to German reunification, and the Americans, having talked for so long of freedom and democracy, were hardly going to stand in the way of a united free Germany.

The French, however, weren't so sure, now that they were facing a much bigger and more powerful Germany, a country with whom they had been at war three times in the preceding 110 years. This new Germany might no longer be content to play the role described by former German chancellor Willy Brandt as 'political pygmy and economic giant'. What if the new Germany was more interested in events further east, diplomats in Paris wondered. After all, their entire post-war settlement was intended to anchor Germany in the EU, where France could remain its political equal.

The process begun in Iceland upset all that. Consequently, French bureaucrats came up with the idea of monetary union as a way of accelerating European integration and tying down Germany financially once and for all.

The genesis of the euro was political, not economic. Forcing together the economies of countries such as Greece, Portugal, Ireland and Spain with those of countries such as Finland, Germany and the Netherlands was an experiment that worked smoothly so long as massive capital flows from the core to the periphery masked the evident competitive differences between the economies.

Lessons of the Gold Standard

For students of economic history, the problems blighting the euro are highly reminiscent of the last time an exchange-rate system was imposed on disparate economies for what were largely political ends.

All the major global economies adhered to the Gold Standard between 1870 and 1914. The countries fixed their exchange rates to one another's, and those exchange rates were maintained by reference to the amount of gold each country had in its reserves. Given that the supply of gold was reasonably stable, this meant global money supply was more or less fixed. Each country could print money only insofar as it had the gold to back it up. This meant credit booms were very rare. It also meant that if one country did start to inflate faster than the others, it would suck in imports. And the only way a country could finance these imports was to sell gold, which in turn would contract the local money supply, leading to price and wage falls.

You might notice two things about this arrangement. The first is that wages had to be flexible downwards for the system to work. If a country wanted to rebalance itself, and to take the heat out of its economy, wages had to fall. It's worth reminding ourselves that there were no trade unions in operation – workers bore the brunt of any economic adjustments.

The second thing you might notice is that the objective of economic policy was to keep the exchange rate fixed; the real economy's needs came secondary to that. This is a bit like the way the euro operates today: competitive differences are reflected in rising and falling unemployment rather than in fluctuating exchange rates.

The Gold Standard worked reasonably well as long as workers didn't stand up for themselves and the countries involved didn't get into a war with each other. Well, both of those things happened in 1914, and as a result the system was abandoned. Governments printed money to various degrees to fight the war and inflation took off. When the war ended, there were attempts to get countries back to the 'stability' of gold. The move to return to gold was prompted by a desire to get back to political normality, which supposedly would be underpinned by the Gold Standard. But things had changed.

Prices in various countries fluctuated dramatically between 1914 and the early 1920s. For example, prices in the US were low because it had never been forced to print money as part of its war effort, so going back to the system at the previous exchange-rate parities would make America very competitive. But prices in the UK had risen dramatically, so locking British industry into a fixed exchange rate would make British industry uncompetitive, unless it devalued hugely ahead of the exchange-rate fixing.

The most terrifying inflation happened in Germany. During the period 1919–23, Germany experienced significant inflation, which culminated in hyper-inflation in 1923. Faced with strikes and starvation in the cities because farmers wouldn't accept worthless paper for crops, the German government realized that something dramatic had to be done. In autumn 1923, Germany decided the only way it could eliminate hyper-inflation was through a new currency linked to gold at the old pre-war level.

This succeeded spectacularly well: inflation collapsed in Germany. But in order to keep the new mark on the Gold Standard, Germany needed to ensure that enough gold flowed into Germany. It could either earn this gold through exports or rent it through borrowing. In truth it did both.

Germany's need for gold was exacerbated by the huge war reparations it was paying. This involved a net outflow of gold from the economy, because France, in particular, wanted to be paid in gold. But from 1923 onwards, America was prepared to lend gold to Germany because it saw the return to the Gold Standard as essential to the return of commercial, and thus political, stability in Europe. Germany therefore had to accumulate huge debts just to keep the economy moving at the prevailing rate of the Gold Standard.

This is similar to the position both Spain and Italy find themselves in today, having to run large current-account deficits to maintain their present standard of living within the euro. These current-account deficits are being financed in large part by ongoing loans from Germany and the other creditor nations of Europe.

At various times during the 1920s all the major economies returned to the Gold Standard for their own political reasons. As long as money moved with reasonable fluidity around the system, there was what looked like a return to stability. Interest rates fell and began to converge, as investors started to believe that normality had been restored to the global financial system.

However, in 1928, in response to the growing stock-market bubble in the US, the Fed had to increase interest rates. Once rates went up in America, everyone else had to raise theirs, or gold would leave their shores and head to the US – after all why would you keep money on deposit in Germany when you could get a higher interest rate in the USA?

As money flowed out of Germany and Britain and into the US, these countries had to start the process of deflation to maintain their Gold Standard exchange rates against America's. This development became particularly acute after the 1929 crash. In the beginning, like the countries of the eurozone, they all followed the orthodox approach of cutting spending and trying to drive down wages. But the problem was that wages didn't fall; as has been the case in Europe since 2008, unemployment just rose.

France and the US both decided to hoard gold rather than to reflate. Had France and the US allowed the inflows of gold to be reflected in an expanding money supply, and therefore lower interest rates and more economic activity, they could have acted as the loco-motive for growth. Equally, had Germany in the euro decided to use its huge current-account inflows to expand its economy with large tax cuts and higher inflation, the periphery would at least have had a chance to sell into a booming Germany.

In the period 1929–31 Germany tried to keep deflating and de-leveraging, as Ireland and the other peripherals are doing now. Tax revenue continued to fall and expenditures were cut. Yet Germany carried on following the orthodoxy. While this helped Germany to qualify for the loans that financed the budget deficit, it made the economy weaker and weaker.

Today Ireland and the other countries of the periphery are being asked to cut current expenditure, to raise taxes and to pay back all our debts – in our case, the odious bank debts. Germany was being asked to cut and cut, while still keeping up the reparation payments. As things got tighter, in 1931 the Germans declared that in order to stay on the Gold Standard they would have to abandon the reparation payments. It was one or the other.

The subsequent run on the mark depleted reserves: Germany didn't have enough gold to retain the gold parity. But, instead of abandoning deflationary orthodoxies, Germany imposed capital controls: the mark would no longer be freely convertible to gold. In so doing, Germany shattered the essence of the Gold Standard. Although the government declared the mark to be worth a certain amount of gold, this was meaningless, as it could not be exchanged freely. And it was the ongoing contraction resulting from Germany's deflationary policies that helped to create a political platform for the Nazis.

In Britain, the decision to take sterling off the Gold Standard was made by the prime minister – and he didn't even tell the governor of the Bank of England. Britain by 1930, like Ireland today, was constantly borrowing to maintain living standards and to maintain the currency peg. The resulting drop in the value of sterling allowed UK exports to move ahead, and Britain emerged out of the Depression quite quickly.

The US, under the newly elected Franklin Delano Roosevelt, abandoned the Gold Standard in 1933 because deflation and unemployment in the US had got to a level where social peace could no longer be guaranteed. Economic misery and political tensions prompted the president to act against all the advice of his advisers.

Roosevelt broke with the orthodoxy and engaged in a vast set of relief and stimulus programmes called the New Deal. This was made possible only by America's having left the Gold Standard: it could now print dollars without reference to gold or gold parities. Within a matter of months, agricultural prices in the US started to rise, coaxing farmers into more production and raising agricultural incomes. Industrial prices began to rise too, and production ultimately reacted positively. Abandoning the Gold Standard, together with the expansion of the government works programmes, allowed the US economy to begin to recover – a recovery that had evaded it when it was adhering to the strict deflationary imperatives of the Gold Standard.

Every financial or economic crisis is unique; there is no one-size-fits-all solution. But the story of the Icelandic recovery, and that of America's abandonment of the Gold Standard and its embrace of the New Deal, are suggestive for Ireland and other eurozone countries struggling under the yoke of debt and austerity today. These examples serve to reinforce the idea that there is an alternative. There is always an alternative.

10. Twenty Weeks

In the weeks since what Barry called 'The Alamo', something had changed inside Olivia. She realized she had no regrets. Her baby was growing, eating, moving, kicking and swimming around, all warm and safe. This was all that mattered. She felt brilliant, even though she had turned into the tummy-monster and looked like she had a donkey stuffed up her jumper. She didn't care. She was happy to rub her bump in the same nonchalant, what-the-hell-are-you-looking-at way men rearranged themselves publicly at every opportunity.

Olivia was – almost – carefree about the prospect of her conversation with Dick Murphy. She knew she needed to tell him the news before someone texted him to say that his history and Spanish teacher was pregnant. But she'd long-fingered it for ages. She couldn't stand the effect he had on her. She felt unnerved when he was around. He had too much power over her and her life. She'd feared she would begin by apologizing for being pregnant and then he'd wait in silence until she blurted out something about how quickly she'd be able to be back in school.

But now, instead of worrying about her job, husband, mortgage or little neglected Sam, who had started playing rugby for the local club and sleeping head to toe in Leinster colours, she was calm. Every morning the boy was there, right beside her, kissing her and telling her he loved her. She was so tired that she rarely heard him come in. But seeing him first thing in the morning, smelling of little-boy sleep, warm and vulnerable, right up beside her, arms around her neck, helped her feel that everything was going to be OK.

She had two free periods this afternoon, and so, as she often did, she went for a walk on the beach, making plans for the bump.

The tide was out at Sandymount Strand. It was one of those days when you felt you could walk to Howth. She took off her shoes – it was unseasonably warm for March.

She loved the crunch of the hard wet sand on the soles of her feet. The corrugated bed massaged her toes as she wandered, breathing in the pungent sewage-scented air, towards Ringsend. Her back was to the Martello tower, Howth was away to the right and the gulls were making a ferocious racket.

Half twelve and no one was around, bar a couple of ould fellas with metal detectors.

A lone figure, looking as if he was walking in from the sea itself, advanced in her direction. His stride was metronomic. She paid no attention – just another jogger – and continued chatting away to her baby.

She was worried about Sean. He had been scraping around with his part-time TEFL work, but there was still no sign of a permanent job.

The figure was much closer now. Olivia thought he seemed familiar, but the stride was a little odd. The purple windcheater and bedhead added to the strangeness. But once they had come within ten feet of one another, she knew who it was.

He spoke first.

'Hello, Olivia.'

He sounded oddly formal; like a job interviewer. But that's how she remembered him from university. He was always going somewhere, fast. Never hung around; friendly, civil and nice, but never more than that. In the library he'd always nod and chat. He was cute in a straight-boy-next-door way, but always a little bit distant.

'It's Damien,' he said, looking as though he expected her to have forgotten him. 'Damien D'Arcy.'

She smiled. 'Hey, I know. How are you?'

She knew things were awful. He was one of the public casualties of the crash. His imploding marriage had been in the back of the *Sunday Independent* because his missus had pushed the charity-ball thingy in the boom and was rarely out of the Four Seasons on her charity-lunch circuit. He'd appeared uncomfortable with the attention on the way up, but things were obviously even harder for him on the way down.

'OK,' he said, shrugging. 'You know the score, I'm sure. Dad's probably told you.'

Mike, his father, rarely mentioned anything, actually. He was courteous, like his son. He'd never bragged about Damien in the good times, and never sought sympathy afterwards.

'He mentioned you'd moved back home.'

Olivia imagined this man, who'd been on top of the world a few years ago, back sleeping in the same box room where he'd plotted his rise twenty years ago.

'Yes, well, there wasn't much choice, I'm afraid.'

Olivia didn't know the exact details, but the papers were full of it and he was the one who'd taken the rap.

'How are things now?' she asked.

There were so many like Damien. Guys her age who had soared, then crashed. Maybe nobody else she knew had done so as publicly as he had, but they were all broken.

'Pretty shit to be honest,' he said. 'Fucking shit, actually.'

Olivia was taken aback. This was the first time she'd ever heard him use such language. But 'fucking shit' gave her permission to engage, to be properly friendly and concerned. Irish people swear when they are comfortable with each other – it was something that the English people she used to work with years ago couldn't get their heads around. Cursing wasn't a sign of anger; it was a sign that you knew you were amongst friends.

'Yeah, I heard you'd been through the mill,' she said. 'This is a small enough town. I don't know what happened, but I had the impression you took the fall for something much bigger.'

She was surprised to hear herself saying this. She had no evidence to back it up. But Damien had always behaved well and seemed decent, like his dad. She had read in the hairdressers that the ex-wife had shacked up with the heir to a luxury-car franchise.

'Thanks, Olivia, that's really kind of you.' His voice softened and a hint of his cheerfulness returned. 'Everyone has their version of the story. Let's just say when those types of corporate giants collide, there are always casualties.'

Olivia didn't quite follow, but she nodded. The sand beneath her feet was cold all of a sudden.

'Why don't you head off to London, like everyone else? The whole of college is over there. No one cares in London what the hell happens in this little shithole. You could reinvent yourself easily. Jesus, Damien, we're still only young.'

Why was she being so intimate? They walked together in the opposite direction, towards Dun Laoghaire pier. She could see the sky darkening over at the Hell Fire Club, towards Three Rock. With the wind picking up, it would be lashing soon.

'Can't leave. Well, I don't want to. Our son's only five and he lives with Sonya. If I headed to London, I'd never see him. Things are bad enough already.'

Yes, Sonya, that was her name. She had been so beautiful in university, smart and tall – American tall, not Irish tall. They were the perfect couple. Of course that was until the shit hit the fan. She'd skedaddled pronto when it all went belly-up.

When the question came out, Olivia wanted to grab it and stick it back into her big gob. But it was too late. She'd said it.

'Do you come here often?'

'Only for the slow sets.'

They both laughed. 'C'mon, let's head back,' he said, 'it's gonna pour any minute. By the way, congratulations. Number two? You're very neat. Dad keeps me up on school gossip,' he explained.

Olivia found this intrusive, although it wasn't meant to be. It was strange to think Damien D'Arcy had been talking about her. He was the person who was talked about. Normal people, like Olivia, did the talking. Was it that, or the 'very neat' that threw her?

'Not so sure about the neat bit, but, yes, can't wait. We were just having a little private chat when you came along.'

'Lucky you.'

They were at the Martello tower now. Her feet were purple. Wet sand was wedged like sloppy cement between her toes.

'Great to see you again,' he said, zipping up his windcheater.

'You too,' she said. 'Might see you here again?'

'Please God. Take care of the pair of you now. Don't catch any colds.'

'You too, Damien,' she said. Like an eejit.

'Hey, if you ever need a cheap, second-hand, but decent lawyer, a bit down on his luck, you know where I am,' he said.

'You'd wanna be bargain basement, given my prospects,' she replied.

She tapped her bump and they both laughed. 'God bless,' he said, heading off into the drizzle.

11. The Good Room

Did your granny have a good room? My granny had a good room, which was so good that I wasn't good enough to enter it. Come to think about it, none of our family was good enough to enter it, except when very important people came to visit.

To avoid temptation, Granny kept the key hidden. As a child who'd overdosed on scary films, I was sure Damien from *The Omen* was hiding inside, festering away behind the locked door.

These 'very important people' were obviously better than us. They ranged from the local doctor or priest to the strong Fine Gael farmer with the good land over in the next parish. Whoever they were outside, if they made it to the good room they were definitely better than us.

There were obvious signs in the parish as to the type of people who might be worthy of entry. A great indicator was the position of one's pew at Mass. In suburban Dublin you grabbed any pew you could find. Not in Ovens, County Cork, though. A rigid pecking order existed there, and woe betide any who ignored it. The first three or four rows were reserved for the 'decency' of the village: the local doctors, the teacher or creamery owner, as well as a few big farmers and one or two others. My granny was well up the church. Given that she owned the local bar, her exalted status reveals something about local priorities.

As you moved away from the altar at half-eleven Mass, the social pecking order asserted itself ferociously, until you were left at the back with the poor labourers huddled around the *Sunday World*.

When the small-time dignitaries had been ushered in to the good room on a Sunday after Mass, china and cut glass were produced. My sisters and I and any cousins who may have been billeted to Granny's for the holidays were lined up like scrubbed little soldiers, our hair matted down with spit and our cheeks rubbed off us with wet hankies. The inspection of the guard started and we stood to attention.

Granny looked down on us with a face poised between pride and mortification.

Then the whole charade kicked off. My family pretended that it was totally normal for us to eat from delicate delph and sip our tea from china cups like little birds. The good room was infested with crocheted doilies – under cups, plates and ornaments, or just lying strategically beside teapots, reminding us that this was a strange foreign land where tabletops bruised easily.

The minute the decency got up to leave, all the china and cut glass were whisked from the table, washed and covered reverentially in old copies of the *Irish Independent*. The good cutlery was returned to the press until the next time the good room might be opened. The doilies were corralled into a press, which was locked, and the key put in an ornamental antique teapot.

Looking back, it was like a domestic Monopoly board. The couch, the unused piano (a very effective passive social statement), the drinks trolley and of course the bragging wall all added to the glory of the room and its owners. If we had a grainy photo of some distant relation who had gone to university in the age of silent movies or even earlier, we'd score extra points. Consequently, a relative in New Zealand, degree in hand, gazed out from our bragging wall for years.

In the good room, my granny's lovely, singsong Cork accent disappeared. In its place a weird noise came out of her, something like a cross between the Queen Mother and Marty Morrissey. For a child, it was terrifying. Some social-climbing alien had replaced my granny – more usually a country publican, always great fun and well loved in her navy housecoat. This alien was a creepy changeling who smelled of lipstick and talc and spoke as though her mouth had been replaced by a beak.

The good room and its affectations were in no way specific to my granny. I'm prepared to bet your granny or even your parents had a good room too. It was part of a big game of 'Let's pretend', driven by insecurity and self-loathing, that afflicted huge numbers of the Irish population. It was a desperate bid by the socially insecure to level the playing field and a sad admittance by self-loathers that they felt they were not quite good enough.

One rule of the game was not to embarrass anyone – not least ourselves – by admitting who we really were. So we play-acted.

Granny put out food she thought posh people might like. In the décor of the room, she adhered to an inexplicable symmetry: two china King Charles spaniels, two matching potted plants, two mounted plates with images of steam trains in North Wales on the bragging wall. Why have one of something when you can have two?

We weren't to know that having one of anything was not only acceptable but quite stylish or that being untidy was a sign of class – or even that plainer food is often posher. How could we? We thought it was precisely the opposite on all three counts. But then we also figured furry toilet seats were the height of style.

The good room allowed us to let on that we were posher than we were. Granny must have thought her resourceful pretensions made us somehow feel equal to 'our betters'. In reality, the good room only reinforced class divisions. The people we were trying to impress – the solicitor or the doctor – played along. But we all took part in the charade – them and us. The rules must have been handed down the generations like freckles, because they came so naturally.

Certain touches were initially perplexing until you understood the subtleties of the good room. For example, one of the first things I noticed in my granny's was an untouched bottle of Beefeater gin in the corner. The Beefeater and I would stare at each other as I necked MiWadi obediently in the corner after the Trooping of the Colour. But the bottle of Beefeater wasn't there for a regimental gin and tonic; it was playing a precise role. In Granny's head, the Beefeater gave the place a slightly British feel – because, despite all the nationalist rhetoric of West Cork, ours was a typical secretly royalist family. We might have spoofed about Easter Lilies, but we listened to the Queen's Speech on Christmas Day, were glued to Charles and Di's wedding as if they were our own cousins and loved the monarchy almost as much as hurling.

The good room was a remarkable waste of space. It wasn't as if my granny could easily set aside a third of the total floor area of the house just to impress the neighbours. But what the neighbours might think mattered tremendously.

The new good room

The good room is becoming rarer and rarer in Irish homes, but its spirit lives on in the way the Irish establishment has handled the financial crisis. For years, Irish and European interests were broadly in alignment – or at least they appeared to be. Those days are over. If Ireland doesn't get a comprehensive debt-forgiveness deal, the country will not recover. This puts us on a collision course with the mainstream EU position, and it also tests our abilities to put the country's interests first. As the Americans say, 'You don't get what you deserve, you get what you negotiate.'

Now swap my granny for our ruling establishment, and replace the posh local dignitaries in rural Cork with the richer countries at the EU negotiation table.

Why do our politicians get such bad deals in Europe? Why, when it comes down to the wire, do our senior civil servants seem to play such bad hands? Take the Anglo promissory note: why are we paying for an IOU given by a bust government to a bank that has closed down? And now that the Greeks and the Spaniards have given the EU the two fingers, why do we remain so pliant? When we do get a deal, it's because others such as Italy and Spain have done our work for us. If the Italians and the Spaniards hadn't mugged the Germans at the July 2012 summit, there would have been no result for Ireland.

At pivotal moments, it appears that Irish negotiators behave rather like my granny when faced with the local doctor: they adopt a sub-servient position and cling desperately to a notion of respectability.

We would rather default on future Irish generations than on foreign bondholders who didn't even expect to get paid. It is as though we don't want to embarrass our neighbours by reminding them that we're bust and that they actually lent money to banks like Anglo and expected to get it back.

Could it be that we are more concerned with the perception of respectability than with reality, grubby though it may be? Why, when we were evidently bust, didn't we call it like the Icelanders and tell the creditors where to go? We knew they had no choice but to come back to us, cap in hand, to take whatever deal we decided to give them, but, out of a desire to please the EU and the markets, we pledged to pay back every penny.

Or why, when it became apparent that banks had been lying about their underlying position, didn't we rescind the guarantee and force the creditors to take equity in the banks? This is how the Americans solved the massive Savings and Loans bank crisis in the early 1990s. They forced creditors to take stock in the banks. Their attitude was, 'If you were prepared to lend to these banks you now have to be prepared to own them.'

The chances to do better for the Irish people kept coming, and our masters continued to pass them up. Why didn't we – like the Greeks – force a debt deal that would eventually see the bondholders asked to cover part of the cost of their reckless lending? We paid, and are still paying, unsecured bondholders in Anglo and the other banks, even though the whole point of unsecured debt is that it will not be repaid if everything goes belly-up. What were we thinking? What bit of the word 'unsecured' don't we understand? Why do we wrap ourselves up in knots with all sorts of promissory notes, incurring yet more debt, when the problem is too much debt in the first place?

Could the reason be that we haven't really left the good room at all? What if our negotiators' overriding concern is to avoid upsetting the swankier neighbours who, we suspect, are better than us? What else could explain the behaviour of the past four years? At every stage the interests of the Irish people have been subservient to the institutional concerns of our neighbours in the EU.

In fact, not only have we stuck rigidly to the mantra that we'll pay every single one of the debts we ran up at home, but we've said we'll help to pay everyone else's debts too, so keen are we to pay creditors. Thus, even when faced with national bankruptcy, our finance minister wrote a €1.3 billion cheque for the first Greek bailout.

The purpose of the bank guarantee ought to have been to prevent a bank run and then to give all the chips to the government: announce a guarantee, but one limited in time and scope and subject to whatever conditions the government might wish to impose. This would have allowed the state to use the period of the guarantee as a negotiating window with creditors, while simultaneously stopping the bank run that was under way in September 2008.

But, instead of doing this, the government decided to extend the guarantee and to pay everything.

In addition, in October 2010 the ECB bullied the Irish government into paying all bondholders, both secured and unsecured. It threatened to withdraw access to the ECB's discount window for Irish banks if we didn't do this. At this stage, we could have easily stood up to them and just said no. We didn't. Trapped in the psychology of the Good Room, we didn't want to admit that we were bust, so we bluffed and blustered like my granny would have done in the presence of her betters.

The referendum in May 2012 wasn't about whether to have a law saying that the state can or can't borrow money. The government's tactic was to lecture us about the shame of embarrassing ourselves in front of our betters. The 'Yes' campaign suggested that voting no was the equivalent of handing the chipped mug used for toothbrushes to the priest instead of the fine china. Our politicians wagered that we were worried more about mortification than about amortization. Even as our growth rate plummeted and our rate of unemployment rose, it seemed that our main political concern was to be seen to tolerate any privation in the name of respectability. Politicians came back again and again to the word 'reputation'.

On the campaign trail for the Fiscal Compact, Enda Kenny warned, 'I do not want to see any damage done to our reputation; any lessening of the confidence that we have from foreign investors coming in here.' Matthew Elderfield, deputy governor of the Central Bank of Ireland, said much the same thing: 'It is vital that we do whatever is necessary to protect and improve the reputation of Ireland as a financial centre.' Michael Noonan's choice of metaphor at the Bloomberg Ireland Economic Summit in Dublin was perhaps the most revealing. Likening Europe to – what else? – a golf course, the minister for finance said he didn't want Ireland to be a pavilion member, 'allowed to drink in the bar, but not play the course'.

Clearly a country's reputation matters. But when you are in an IMF bailout programme, you've lost your reputation. Perhaps the best solution to the dilemma of the Good Room is to have no need for one in the first place, to refuse to endure the charade and to stop being obsessed with what others think of us.

The EU has become the diplomatic equivalent of the local swanky solicitor – the Dick Moran-in-*Glenroe* type. Once we're in the good room with such a figure, we pretend everything is fine rather than admit how dire our straits are. Ah, yes, sure a bit of austerity will do us just grand, we say; even though all the objective evidence from economic history indicates that austerity without debt forgiveness simply cannot work. We smile helplessly, taking solace in being the poster boy for austerity, even as our national economy judders to a halt. Our political leaders and negotiators in Europe do the bidding of their real masters rather than looking after the interests of the eejits paying their wages.

My personal experience of this dynamic was in the early 1990s, while working at the Central Bank of Ireland in Dublin. We would prepare reams of briefings for the central bank governor so he could use them to make the Irish position heard at EU meetings in Brussels.

But what actually happened? He said nothing. The detailed minutes of the meetings revealed that the British and the Danes, in particular, queried and questioned everything in the run-up to the Maastricht Treaty. Our delegation rarely spoke up for Ireland during the negotiations in the run-up to the creation of the euro.

Rather than weigh up the options in the Irish national interest, we opt for being what is called good Europeans. We ignore basic economic realities and, in so doing, behave like my insecure granny in the good room. Our horror of being awkward and honest in assessing our own position – as the British and the Scandinavians were when they decided to stay out of the single currency – meant we turned the discussion against ourselves. We asked: 'Are we good Europeans?' Only good Europeans, we believed, could be admitted to the good room. Standing up for ourselves might mean being bad Europeans, and we couldn't have that.

We also worry about what the neighbours think whenever the Irish state tries to raise money on the financial markets. Remember, we are only borrowing: refinancing old debt or taking on new debt. That's all a bond issue is. The favoured short-hand for a successful Irish bond auction is 'The issue was oversubscribed.' What does this really mean? It means that at that price, there was more demand than could be met by the available supply. Think about selling a car. If you put the price at €5,000 and loads of punters turn up with offers, what is that telling you? It is telling you that you are selling too cheaply, so you should increase the price.

Now consider the notion that oversubscription on a bond auction should be regarded as a sign of success. Yes, it means you look good and people are interested in your bonds – but only because you are giving them away too cheaply.

Look, for example, at the bond auction on 5 July 2012. Ireland sold €500 million in three-month bills in the first bond sale since 2010. Our finance minister, Michael Noonan, was over the moon. He called it an 'important milestone on Ireland's continuing path to recovery'. The bills yielded 1.8 per cent. The issue was, the *Irish Times* reported, 'healthily oversubscribed'. Rather than being relentlessly commercial and achieving the keenest interest rate for the Irish people, the state's official ambition is to have an issue oversubscribed. In the real world, this is a sign not of success but of relative failure, because the bonds have been pegged at a giveaway price.

But it sounds good and that is what counts.

Because of the Good Room mentality, we think keeping the head down will curry favour with our new masters. We take pride in the fact that the Germans don't regard us as being as bad as the Greeks. Instead of doing a deal on our own terms, we are waiting for the German people to give their politicians the permission to treat us favourably.

Over the past year, Ireland had plenty of opportunities to seek common cause with Greece, Portugal, Spain and Italy – but didn't. We didn't want to be associated with them, even though an alliance with these countries would have made lots of sense. In terms of the Good Room mentality, aligning with the Mediterranean countries would have reinforced the accurate but unpalatable idea that we are second-class citizens. Like my granny, we preferred a frosty reception from our betters to a generously warm hug from our equals.

In the end we are happy for other countries to do the dirty heavy-lifting, while we keep our hands clean in the good room.

12. Twenty-four Weeks

Hail Mary, full of grace, the Lord is with thee,
Blessed art thou amongst women and blessed is
   the fruit of thy womb, Jesus
Holy Mary, Mother of God, pray for us sinners
Now and at the hour of our death
Oh Sweet Jesus, make sure we all do the right thing

There had been a run on devotion candles. Patsy Vickers groped around, elbow deep in the candle drawer, but there wasn't a single one left. The butcher and the baker might be down on their luck these days, she thought, but the candlestick-maker is earning a bomb.

'Ah, Patsy, sure you mightn't be going to Mass,' chuckled Father Declan half accusingly as he met her in the aisle, 'but you're still saying your prayers.'

Our Lady of Good Counsel, one of those enormous 1970s churches, figured in the background of most of the photos on Patsy's mantelpiece at home. Hairstyles came and went – mullets, bobs, mop-tops, backcombed frights, shaggy perms, spikes, fins – and, to judge from the photos, the Vickers were as good a fashion barometer as any. But the local church remained a constant through the decades.

There was Patsy in 1980, doing her best Purdey, Olivia just baptized in her arms and Dermot grinning dementedly, like Eddie Gallagher crossed with Rory Gallagher, as if the whole baby thing had nothing to do with him. A year later Patsy stood with her backcombed Kim Wilde do, squeezing Vivienne.

On to the summer of Jack, when Ray Houghton put the ball in the English net, while the Vickerses sweated at Olivia's first communion. There was her daughter, a gap-toothed child bride clutching a pink Sony ghetto blaster, ready to beg shamelessly. And behind her was Patsy, now all shoulder pads and big hair, while five-year-old Barry, with a big orange 'fro of his own, wore the smallest Liverpool FC kit imaginable and squinted, face full of freckles, into the Kodak. Sticking with the Scouser theme, Dermot was now a cross between John Aldridge and a Latino crim in *Miami Vice* – sleeves rolled up and big 'tache.

Through it all the church remained the same. You never have to paint over brown sandstone. Even when they moved up to a detached new house around the corner from the old house at Carrickmelton Lawns, they still usually made it to half-five Mass, until, eventually, like almost everyone else, they stopped going altogether.

Patsy had been on the way to her mother's, but for some reason had pulled in to the church. Maybe it was hearing on the car radio the news of more redundancies at the banks, but, whatever it was, she walked up the aisle with the confidence of a daily communicant.

She crossed herself, and felt her knees creak as she knelt in the quietness. In the light from five candelabras blazing in the darkness, Patsy considered the general upheaval in their lives. Olivia was pregnant and broke; Vivienne's job at the bank might be in danger; Dermot owned two empty holiday homes in Wexford; Barry – the only sane one, the only solvent one – was about to plough all his money into yet another business venture. And of course her mother was still there, interfering and giving advice. Better get it over with, she thought, leaving Father Declan and his candelabras to their devotion.

The little houses of St Patrick's Crescent were spick and span. The Blessed Virgin Mary stood spotless, the lawn around her full of forget-me-nots. The chipper was still there, with a different Calabrian surname over the door. Mr Mooney's shop was now a Spar with automatic doors, but, apart from that and the 4 × 4s clogging up the pavements, the Crescent hadn't changed much since the 1960s.

Patsy's mother, Bubbles Fagan, née Lockhard, was putting food out for the cat on the sill when she arrived. The rant commenced with no preliminaries.

'I mean, what in God's name is the child doing in a Protestant school? My great-grandchild! Are her own not good enough for that child of yours?'

'Mam, it's her life. Olivia is a grown woman,' Patsy said. 'And she'll be here any minute. If you have anything to say, say it to her face.'

If she heard, Bubbles didn't show it. 'And she's going again, did I hear you right? What'll it be this time, a Methodist? At least it's not going to be black. Have you seen the young wans waddling around in Tesco's with their wild little half-castes hanging out of them?'

Oh, Jesus, Patsy thought. Her mother was warming to the theme.

'Mam, Olivia is an adult. She has her own life to lead.'

'Well, why do you be babysitting the children?' Bubbles was triumphant. 'If they are all so adult, can't they look after their own children, like we did?'

'It's different now, Mam, they have to work.'

'Work me eye, sure they're all on the labour. Teresa, meself and Ann were down in Our Lady's, you know the hall, on Thursday and there is hardly a grandchild working amongst us.'

'Do we always have to have this argument, Mam? Olivia's working, Vivienne is in the bank and Barry's starting his own business. You know that.'

Bubbles brightened. 'How's Barry?' She'd always had a soft spot for him. 'Any sign of anything?'

This was her mother's shorthand for meeting a nice girl and settling down. But Barry was not the type. Not yet, anyhow.

'Here, at his age your father and I had our children almost reared. Did you tell me he's moved back home? Sweet Lamb of God.'

'He's just getting his own place done up, so he's back with us for a few weeks. You know Barry, always on the go.'

Barry was plotting his new venture, always at the computer, making a website or whatever. It was something to do with puzzles and furniture. Barry was good with numbers; nothing fazed him. He'd be fine, but it still annoyed her that the fridge was always empty, his clothes were everywhere, and his friends seemed to have moved in too. Patsy and Dermot had just got used to having a bit of time on their own for once, and, much as she loved him, the house was starting to feel like a youth hostel crossed with a crèche. Now it looked like it was going to be an old folks' home too.

Patsy sat in her mam's kitchen, where they used to sit around the Superser when she was a girl, watching Jimmy Savile on the HP telly every Thursday introducing *Top of the Pops*. She steeled herself to say what she had to say.

'Mam, you can't stay here on your own.'

'Who says?'

'Doctor Leary.'

'Don't you Doctor Leary me. Sure, he thought your father had indigestion when he was dying.'

That wasn't true. Doctor Leary had told Daddy his chest pains were serious. It was Joe Fagan who said it was only the dinner he was after having. But in the family folklore, usually written by Mam after the event to suit herself, Doctor Leary, the nicest man you'd ever meet, was guilty.

She'd never say this to Doctor Leary, mind.

'He'll have to take me out of here in a box.'

'But, Mam, one more fall and you're a goner. You can barely get up the stairs. And would you ever charge that mobile I bought you?'

'What's wrong with the phone on the hall table? Forgotten the number?'

How could she forget her family phone number?

'I remember your father said he could time his watch by the phone call every Saturday night when you and Dermot were courting out there in –' She stopped for a moment, jabbing her finger at Patsy. 'What was that place called again? The Grail? The Garden? The Grove. Yes, that's what it was.'

Mam was in full nostalgia mode now. 'And your father would get up and drive you in the Sunbeam – only decent car on the road, mind you – and the three Clancy sisters home. That Dermo always smelled like St James's Gate. You were no better – a walking ashtray. But those Clancy girls were a sight dressed up like Five Lamps brazzers, God knows how Winnie Clancy, Lord have Mercy on her, let them out like that. Anyway,' she sniffed, 'the mobile's only a cod with all that charging and plugging in. You'll want me texting next.'

'What about the leg, Mam? You can hardly walk.'

'I can walk fine.'

'No, Mam,' Patsy said gently. 'You can't. You haven't been out in days.'

'Not true.'

'Mam, come home with us. We have loads of room. The garage is extended downstairs. You'd have your own bathroom, hall door and us – all of us – around you.'

'This is my home. Didn't I bring you all up here?'

Patsy sighed. She could see why her mother didn't want to leave this place: the spotless kitchen that she ran like a sergeant-major; the Sacred Heart that had scared the life out of her as a girl; the child of Prague; the good room with its brass coal bucket, brush, shovel and tongs. This house was her mother's creation, her domain.

But the redoubtable Bubbles Fagan, née Lockhard, was faltering. The past few winters had put years on her.

Patsy watched her as she made the tea. There was still the same heart, the same humour. She was still full of life, her soft brown eyes still alert, but her body was worn out. Her strapped ankle was bothering her more and more these days. Patsy knew she was hiding the limp.

Bubbles tried to change the subject. 'Anyway, how's Olivia? Having another babby. Isn't that great.'

'She's OK,' Patsy said, 'but she nearly destroyed Viv's wedding. Sure you were there, but you didn't hear the half of it.'

'Oh, I did, Barry told me.' Mam grinned. 'He couldn't wait. She's a spiky young wan, that Olivia of ours. Didn't lick it off the ground but. Like my own mother, the same Eyetalian black eyes on her. But you know where you stand.'

Patsy only vaguely remembered Nanny Lockhard – daughter of a Dublin Fusilier who had married a staunch republican, Frankie Lockhard.

'She's got terrible cramps in the legs, Mam. Has her up in the night. She's anxious about the bank too, so she can't get back to sleep, or so she tells me.' Patsy was very worried about Olivia. She and Sean seemed to be so up against it. They were due a bit of good luck.

'What's she worried about the bank for?'

'The young ones are all the same, Mam, they're up to their gills in debt. It has them up the walls.'

'Debts? For what?'

'For the houses, Mam.'

'Houses? Sure aren't all the houses still there? Aren't they still in them?' Mam squared her shoulders. 'They should tell the banks where to go. If your father was around today he'd have run them. He'd have given them a bunch of fives. Bloody moneylenders.'

Mam warmed to her theme. 'Sweet Lamb of God, is this what the bould Frankie Lockhard was holed up in Boland's Mill for with Mr De Valera? He only a young fella and the Brits taking potshots at them. Is this what he and them patriots fought for?'

The brown eyes were alight now, dancing.

' "There's no diehard like Frankie Lockhard," that's what they used to say. Did you know that, Patsy?'

Of course she did. How could she not? Mam had only gone on about it for her entire life.

'It's not that easy any more, Mam – not as black and white as it was back then.'

'More Black and Tan than black and white in them days. It wasn't easy then, love, but you knew where you stood. Tell Olivia her nan says she should tell the banks to go and jump. Mr De Valera, God rest him, wouldn't have put up with this codology. Young people slaving away to pay off moneylenders for the rest of their working lives and their children brought up by their nans because of it. That's not right, Patsy.'

She paused to scald the pot.

'Tell Olivia to stay where she is, look after her young lad and look after her new baby. Tell them banks where to go.'

Bubbles Fagan stopped under the Sacred Heart and smiled at her daughter, soon to be her landlady.

'But also, tell her from her nan, who will be eighty-three this year, enough of that Protestant malarkey for the young lad. Isn't the world mad enough as it is, without that class of carry-on?'

She put the pot down.

'There's no call for it. Now, get the door, would you? Like a good girl.'

Olivia was mortified. Not merely by the size of the knickers she had just bought in Penneys but by the fart that announced her arrival at the back of the queue at the checkout. She couldn't help herself – with the baby everything was squashed together: the slightest move squeezed something somewhere. She was a walking whoopee cushion.

People who hadn't had children – like the two teenagers in front of her – couldn't believe their ears.

She thought she had perfected the silent release, followed by disapproving nose wrinkling, as if to signal that it couldn't possibly be her, the fragrant lady with child. But stuck in the queue, after the shock of buying knickers that could double as duvet covers, she couldn't stop it. Now she had to move swiftly, which at twenty-four weeks is impossible to do in a dignified manner. Sneaking off discreetly isn't really an option when you move with the grace of a yeti.

Later, on the way to her nan's, she heard the redundancy news about the banks on the radio while she was rearranging the cushion, making sitting slightly more bearable. The seat belt didn't do a good job at anything other than accentuating her bump.

All set in there, baby? All good, Una?

For some reason, she'd started calling the baby Una. Sean quite liked it. She'd thought she hated the name, but something about it was beginning to stick.

When she got to Nan's she saw that Barry had beaten her there, and was unpacking the messages when his sister came in. Their mother had asked them to join her and Bubbles for dinner.

'Here comes the cookie monster,' he announced, as Olivia waddled into the cramped kitchen.

'Triplets, Nan,' he smirked.

'Up yours, Jaffa-head,' she replied.

'Now, now,' Nan said. 'Your little Sammy has the red Vickers gene too.'

The Fagans and Lockhards were all, as Nan used to say, 'a bit Eye-talian'. 'Touch of the tar brush' was how Grandpa used to put it. Like De Valera, the best Irishmen were all a bit foreign.

When Patsy was young, the other kids in St Patrick's Crescent used to slag her off with 'Two smoked ray and large please, Patsy.' She and her twin brother, Josey, were known as 'Salt and Vinegar' until they were nearly out of school.

Olivia wondered if the dark genes would dominate this time. A Fagan or a Vickers, red or black, brown or blue, freckles or moles. She didn't care, really.

'Now sit down there and take the weight off your feet, love.'

Nan was in her element, with lots of bodies to command. 'Barry, get up and let your sister sit down and make us all a cup of Rosie Lee. Now, love, your mother tells me you're worried about them banks.'

'It's just the mortgage, Nan,' Olivia said. 'It's going to be tricky when this one arrives, but it's grand, don't worry.'

Everyone glanced at the bump. Bubbles put her hands on her granddaughter's tummy, the way you'd hold a basketball. She was delighted. Another great-grandchild was always good news.

Looking at her nan, but talking to her brother, Olivia continued. 'Our mortgage is moving to a variable rate. The rate is actually going up, even though interest rates are supposed to be at an all-time low.'

'Crooks the lot of them,' said Nan.

Patsy had had it up to there about the bloody mortgages, houses and banks, but secretly she felt guilty. She remembered the night she had urged them to go the extra few grand and stretch to Wicklow. Before Barry could answer, she said to no one in particular, 'They said they always went up. We thought prices would only keep going up.'

Bubbles turned to her daughter. 'Why did you believe that tripe, Patsy? I've lived in this city for over eighty years. Houses have gone up and then down. Sure remember when you moved into the swankier house out of Rory O'Connor Park, when Barry was only a bonnyer? The houses were cheaper than when they had been built, what year was that again?'

'1983,' Patsy answered.

'Right. So them houses were built in the 1970s, by Whites the builders out of Baldoyle, and they were cheaper ten years later.'

Barry made four cups of milky tea.

'But the interest rate going up must be a mistake, Barry, right?' Olivia asked.

'I doubt it, Liv. Here's the deal.' Barry rubbed his thumb and forefinger together. 'The banks have to raise money to cover their losses on the loans that have gone south. If you read the paper, you'll see ads of 4 per cent interest on big deposits. So if the banks are giving some saver 4 per cent on deposits, they've got to charge you 5 per cent for your borrowing. Otherwise they'd go bust.'

Patsy spoke up. 'What about the interest rates being the lowest ever?'

'The ECB rate doesn't matter a shite when the banks are bust. Sorry, Nan. They need to get in as much in the way of deposits as possible and charge as much to borrowers as possible. Now don't get me wrong, this won't go on forever, but it could be at least another five years.'

'Five years? Fuck's sake,' Olivia said.

'Language,' Bubbles said. 'And you a schoolteacher and all.'

Barry continued, 'Or however long it takes them to pay back all the money they borrowed or until they can get their house in order.'

Patsy looked resignedly into her tea. All their hard work, herself and Dermot saving and scrimping and doing without, for this. Jesus, they'd even sent the girls to elocution lessons. Now they were all back in her mother's kitchen in a proud little 1940s corporation house that no one had ever owned, and everything was falling apart.

Bubbles, though, was beaming. 'Telling you, Patsy, I always said Barry's the smartest Fagan we ever produced. Remember when they were calling him queer on account of the words jumping all over the gaff when the little cratur had to read them? Smile's on the other side of their smart-alec faces now? Right, Barry?'

She gave him her wink, the kind of wink that would make you ten foot tall, even when you were all grown up and your nan had just embarrassed you about being dyslexic again. Only she could get away with it, he thought.

'Now, Nan, when are you moving in?' he quipped, sensing his chance. 'Sure I'm there too, just for a few more months, until the real bargains kick in.'

Olivia was at the sink, looking out at the small back garden, through the line of hanging baskets. She felt stunned, defeated.

'So it's not a mistake, Barry?' she asked. 'The interest rate. It's not an error?'

13. A Long War

Olivia and Vivienne – indeed, the entire Vickers family and thousands like them – are living through the consequences of an excessive build-up of debt. The difficulties they face are a microcosm of the pressures afflicting the entire eurozone project.

The path out of the euro-debt crisis is not straightforward. This is partly because each European country cleaves to its own political imperatives. The Germans want the opposite of what the Italians want. The Finns go one way, the Spanish another. As long as European countries pull in opposite directions, a solution remains remote, and it becomes ever likelier that the entire project will implode.

Victory has been declared in EU summit after EU summit. Why does the euphoria dissipate so quickly? If the remedies thus far have proved unsuccessful, why are others not being considered?

One clear obstacle to alternative solutions is that vast quantities of political capital have been invested in the status quo. Any suggestion that there are cracks in the European structure is often taken by the policy-making elite as an attack on the entire project. As John Kenneth Galbraith observed, 'When faced with the choice between changing our mind and proving that there is no need to do so, almost everyone gets busy with the proof.'

Mainstream economic thought has been slow to accept the possibility that the euro might break up, but the edifice of conventional wisdom is beginning to crack. Slow acceptance may not be ideal – it may yet cause much distress – but it is far preferable to utter denial. In July 2012 the Institute for New Economic Thinking warned that Europe was 'sleepwalking into disaster'. In this chapter, we will begin by exploring the 'sleepwalking' idea. Is it true? If so, why might the

EU – and the Irish political class – be sleepwalking into the path of major catastrophe?

Manufacturing conventional wisdom

In the second chapter of his study of 1950s America, *The Affluent Society*, John Kenneth Galbraith wrote about what he called 'conventional wisdom' – a way of looking at the world that has become so ingrained that reasonable people view any challenge to it with a sort of contempt: 'The defenders are able to say that the challengers of the conventional wisdom have not mastered their intricacies. Indeed, these ideas can be appreciated only by a stable, orthodox and patient man – in brief, by someone who closely resembles the man of conventional wisdom.'

Let's examine an idea that became entrenched in Ireland not very long ago: the widespread belief that the Irish property market would achieve a 'soft landing'. There was a great deal of evidence, widely available, that suggested when house prices go up at a spectacular rate, they usually fall violently back to earth. But the 'soft landing' fantasy hardened into an ideology that persisted until the horse had well and truly bolted, trapping many people in debt prisons they might otherwise have escaped.

Why did this peculiar idea take hold so firmly? Fashion chains such as Hollister make millions every year by betting that teenagers will go to great expense to avoid looking different from their peers; and in the same way the acceptance of conventional wisdom by academics, economists, civil servants, journalists, lawyers and politicians creates an atmosphere in which differing views are seen as untrustworthy and socially reckless. In this instance, familiarity breeds respectability; and it also breeds profit, at least in the short term. The talk of a 'soft landing' allowed the various interested parties to stick to the policies and approaches that had created vast profits for the banks and estate agents, and massive tax revenues for the state.

If an idea is repeated often enough by the pillars of society, it becomes conventional wisdom. Once this point is reached, wild ideas – such as 'Ireland's boom is based on sound fundamentals' – are seen as axiomatic.

A number of Irish institutions help to produce the sort of citizen prone to this way of thinking: a type of groupthink that makes bizarre propositions seem like the simple truth. One such institution is the Leaving Cert.

A standardized exam tends to reward the standardized answer. My memory of the Leaving Cert is of an exercise in conventional think-ing, rote learning and mass regurgitation. Students who thought a bit eclectically or laterally, or who questioned a bit too vigorously, were strongly discouraged from doing so. The student who found easy rewards was the one who possessed a certain type of cleverness – a linear cleverness – that facilitated the absorption, stacking and repro-duction of information in a conventional way. By making a young person's educational future wholly dependent on the score he or she receives, the Leaving Cert gives a huge leg-up to those with a par-ticular kind of intelligence, while penalizing other kinds.

The Leaving Cert is a big part of the problem, but it is not the whole of it. We can't blame the Leaving Cert for the disproportion-ate prestige of the professions in Ireland. The 'my son, the doctor/ lawyer/accountant' complex is a second cousin of the Good Room phenomenon; it is not, of course, unique to Ireland, but it remains particularly virulent here. The prestige of the professions is both reflected in, and fed by, the remarkable financial rewards on offer. Compared to their counterparts elsewhere, Irish lawyers and doctors make ridiculous amounts of money. Another bastion of convention-ality, the civil service, is also extremely well paid by international standards.

It might sound harsh, but there is an element of well-heeled loot-ing in this. The professional classes tend to be what economists call 'rent-seekers'. They don't create wealth themselves, but they find highly respectable ways of looting the wealth created by the product-ive elements of society.

The system of rewards in a society is crucial, because it is a concrete expression of society's values. It also incentivizes certain types of behaviour and specific ways of looking at the world. The system of rewards that prevails in Ireland creates disincentives to challenge the status quo; it also provides a comfortable safety net for the elite when things go sour.

As the German philosopher Arthur Schopenhauer supposedly observed about the three stages that must be suffered by those who challenge orthodox conventions, 'The first phase is ridicule, the second violent opposition and the third phase is when everyone pretends they were on your side all the time.' And when the old thinking has finally been rendered completely ridiculous, another bit of conventional wisdom arrives to take its place.

This process has nothing to do with reason. The conventional wisdom about the Irish housing market was not blown away by the force of superior ideas. What destroyed it was, quite simply, falling prices. The current conventional wisdom – that the Irish economy can recover, people can pay all their debts and the euro can survive if we adhere to the austerity policies enshrined in the Fiscal Compact – is now seriously threatened by events. However, there's not much evidence that our rulers are conscious of, or overly concerned by, these threats. Will there be a two-speed euro, a default in Spain or Italy, or even a rapid push for European federalism, the last forcing Ireland to offer up its advantageous corporation-tax rate on the altar of harmonized taxes? The Irish ruling class does not appear to be adjusting its thinking to allow for such possibilities. This is not surprising, given its attachment to the conventional wisdom of our European masters. The nature of conventional wisdom is that it doesn't adjust itself until a fresh crisis renders it untenable.

Our political leaders, while pretending to take the sober, responsible course, have in fact taken a wild gamble: that the present austerity policies will work and work quickly. In brief, they are gambling on a short war.

History is littered with the political corpses of politicians and their followers who gambled on short wars.

The ghost of John Redmond

One grainy photo that didn't make the bragging wall of the good room was a snap of my mother's uncle in British uniform. People didn't boast about that sort of thing. Missing too were the yellowed photos of my father's relations in their Dublin Fusiliers garb on Dun Laoghaire pier, smiling into the lens before they headed to the Front. The extraordinary fact that close to 260,000 Irishmen fought and 50,000 died in the Great War never became part of the national narrative, and had largely been forgotten by the time I started asking questions about the photos of young lads in khaki. Why did they look so happy – and where were they going in such a hurry?

We forget, or never knew, that one hundred years ago the broad Irish nationalist establishment supported Britain's war effort.

Over the next few years, it's a safe bet that the various centenaries of the events leading up to the creation of the Irish state won't devote much time to what might have happened had the First World War been 'over by Christmas'. John Redmond, the leader of the Irish Parliamentary Party, which pressed for home rule, will not figure prominently in the pantheon of nationalist giants. Yet it might all have been so different.

After an epic parliamentary struggle, the Government of Ireland Act was on the verge of being enacted when war broke out in Europe in July 1914. The legislation, which would have given Ireland home rule, was suspended upon the commencement of hostilities. The conventional wisdom at the time was that the war would be short. Hoping to position his party advantageously for the final implementation of the Act – and to avert the possibility of a revolt by the Ulster Unionists – Redmond got behind the British war effort.

If, in 1912, you had told the constitutional nationalist elite of the Irish Parliamentary Party, in its fourth decade of political dominance in Ireland, that they were on a kamikaze course to obliteration, serious people would have laughed at you. If you had forecast that by

1918 Redmond's party would win only one seat in the south of Ireland, and that Sinn Féin would be by far the most popular party, you would have been looked on as mad.

But the war did not end quickly, and as it dragged on, the political dynamics of Ireland changed dramatically. Redmond's support for the war effort became a political liability. The execution of the leaders of the Easter Rising in 1916 caused a dramatic shift in popular opinion away from the patient approach of the Irish Parliamentary Party and towards the irredentism of Sinn Féin and the various forces it represented.

This is a wonderful example of what can happen to conventional wisdom when events move against it. In fairness to Redmond, any political leader would have struggled, having been dealt such a hand. His position demanded that he carry nationalist Ireland along with him while avoiding a sectarian civil war; and that he make a naturally distracted Britain focus on Irish constitutional issues when it was involved in a world war, the outcome of which was very much up in the air until the German collapse in late 1918.

Our own present-day politicians and policy-makers occupy a much stronger and more straightforward position than Redmond's. They have no excuse. They needn't try to guess the course of a world war, and they don't have to deal with an event such as the Easter Rising. Redmond was flying blind; by contrast, our leaders have access to reams of financial and economic evidence – from the Asia crisis to Latin America and Iceland and Japan – to help guide our path. We know what happened in the Great Depression, and we understand how the economy works. Yet Ireland and Europe seem to be hell bent on following a course of action that almost guarantees the recession will be epic.

The wrong medicine

The main – and arguably only – reason that no permanent solution has been found to the euro's travails is that every time the politicians sit down to debate the issue, they find the right answers to the wrong questions.

In the past, when a European country was running a large trade deficit in comparison with other European countries, the imbalance was rectified by a devaluation of that country's currency. The devaluation made imports expensive and exports cheaper. People stopped buying more expensive imports; domestic companies exported more; and the trade gap narrowed.

But if, like today, you don't have your own currency, the only way to force your own people to spend less on imports is to cut their wages. This is called 'internal devaluation', and it is the mechanism currently being relied upon by the policy-makers of the eurozone.

To give some idea of the current-account gaps at present in the eurozone, Germany has a current-account surplus of €41.1 billion, while Spain, Italy and Portugal have deficits of €14.4, €13.1 and €9.6 billion respectively. These trade imbalances, which occur when a country imports more than it exports, are made up by borrowing. So a country like Germany lends to a country like Spain. This allows the Spanish to buy the Mercedes they want; but obviously the Spanish have to pay that money back at some stage.

In order to repay the debt, Spain must export more stuff to Germany and buy fewer German goodies in the future. The quick way to do this would be via a devaluation of the Spanish currency. But, because that's not possible in the eurozone, the only alternative is for Spanish wages to fall.

Theoretically, grinding wages and prices down for years will force costs down, until the point is reached where Spain, or Ireland, will be able to compete with Germany. This – we are told – will eradicate the current-account imbalances in Europe over time.

However, there is one problem: there are no instances, anywhere in the world, of this strategy succeeding.

While slashing wages looks good on paper and in first-year economic textbooks, it is very hard to do in real life, where trade unions protect their members and politicians vie to get re-elected. The basic truth is that wages are what we all live on and we don't like them to fall. What actually happens during a downturn is that wages don't fall to any significant degree: instead, the labour market splits between insiders and outsiders. Employers, faced with a choice between laying off workers and cutting wages, generally choose the former. As a result, unemployment increases, but wages don't change very much. This tends to be the case in both the public and private sectors alike.

Fundamentally, the interests of the unemployed and the employed are in conflict. Unemployed people want to get back into work and, typically, are prepared to accept lower wages. They would be happy enough to see the general wage level drop. But it is not in the interests of the people still in work to see wages fall, because they will lose out. Those in work, therefore, use all their efforts to keep wages high.

The evidence in Ireland, despite all the shouting and roaring on talk shows, is unambiguous. Let's take 2008 as a starting point, with an index of wages at 100. Even though the economy went into a nosedive from that year, wages in manufacturing actually rose, peaking at around 106 at the end of 2009, before falling to a low of 102 in 2011. Since then wages in manufacturing have stabilized at a level higher than that of 2008. Even in the construction sector, where employment collapsed in the wake of the building bust, wage rates declined by only 6 per cent between 2008 and 2011. Overall, average wages in the public sector in Ireland have fallen by just over 1 per cent since 2008, while general wages in the private sector are down just shy of 6 per cent.

When we compare Ireland's competitive position to the rest of the world's, we see that the vast majority of our gains came not from decreasing wages but from recent falls in the euro against the currencies of our major trading partners, the UK and the USA.

Unfortunately, despite this evidence, the conventional wisdom of 'internal devaluation' continues to hold sway. Whether the economists within the IMF actually subscribe to the idea that countries can force down wages is debatable, but in its public utterances the Fund still champions the internal-devaluation notion and is prepared to clutch at any straw it can to substantiate this view.

For example, on 5 June 2012, IMF chief Christine Lagarde showered Latvia with fulsome praise. Latvians, she said, had shown 'collective determination and resilience' by their decision 'to bite the bullet' and pursue a policy of internal devaluation. She and the top brass of the IMF saw Latvia's efforts as 'a real achievement, a real tour de force'.

But the victory was fictitious. A report by Mark Weisbrot and Rebecca Ray for the Center for Economic and Policy Research (CEPR) found that not only had Latvia failed to follow the route of internal devaluation, but that its recovery was due to luck and to the determination of the EU to have a success story at any cost. As Weisbrot wrote in a subsequent article:

> They had promised to tighten their budget by a huge amount, but they didn't do it. And they also got some help from unanticipated inflation, which gave them a more expansionary monetary policy than they had planned, and reduced the growth of their public debt. Latvia also got a lot of money from the European authorities, which wanted to make sure they didn't devalue their currency, as that would have left the Swedish banks with big losses.

The bottom line is that trying to grind down wages is as effective as chipping away at Mount Everest with a teaspoon. The only way wages and costs in a country can fall dramatically is through changes to the exchange rate. Since monetary union prevents this from happening, the peripheral economies are stuck in a cycle of perennial deficits in relation to Germany.

Investors looking at the peripheral countries have figured out that the internal-devaluation solution is not likely to work because wages don't fall; and that if unemployment rises because wages haven't fallen, the social-welfare bill will rise and the income-tax take will fall. This presents a serious and possibly insurmountable problem for the process of getting fiscal deficits down – as required by the Fiscal Compact we voted for. The governments will therefore have to cut back even more in order to hit their deficit-reduction targets.

It is not difficult to see how this process can become self-defeating.

The logic of the Fiscal Compact, largely driven by the understandable fear in Germany that without legal commitments peripheral countries would never get their budgets sorted, rests on the premise that government spending is at the root of these trade and current-account imbalances.

But we know that's not the case.

If the Germans were really being honest with themselves and with us, they'd say something like this: 'Listen, we don't trust you guys and that's why we need you to sign up to these rules. We know that the root of the problem isn't (with the exception of Greece) profligate governments but rather too much cross-border private-sector borrowing and lending – and that these rules will tend to depress the economy further. Yet we need you to sign up in order to show the German electorate that monetary union is underpinned with firm rules.' Such a declaration would beg a great number of questions about how we're going to get Europe working again – a question for which the Germans have yet to propose an answer – but at least it would accurately characterize the rationale for the Fiscal Compact.

Prescribing government deficit reductions to fix private capital imbalances is like prescribing chemotherapy for heart disease. Today's large fiscal deficits are the result – not the cause – of Ireland's and Spain's crises. Both countries' public-debt ratios were actually lower than Germany's in 2008. Since Ireland adopted the euro, its household debt-to-income ratio has exploded. Ireland's public finances were broken by its recapitalization of the banks (in keeping with the eurozone orthodoxy that banks and their bondholders will be protected at any cost), and by the normal consequences of recession: lower tax receipts and a higher need for social-welfare payments.

With the Fiscal Compact tying the government into reducing deficits and bringing down the public debt-to-GDP ratio irrespective of the business cycle, fiscal policy in the eurozone will be pro-cyclical and spending will be cut in the periphery at a time when these countries most need help. The result will be lower growth, higher unemployment, more political instability and more capital flows of frightened money from the periphery to the core. This is all being done to make the eurozone more credible. But it won't work.

14. Twenty-seven Weeks

It had been raining for days. The Met Éireann girls were solemn as they announced another front coming in from the Atlantic, a big swirl of menacing grey. Not even Jean Byrne's red leather numbers could break the relentless nightly depression. The farmers were terrified, going mad on the radio about silage. Big matches played to small, drenched crowds; the first dance festivals of early summer turned into giant mud baths. Quick to see an angle, travel agents tantalized the broke population with sun holidays in cheap countries with Cyrillic alphabets.

In small towns all over the country, angry swollen rivers burst their banks, crippling insurance companies with claims. Sodden IKEA furniture, breaking asunder, floated down submerged quay-sides, past excited RTÉ reporters in galoshes.

Local know-it-alls paddled smugly in inflatable dinghies down the uninspiring streets off the main drag, those streets named after lesser patriots and second-rate saints, places close to barracks, built in hollows.

Estates out in Trackerville, thrown up by cowboy developers on floodplains, were under water. The radio was furious with finger-pointing.

Is there a pike in that thatch?

Could you credit it, Joe?

In this day and age?

All over the country, people were fidgety, annoyed and fed up with the whole thing. Everyone, that is, except Damien D'Arcy.

Damien was the picture of calm. He took the panic in the face of the elements as yet more evidence of the frailty of Man, in contrast with the awesome might of God.

★

He parked carefully – it was his mother's car – at the edge of an enormous puddle. Once the engine was off, he could hear the gutter gurgling as water swirled violently down a dead end and found its way back to the top. Two lads from Dublin Corporation in hi-viz jackets looked on, bemused.

Rathmines, whatever its other charms, doesn't suit rain, he thought.

Damien picked up the Book, which he had marked the night before: Deuteronomy, Leviticus, Amos and Ezekiel from the Old, and Luke and Matthew from the New, and headed towards the entrance of the church. The young pastor arrived as the congregation were gathering just before twelve for a quick coffee and a natter. Damien had been relieved to see, on his first visit, that there were all sorts here, not just the 'happy clappy' types you'd expect. The church filled up with children and young parents, as well as plenty of singletons.

Damien was one of them, these people of faith, the members of the New Voice evangelical family. Six months earlier – only three months after Sonya had walked out, taking their son with her – he had arrived at this church for the first time, a broken man.

Now he was reborn. The past was truly a different country. All the nasty headlines, the vicious gossip, the social shunning – they counted for nothing here. In fact, Damien's first task was to forgive. In order to do this, he had to dispense with his anger, which, his pastor explained, was only the flip side of impotence. Rage is an emotion sourced in the lack of control. Damien had to learn to be in control again. This meant replacing anger with forgiveness and humiliation with openness and generosity. He had to move from self-pity to concern for others, to see his story as part of a greater tapestry.

Of course it was difficult to quell the look-at-me impulse, to cease striving to be Number One. His outward humility had always been false, and he knew it. The secret satisfaction of knowing that people were talking about him, that he had the most Leaving Cert points, was the best sportsman, had the prettiest girlfriends – it was addictive.

His first and most difficult battle was to let in God. Although he knew his vanity and conceit left him weak and exposed when he fell from grace, letting go wasn't easy. But now he had a new mission. He, a man who had always understood power, recognized this real missionary power immediately. If people saw him now, they would see the transformation writ on his face. He would walk amongst the weak and make them strong, stronger than the supposed strong could ever fathom.

Damien D'Arcy stood in the seventh pew, his hands outstretched in the air, singing along to the choir's rendition of Glen Hansard's 'Falling Slowly'. The rain clattered on the roof.

The rest of the congregation swayed to the rhythm. You could always tell the new members. Initially, they were reserved, unused to showing their feelings in public, but, as the music infected them and their neighbours began to raise their hands, the rush of joy and community dispelled their inhibitions. They were united in the light of the Lord.

Singing together brought them closer. The congregation was overwhelmingly Irish, bar two or three Asians and one African in full hip-hop regalia, complete with outsized basketball shirt and baseball cap cocked sideways. Most were young men and women. Damien felt honoured to be amongst such people. This was their communion.

He sang for his son, his world. He sang for Jesus. He loved and he felt loved. All vulnerabilities were strengths, his past was someone else's. He had been born again.

The pastor nodded to him and beamed. He had made Damien welcome. From the first 'newcomers' meal' at his own house, he had listened, not judged. For the first time in two years Damien wasn't wearing a hunted expression; he wasn't the guilty one. He was just a man, nothing more or less, equal in God's eyes and under God's law. Inside he was healing – and he would heal others.

The children went up to the altar before leaving for Sunday school.
How many sons did Jacob have?
Where did the Pharaoh take Joseph?
The children scrambled to give the answer: *Me, me, me, me, please, please.*

Damien would have loved to bring his son here, but Sonya wouldn't hear of it. She thought the Dundrum Shopping Centre on a Sunday morning was an acceptable place for children, and many respectable people seemed to agree with her.

When the children left, the pastor called Damien up to the altar.

'You all know our friend Damien. Today he will share with you. He will share some thoughts and reflect on God's will. Thank you for sharing, Damien.'

Damien D'Arcy stood behind the lectern and looked down on his new family. The confidence was back, a gentle confidence. He smiled and they smiled back – people and families for whom the world made more sense when they saw themselves as part of something greater.

'You are all aware,' Damien said, 'that the country is in enormous debt, and you all have family members or friends who are struggling under this weight of debt. This debt is squashing them. It is the legacy of the so-called boom, and we know that many of us will be years paying off debts on houses, bricks and mortar now worth a fraction of what they were bought for.'

The audience nodded their heads, because they knew the score. Everyone in sodden Ireland knew the score, he thought.

'Sometimes, when we discuss these issues, we make a mistake. We think that things like mortgages and credit-card debts, to finance the lifestyle that we thought we wanted, are new things, new dilemmas, but they are not.'

He focused on the back of the church, picking a spot slightly above the heads of everyone and talking to it. An odd glance down at a face or two every now and then gave people the impression he was talking directly to them. This was the art of persuasion. You can make everyone feel loved only by being slightly aloof. People need to want you, to covet you, and you need to be their Messiah. Damien's vanity was still there. But he knew it. He recognized it. He could harness it now for good. Call it charisma.

'Debts are as old as the Good Book itself. Today I'd like to talk to you about the morality of finance and economics, and how God wants us to deal with them.'

The Book empowered him. How can you doubt a man with one arm outstretched and the other holding the Bible? It gave you permission to leverage thousands of years of wisdom. He raised his head up to the ceiling, exalting a greater power, a greater understanding, and felt himself free.

'The Lord's word is that we forgive the debts of our neighbours after a certain time. Deuteronomy 15, Verse 2, written 1,500 years before Christ our Saviour brought the Good News, makes it explicit. "This is how it is to be done: Every creditor shall cancel the loan he has made to his fellow Israelite. He shall not require payment from his fellow Israelite or brother, because the Lord's time for cancelling debts has been proclaimed."

'*When shall he do this?*' Damien demanded, the pitch of his voice rising. 'In Deuteronomy 15, Verse 9, He says, "In the seventh year thou shalt make remission; he to whom anything is owing from his friend or neighbour or brother cannot demand it again because this is the year of the remission of the Lord."'

Damien paused, then continued: 'This is the Jubilee year, the year we forgive the debts of our neighbours. And what should we do after that?'

The crowd was expectant. He had them in his outstretched palm.

'Let's turn to Leviticus 25, Verse 12.'

He read solemnly: ' "For it is a jubilee and is to be holy for you; eat only what is taken directly from the fields." In other words, we live within our means – eating only what is taken from our own fields, using our own resources, and the cycle starts again.'

'Praise him,' said a man in the congregation. 'Listen to his word.'

'These rules are old and wise. The prophets knew that if you subjugate one part of the society through debt, these people, your brothers and sisters, will eventually rise up in violence against the creditors. It is human nature, understood by the ancients, but forgotten by the modern age.'

The congregation understood that the Bible couldn't be taken literally at all junctures, but they could see the parallels. They could understand the wisdom.

'Debts and too much credit, boom and bust cycles, were there in the Old Testament days, as far back as Genesis – the first book. In the beginning there were economic cycles.'

'Hallelujah.'

Damien flicked to Genesis 41, verses 30 and 53. His voiced bounced off the back wall of the church and filled the space. It was round, rich, mellifluous and reassuring.

'The seven years of abundance in Egypt came to an end, and Joseph predicted that seven years of famine would follow them. Then all the abundance in Egypt would be forgotten, and famine would ravage the land.'

'Ladies and gentlemen, good people of faith: Joseph, son of Jacob, was the first ever minister for finance, telling the Pharaoh that seven good years would be followed by seven lean years and he should save in the good times to have money in the bad years.'

'Praise his name!'

The congregation was ecstatic. There was nothing new under the sun; all that was missing was wisdom.

'Everything repeats itself. These problems are as old as the hills. People borrowed and lent too much more than a thousand years before Christ. And the resulting tensions between creditors and debtors were recognized by the scribes, the prophets and the holy men, even back then.'

'Let Him in.'

In a rapid-fire sweep of the scriptures, Damien deployed the dreary Ezekiel 27 on Tyre, and the upbeat Luke, reporting the words of Jesus himself. He switched back to the prophetic Amos, before bringing the audience right up to the evangelist Mark, telling them not to be vengeful but moral: Jesus walked up to the creditor and 'Jesus loved him.'

Damien ended with Matthew 18, verses 21–35. Matthew, the tax collector, told the tale of the wise king who forgave a servant his debts, only to find the same servant refusing to forgive a much smaller debt owed by a much poorer man.

'When we bailed out the banks, were we not forgiving them their debts and preventing them from going bankrupt? Yet do they not, like the wicked servant, chase the weakest of us for mortgage debt? Friends, what would Jesus have done?'

Olivia was at the Coombe for her third-trimester examination. The place was jammed.

'You'll be grand, love, you look fit as a butcher's.'

'Thanks.' Loving this, she thought, being mothered by a seventeen-year-old.

'Who are ye havin' it for?'

'Sorry?' Did she just say what I thought she said?

'Second for me, both Crip's an' all – lad over there.'

'Cool.' Nice sovereign-and-choker combo, Crip, respect.

'Lovely to see the little yoke swimmin' around inside you. Got the jaysus thing on me phone's screensaver.'

'Sharon Larkin, please,' bellowed the midwife, and Olivia's new friend rose to her feet.

Her phone beeped.

Yeah of course

You OK?

The Coombe

See you in Fallon & Byrne in half an hour so

Vivienne should have copped when they stopped including her in those run-of-the-mill morning meetings. She had shrugged it off, telling herself she was busy anyway, what with that file in Carlow. These meetings took up precious client-facing time. But she was a bit hurt, because she knew that the bank was run on the basic idea that knowledge is power. Access to the font of knowledge was a clear marker of seniority. In the bank, there were the types who went to everything, not only to be seen, but also to gather information, even trivial stuff, like the fact that the staff car-parking numbers were changing.

She'd known there would be a cull. It had been all over the papers. But she'd always felt she might be one of the lucky ones. She believed that the head of credit – who had promoted her only last year – would protect her.

Towards the end, she had waltzed towards her corporate execution as if in a dream. The younger colleagues who had survived the cut seemed embarrassed by her presence.

Vivienne had missed birthdays for the bank, even lied for it. Now the bank had cast her aside, along with several hundred of her colleagues.

In truth, the bank had not been a happy place for the past few years. Its whole world had been turned upside down: because of the bailouts and the nationalization and the earlier rounds of layoffs, and because of the sudden switch from lending freely, almost messianically, to pursuing debtors for arrears. No group in Ireland believed the property hype more fervently than the ordinary bank workers. They had been disciples of the elixir of cheap money, and lots of them had huge mortgages themselves.

Vivienne knew her boss had been given a quota to get rid of. She knew her own rise had scared him. If he could surround himself with mediocrity, he might stay in the corner office until the carriage clock was awarded to him.

She had to talk to someone. Her husband was in an all-day meeting, so she texted the person in the world who knew her best, even though she still hadn't forgiven her for ruining the wedding.

Sitting in the window of Fallon & Byrne, Olivia could see her sister coming up Wicklow Street, hassled.

'Jesus, Viv, stupid fools.'

'I should've seen it coming.'

'The banks are screwed anyway. You would have had to move sometime. How much did they give you?'

'The package is OK.'

'Sure, John Paul is doing well anyway.'

'It's not that easy, Liv. Don't tell anyone, especially not Mum. JP was caught up in a deal for this hotel in Cork. They all ploughed money into it. Now it's a shell, and they still have to fork out for the difference. It's thousands a month. That's why he's working so much.'

'I thought he was on the NAMA gravy train.'

'He is, I suppose, but it's all going in and coming out. Everything looks OK from the outside, but we're up to our gills in debt.'

'What about the parents? Aren't they pitching in?'

'It's all show. They're barely clinging on. They had loads in AIB shares. That's all gone. They remortgaged the big house to buy that place in Portugal; now that's worth nothing too. They've got nothing at the end of the month, believe me. It's just keeping up appearances. Half of Dublin is at the same game. I know, I've seen it from the inside.'

Olivia was beginning to feel less of a failure, less of an outcast.

'Listen, Liv, I was thinking about you and the mortgage. Just before I left, when I was sorting things out a few days ago, I went over a few details, just to make sure it was all above board. In case there was something I could do. I assumed I'd be locked out of the bank's systems as soon as I got the bad news, but the IT heads at our bank aren't the smartest.'

Olivia was amazed: her sister, having just lost her job, had become energized. It was the old Viv, not the walking corporate bore who had begun her career lending money to people and then, for the past three years, been the one charged with getting the money back when those people couldn't pay.

Her brown almond eyes were almost black now.

'Liv. I've got your file on a memory stick. Maybe you can find something useful in it.'

15. Meet the Germans

The morality of it all

The first time I was in Germany, I was weighed down with a football sock full of 5p pieces. We were on a teenage schoolboys' football trip. One of the big lads on our road had told us that the German mark (then worth about thirty pence) was the same size as a 5p piece and that the vending machines in Germany couldn't distinguish between the two. It cost three marks for a packet of smokes. The illicit exchange rate meant we could get twenty Rothmans for fifteen pence in the Fatherland.

So, laden down with as many 5p pieces as we could put our hands on, we headed to Germany to chain-smoke, defraud the locals and play the odd match in between. We had a ball.

Imagine German teenagers doing the same if the roles were reversed – if Irish people had generously opened up their houses to them. Don't tell me culture doesn't matter. Culture is everything.

One of the ideas at the heart of Germany's post-war culture is the idea that inflation needs to be avoided at all costs. In other words, the central bank's primary function is to make sure that the money supply of the country does not expand in such a way as to drive up prices. The central bank of the USA, the Federal Reserve, has an obligation to keep inflation down but also to keep an eye on the growth rate of the economy. The German view is that controlling inflation is a central bank's only legitimate role.

Vigilance regarding inflation is seared into the German DNA. This bias stems from the crushing hyper-inflation that peaked in the middle of 1923. It has become an article of faith in Germany that hyper-inflation destroyed the wealth of the German middle class, radicalizing them and paving the way for the rise of Nazism.

The Federal Republic's Bundesbank executed its brief efficiently during the course of its five-decade reign. The Deutschmark was a symbol of the new Germany – strong and stable. Germany's currency was also a key tool in subsequent moves towards greater European integration. From 1979 to 2000, national exchange rates in Europe were tied to the Deutschmark through the European Monetary System. It was hoped that the lack of exchange-rate volatility would increase the incentive for countries to trade together: the more they did so, the lower the barriers between them would become, meaning that they would be more likely to move in step with one another. This was seen as a precursor to political integration, the logic being that the more dependent and interlinked the economies were, the less domestic political opposition there would be to giving up sovereignty altogether.

In terms of European integration, nothing underscored the importance of the Bundesbank and Deutschmark more vividly than the decision in 1982 by the French president, François Mitterrand, to fix the French franc to the Deutschmark through the *franc fort* policy. This signalled that even France was prepared to allow the Bundesbank to be its de facto central bank.

There were, however, significant costs attached. Long-term unemployment rose rapidly in Western Europe in the 1980s and particularly in countries like Ireland. Many, many Irish manufacturing companies went to the wall in the 1980s because the Irish currency, tied to Germany's, was too strong.

In the late 1980s I did a post-graduate course in the College of Europe in Bruges, which was dedicated to training the future functionaries of the EU. There, it became clear to me just how significant German financial culture would be to European integration; professors and EU officials alike drummed home to us the centrality of the Bundesbank in both facilitating and tempering political aspirations.

My first real job, working as an economist in the Central Bank of Ireland, afforded me the opportunity to see at first hand the extent to which, by common consent, the Germans ran the show in Europe. During the 1992/93 currency crisis, I witnessed the fanaticism with which the Irish policy-making elite reacted to the notion of devaluing the currency, as the United Kingdom had just done. Interest rates were increased to 100 per cent overnight, to affirm our commitment to staying with the Germans. That was just silliness – a denial of the inevitable – and ordinary people knew it. As the elite hunkered down in Dublin, or shuttled back and forth to Brussels, the real death-knell for the policy of maintaining an artificially strong punt was signalled by the queues of Toyota Corollas backed up outside Newry. The average punter realized that the chance to buy cheap booze priced in sterling would last only so long before the punt would have to be devalued – which it soon was.

British commentators constantly underestimated the strength of the European will to keep the political-and-monetary integration show on the road. Later in the 1990s, working in the City of London, I watched as this British misunderstanding cost lots of people a lot of money, as they bet heavily on the disintegration of the European project. However, just because the British have been wrong up to now doesn't mean that they will be wrong forever. In the years ahead, Germany will need to accept, at the very least, a dilution of its monetary culture if the euro is to stay intact.

The first ten years of the euro were more or less successful because of massive capital flows from the core to the periphery. This led to an inflationary boom in the latter, most dramatically in Ireland – which in turn allowed the German economy, in trouble in the late 1990s after the costs of unification had spiralled out of control, to experience a big gain in competitiveness. The Germans could pay themselves well and still export because the periphery was booming. At one stage there were more Mercs per head in Dublin than in Frankfurt.

Now that the credit bubble has burst and capital is fleeing the periphery, all this has changed. To prevent the euro from imploding, there needs to be an inflationary boom in Germany, so that the periphery can regain competitiveness without suffering devastating levels of deflation. A higher rate of inflation in the euro as a whole, and in Germany in particular, will be the result. Which is why culture matters, particularly German culture.

The euro question is really a German question. If Germany wants the euro in its current form to survive, the euro will survive. If it decides it would be happier with a narrower currency union of the northern creditor countries, which share its monetary values, that is what will happen.

So: what does Germany want?

The eurozone housing estate

One way of imagining the euro crisis and the position in which Germany finds itself is to think of the eurozone as a housing estate.

Germany is the good, house-proud homeowner in a neighbourhood that has taken a turn for the worse.

France is the neighbour who copies the German lead, trying to match the German hanging baskets and freshly swept drive. If you've ever had a neighbour who copies your home improvements, you know how annoying this can be. But at least they don't bring down the tone of the area.

The countries of Europe's periphery are the bad neighbours, and they are getting worse by the day. For a while, they clipped their hedges and washed their cars. They even put a fresh lick of paint on the house every few years. But now they are like extras from *Shameless*. The gardens of the peripheral Europeans are full of weeds, overgrown and tatty. The paint is peeling off their porches and the slates have not been fixed. Some of their houses have boarded-up windows.

Germany's problem is that the value of their house is more dependent on the condition of the rest of the estate than it is on the neatness of their own manicured hedge. As time passes, the estate worsens. Youths in hoodies menace passers-by, and the value of Germany's house plummets. They now have a massive personal stake in cleaning up the neighbourhood.

Will they pay to have the other houses tarted up, to get the delinquent kids off the street? If so, how much will it cost?

In the past, Germany could at least enlist the support of France in its effort to improve the area. But now even the French are threatening to go rogue. The Germans fear it is only a matter of time before there is a burnt-out old Renault up on blocks in the driveway.

They know they can't isolate the bad houses by building a wall, because that will just draw attention to the problem. Potential buyers will always worry about what is happening on the other side and whether delinquents will jump over and rob them in the night. They also know that policing the area with security guards and posting rules on all the lamp-posts won't help, because the anti-social neighbours will either take no notice or renege on any promise to behave.

So Germany is trying to change the estate-management committee's rules, but they need to achieve this voluntarily. They can't just call a residents' meeting and upbraid the delinquents in public. It must appear from the outside that the area has had a change of heart and wants to clean up its act.

If the unruly neighbours tell the Germans where to go, the price of the houses on the estate may fall – but it has already fallen hugely, so the unruly neighbours mightn't really care. At least, they don't care nearly as much as Germany, which has devoted so much time and effort to its house.

A philosophical clash

In March 2012, I spoke to Arab investors at an economics conference in Abu Dhabi. I was preceded at the podium by Axel Weber, who had resigned the previous summer as head of the Bundesbank and from the ECB's board in what was widely seen as a protest at how the ECB was breaking its own strict rules to bail out the periphery. Weber lost a lot in this principled move: he had been hotly tipped to be the next ECB president.

Weber is an impressive speaker with a large presence and clear views not only about how the world works but about how it ought to work. It is not hard to see why he has got to the top of the global financial tree, where individuals move seamlessly from public to private, and from central banks to investment banks. It is no coincidence that the views Weber espoused were strongly aligned with the concerns of Switzerland's largest bank, UBS, where he was about to take up the post of chairman. Weber is not alone in moving between big investment banks and public authorities. Mario Draghi worked at Goldman Sachs; so too did Mario Monti and Lucas Papademos – the technocrats who took over from the leaders of Italy and Greece in 2011 and 2012 respectively.

At this stratospheric level of influence, huge decisions are taken by a tiny number of people. All these people are in the same social circle. They go to the same gatherings and have similar contact lists on their phones. This narrowing of influence is how conventional wisdom becomes embedded.

I chatted with Weber in Abu Dhabi and found him excellent company. Like many Germans, he has a fondness for Ireland, as a holiday destination and as a breath of fresh air. In the world of business, he regards us as inconsequential and unthreatening.

We should never underestimate how well our finely crafted antipathy to the UK goes down in Europe, particularly amongst the elites, who are often annoyed with Britain's stubbornness and told-you-so glee when things on the Continent go pear-shaped. But don't mistake this fellow-feeling with regard to the UK for an alignment of interests. Germany will not lose sleep over Ireland.

I came away from our conversation with a strengthened appreciation of the fact that the Germans really do think about economics and finance differently from us. It also struck me that there are many at the very highest level in Germany who are prepared to accept that the euro might not survive in its present form. Furthermore, they would even like to see a smaller eurozone, one in which rules and regulations are adhered to.

It is now clear that only by breaking the rules about lending to governments and banks can the ECB realistically hope to keep the eurozone intact. At the highest levels in Germany and in Europe, there is a conflict between those who say that the rules are sacrosanct and those who are willing to bend or change them in order to hold together the eurozone. The Bundesbank is the firmest proponent of the former view. Weber and his Bundesbank vice-president, Jürgen Stark, resigned from the ECB over their fear that the ECB might lose its Germanic identity if it intervenes too much in the bond markets.

This battle is ongoing. In late July 2012, when Mario Draghi stated the ECB would 'do whatever was necessary' to keep the euro together, this was taken to mean that it would buy Spanish government bonds. The Bundesbank was out of the blocks the next day with a statement saying that this would be 'problematic' – diplomatic phrasing for 'over our dead bodies'.

In September Draghi announced that the ECB will open its balance sheet and buy all sorts of assets from peripheral countries in order to keep the euro functioning properly. This constituted a crushing defeat for the Bundesbank.

The Germanic view, exemplified by Weber, sees money as a common good, protected by treaties and laws: the economy adapts to money, not the other way around. The alternative school of thought views money as a tool: the state has a responsibility to use money to achieve desired outcomes, such as full employment, or economic growth, or saving the euro.

It is not hard to understand why the Germans might see the world as they do. After all, during the twentieth century they were first financially wiped out by hyper-inflation, then politically and militarily wiped out by a man who regarded treaties as little more than pieces of paper.

There are many Germans who believe that there is nothing worse than failing to uphold signed international treaties, such as those that underpin the euro, irrespective of economic crises or any other contingencies. There may come a point – another bailout, or another change in the way the ECB deals with the crisis – when the German body politic refuses to bend on grounds of principle. That moment might not be too far away.

The assumption of the Irish mainstream – the prevailing view of our government and that of the Europhiles in Brussels – is that the

Germans will eventually break the rules as necessary in order to save the euro. But, as the crisis gets more and more acute, and the problems in Spain and Italy get bigger and bigger, this assumption needs to be reassessed.

Football lessons

Two months after meeting Axel Weber, I was in Germany for the Champions League final.

Germans are naturally proud of their national football team. They are also very proud of their Bundesliga. Nowhere is that pride more justified than in Munich, where Bayern München, the most successful German club, reigns supreme. Bayern is a proper club, with a wonderful history, great players and an exciting approach to the game. It recruits local talent, so that many of the heroes on the pitch – including captain Philipp Lahm, playmaker Bastian Schweinsteiger and forward Thomas Müller – are local lads from the famous Bayern youth academy.

The club is well run. Its new stadium, the Allianz Arena, is an architectural gem owned by the local municipality, which rents it to Bayern and its rival, TSV 1860 München. The 70,000-capacity stadium cost €340 million to build and is used every week for three-quarters of the year. The contrast with Dublin's Aviva Stadium is stark. The Aviva cost €410 million to build, holds 16,000 fewer people than the Allianz and is used much less frequently.

Sitting in the Allianz as the place filled up with the red of Bayern and the blue of Chelsea for the Champions League final, I felt the difference between the two clubs couldn't have been greater. Bayern is solid, Germanic, book-balancing and local; Chelsea, owned by a Russian oligarch, is all London chutzpah and flash, debt-financed and cosmopolitan. If there was ever a demonstration of how football culture reflects the broader financial culture of the economies of Europe, it was Bayern versus Chelsea in 2012.

Financially, Bayern operates well within its means, much like the

German economy. Its accounts are perfect and its players are paid well but not extravagantly. Bayern is all about tradition and continuity, about meticulous planning from youth development to the professional first eleven. T-Mobile, the local telecoms company, is the main sponsor. The club is owned by the fans and operates as a tight cooperative. Bayern's manager is a former German international. If Bayern were a country, it would be running a massive current-account surplus in relation to the rest of the world, and have a huge savings ratio and low inflation.

Chelsea, in contrast, is everything Bayern is not. Its players are mainly foreign mercenaries who wouldn't know Fulham's Broadway from Manhattan's. The club is debt-financed. It is sponsored by a Korean electronics firm. While the majority of fans are Londoners, the team – like the city – is deeply cosmopolitan. The Chelsea player who stole the show at the final is from the Ivory Coast, whereas the Bayern talisman was born within sixty miles of Munich. The Chelsea manager is Italian; he was preceded by a Portuguese, another Italian, a Dutchman, a Brazilian and another Portuguese. If Chelsea were a country, it would be running a massive current-account deficit. It would borrow where it could and be prone to higher inflation.

The same could be said for the team Bayern knocked out in the semi-finals, the *galácticos* of Real Madrid. Brilliant, overblown and stylish, Real boasts Portugal's Ronaldo, Brazil's Kaka and France's Benzema. The club carried debts of nearly a quarter of a billion euros last year.

On the evening of the final, my son – in full Chelsea kit – and I watched the first half of the Heineken Cup final between Leinster and Ulster in an Irish bar in downtown Munich, then grabbed a cab to the Allianz Arena. We shared our taxi with a Kuwaiti couple, also in full Chelsea kit; neither could name any of the team, much to my son's dismay.

Chatting in the cab, the driver told me things were going well in Bavaria. Unemployment was less than 3 per cent, business was booming, and life was good. I asked him about the rest of Europe and he shrugged his shoulders. 'We don't feel the crisis here,' he said. He paused and then added, 'Maybe there are a few more immigrants, but we don't feel any problem here.'

In the middle of a massive global recession, Germany was thriving. By the end of the summer, the economic news in Germany would be less positive; but in late May unemployment was still the lowest in a generation; exports to the rest of the world were strong; wages were rising; and property prices were inflating in the big cities of Hamburg, Frankfurt and Munich. In a recent poll 86 per cent of Germans said they were happy with their standard of living.

That week in May the feel-good factor was reinforced by the news that people were now prepared to give Germans money for nothing: the government was able to borrow at 0 per cent. This was because billions of euros were flowing out of the eurozone periphery, particularly from Spain, to Germany, because investors and the average citizen believed Spain would leave the euro. In the first three months of 2012, €97 billion left the Spanish economy. That's nearly 10 per cent of GDP, and that was before the crisis intensified in the early summer of 2012.

The taxi driver also talked about the rules governing German football clubs. A full set of documents – covering assets, receivables, cash and bank balances, liabilities and provisions, current overdraft facilities, loan commitments, projected and current profit/loss statements, and cash inflows and outflows – must be submitted each year before a playing licence is issued. These documents are judged by the German football league. All clubs must inject money into a fund to make sure that if a club does get into difficulty, even after all this scrutiny, it won't go bust. No Bundesliga club has experienced an insolvency since the league's creation in 1963. By way of comparison, there have been 92 such events in the top-five divisions of English football since 1992.

Ticket prices are kept low. The average Bundesliga ticket costs €10. The fans feel real ownership, which was very evident amongst the Bayern fans we met. The Bundesliga is the best attended of the big football leagues in Europe, with an average attendance of 45,726 in 2010/11 – 10,000 more than the English Premier League.

The cabbie told me that good management and aversion to debt were the secret to the success of the German clubs. He had a point – but only if German clubs are content to play solely with themselves. The German rules in the German league work because they are in sync with German culture and philosophy; but such rules would be unthinkable in England, Spain or Italy. Without free-spending, debt-financed English clubs, or the brash Spanish giants like Real Madrid or Barça, there would have been no Champions League final in Munich, and I wouldn't have been in that cab, paying my fare. It takes all sorts, all manner of preferences and all types of biases to create the tapestry that is competitive football.

Similarly, without the countries of the periphery inflating their economies in the last ten years, thereby creating the demand for German goodies, the Germans would have had no one to play economics with. Every creditor country like Germany needs a debtor country like Spain. Every budget surplus needs a matching budget deficit, and every current-account surplus needs a current-account deficit.

And therein lies Germany's dilemma. It needs Europe and the rest of the eurozone. But this puts it into an uncomfortable position, because the solution to the euro's crisis in the short term will involve breaking the rules to which the Germans are so attached. And the longer-term solution will necessitate an inflationary expansion in Germany to drag the periphery out of the recession.

On my last visit to Germany, in July 2012, I sat on the banks of the Rhine in the lovely city of Mainz, watching the Euro 2012 final between Spain and Italy on a big screen. It was a warm evening, and the city was buzzing, the river busy with huge barges, propelled by the low drum-and-bass of large diesel engines. This is the muscle of the German economy: exports heading up the Rhine to Rotterdam and on out to the rest of the world. As I sat amongst the locals watching Spain and Italy, I wondered if these Germans had any idea just how much their future would be affected by what happens in those two Latin countries.

There was more at stake than football. Much more.

16. Twenty-eight Weeks

Olivia hadn't slept very well: not just because she was the size of a house, but also because today was D-Day. She was meeting Dick Murphy, the principal, about next year. She was trying to anticipate what he might say but couldn't concentrate because of the heartburn.

Look at what you're doing to me, Una.

Beside her, Sean slept, half snoring, little tufts of hair knotted on his chest. He looked well – lean and disciplined – unlike their finances, which were getting more sloppy and chaotic by the day. He had taken up running to keep sane, and it was working, on his body and brain. Look at the pair of them, she thought: Jabba the Hutt and Jarvis Cocker. As she got bigger, he became slimmer.

If they could only run the debts off, things would be OK.

But they couldn't.

She eased herself to the side of the bed and started to rub her bump with big dollops of moisturizer, hoping to avoid stretch marks. It looked as though she was trying to make yoghurt, lathering on oceans of the stuff in the half-light, with you-know-who stretching and kicking and making herself comfortable.

You quite all right in there, Una? Got everything you need? Satisfied with the service? I hope it's not below your expectations.

Olivia couldn't wait to meet her. By now, she knew, the baby was beginning to look like a real thing, an actual person.

She took her phone from the bedside locker. She punched the numbers in again, as if repeating the calculations would somehow make their budget miraculously add up.

But it didn't.

The new variable interest rate was 5.19 per cent. It wasn't an error.

It meant their monthly payments were now €1,727.75 per month. They could just about scrape it together, but her Gaviscon bill alone might tip them over if Sean had a bad month. There was simply no margin for error.

She'd never been that gone on the house, with its flimsy walls and cramped spaces, but she had come to love the estate. Sam was happy there. He was settled in the tiny local Church of Ireland school – much to Nan's disgust. The Indian dad of his best friend, Arwan, had organized a cricket team for the kids of the estate. The minute he put on his Chelsea kit and headed out to the green, he was master of his universe. The children had a lot of freedom to roam, just as she'd had when she was young, hanging out on the streets with Viv, Barry and all the other local kids, playing Bulldog, Capture the Flag and endless soccer matches.

The family across the road had recently left for London. They were holed up in a small flat. The other day their little boy complained via Skype to Sam that there was nowhere to play. No doubt the parents could reinvent themselves in London, but it was a paradise only for adults. For the children it was a chicken coop. Sam was as glued to Xbox, PSP and Wii as any child, but at least he had a life outside too.

Olivia's problem was that they couldn't afford it.

She stared at her phone. €1,727.75. She held her head in her hands. Her elbows rested on the bump. €52.13 per month extra since they'd moved on to the variable mortgage rate on a house that had cost €350,000 and for which they'd be lucky to get €150,000 now.

There was no way she could get back to sleep. Besides, the cramps in her left leg were killing her. She needed to walk and think.

Olivia moved as gracefully as a heavily pregnant woman with an aching back and heartburn could, easing downstairs and settling beside the IKEA Billy shelf in the 'office'. This was a corner of the sitting room, between the Ektorp pull-out couch bed and the Micke desk – the same collection of furniture that the whole estate seemed to have. Everyone in the estate thought they were individuals, but, inside and out, all the homes were nearly identical. She smiled as she remembered thinking she was way ahead of the curve when they had bought all their bits and bobs in the Belfast IKEA, before the Dublin store opened.

She pulled up myhome.ie on the laptop. Rentals in Wicklow: a few houses on the estate were listed. She could rent an exact copy of their house for €850 a month – the McBrides' from across the road, the family who were off in London trying to make their fortune.

We have to do something about this, Una, she thought. *Otherwise, you're going to grow up a pauper. We can't have that. You're not coming out of Mummy into the cold for that, are you?* She smiled. *I didn't think so either, honey.*

She opened the old CD folder they used as a skip for the bills and started totting everything up.

Her take-home pay was €2,100 a month. Sean was getting €700 from standing in for people at the TEFL school, but that could vanish at any time. Child benefit was €140. That gave them a monthly income of €2,940.

She got out the overdue bills and spread them on the desk. Sean was great at so many things but he couldn't seem to face this mess. The dreadfulness of their situation, and his inability to make enough of a living, made him too angry to focus. So many people were like them, she thought. How many other households around the country were doing the same thing: clinging on, stuck in the no man's land between great expectations and hard times?

She started to make a list of their monthly expenditures.

Mobile phone €80, petrol €160, groceries €500, health and house insurance €225, Dart fares €112, TV licence €13.33, motor tax €31, car insurance €29, house phone €30, internet €29.99, electricity €124, childcare €541, bin charges €12. That made €1,887.32 so far.

She'd put the credit card in a drawer months ago. She was relieved the repayments on the car loan had finished last year, but the NCT was going to be due soon, and they didn't have the money to fix the car if it failed.

With the new mortgage of €1,727.75 a month on top of the other bills, their outgoings were €3,615.07. Right now, they took in €2,940.

So, with nothing going wrong and nothing unexpected happening, they were under water by €675 a month. They had just over €2,000 savings, but that would be gone by September at this rate. And a new baby was coming.

It was nearly morning. The sun was rising over Wicklow bay. Tucked behind the desk, she couldn't see it, but she could sense it.

Upstairs, nothing stirred.

Dick Murphy was a neat little man. Five eight, ten stone, small-shouldered and slim. He rarely missed an opportunity to have a quick double-check if a mirror or reflecting window presented itself – just to make sure everything was in place. In recent years he'd started carrying round a pair of curved scissors for cutting nose and ear hair. His suits, which were taken in at the shoulder and tapered narrowly on the leg, always hung perfectly, just landing on the fourth lace hole. His waist was unchanged since college: 30 in British, maybe a 32 in the more slim-fitting Italian numbers.

He had a fondness for slightly cutaway collars, the kind favoured by pre-Big Bang City-of-London types. His shirts were always starched, double cuffed, 100 per cent Indian cotton. He had a pair of shoes hand-made for him every two years, not expensively, but by one of the few cobblers still in business just off Capel Street. He kept a collection of wooden shoehorses; he never much fancied the plastic versions.

His grey hair was cut short, and he had a military mien, a sort of barracks-room efficiency about him. He was, after all, running a training camp for the next officer class of the Republic.

Nothing mattered more to Dick Murphy than the points race. It was the objective measure of success. He was, unusually for the head of a school steeped in Catholic tradition, inclined towards atheism. He put his faith, such as it was, in the rational, the proven, the scientific.

★

'Come in, Miss Vickers,' he said formally. The voice had a slight hint of the Cork merchant prince. Maybe not quite the RCYC or Glenstal, but no lower than Pres', Christians at a push.

It was obvious to Olivia that her altered form unnerved him. His gaze lingered a little on the bump. She could almost feel him calculating her BMI. It was the sort of sum that would occupy his frontal lobe. Dick Murphy didn't like waste. She could see he was worried about whether she would be able to shed it.

The Newton's Cradle on his spotless desk clicked and clacked, until he stopped it with an abrupt, decisive movement.

'Olivia, sit down, take the weight off your feet.'

Charming, she thought.

'How's everything?'

'OK, considering.' She looked down at her bump.

'Not long to go now?' His nonchalant air felt forced.

'Twelve weeks to go,' she said, 'and then the real fun starts.'

'Yes, I remember when our little Robert was in nappies, Susan was run off her feet,' Dick said. 'Things are different now, I suppose. Men, I mean – they're different now, no?'

Olivia had forgotten he was a father. It didn't seem to fit.

'Well, more interfering,' she joked. 'No, seriously, Sean is a brilliant father. He's always there and carries more than his fair share of the load.'

Dick, well aware of Sean's predicament, decided he'd get straight to the point.

'Olivia, I have some good news and some not so good news for you.'

Here it comes, she thought.

'First, we will hope to see you back here in November, or will it be December?'

Olivia wanted to hug him, but was afraid he'd never recover from the suffocating experience.

'The not so good news is that you'll be on reduced hours. The parents of the Leaving Cert boys wouldn't tolerate a change in teacher in the middle of the academic year. And they are right.'

Typical Dick – direct, cutting, but, in a way, fair.

'You are a wonderful teacher, Olivia,' he continued. 'I'm aware that you'll have a lot on your plate in the coming months. Your grade matrix is excellent. The boys like you and you bring out the best in many of them.'

Nobody could accuse Dick Murphy of playing fast and loose with the compliments.

'So, unfortunately, you won't be teaching sixth years next year. But you will have both second year and fifth. This means your hours will reduce by 36 per cent. Unfortunately, your salary will reduce as well, pro rata. However, we have no hesitation in keeping you, Olivia.' This last was delivered with what Dick Murphy believed to be a supportive smile.

Olivia tried to take it all in. The optimist in her was thankful because there could have been truly dreadful news – she might have been let go altogether. But she knew their already fragile financial house of cards was about to be hit by a real wrecking ball, not like the pretend yoke sitting on Dick's desk.

'Olivia,' he said, 'I will try to boost your income by making some of the grinds that parents insist on available to you as they come to me. It's not school policy to encourage these adventures, but who are we to contradict the will of fee-paying parents?'

He summed up, clearly pleased that Olivia hadn't made a scene. 'The paperwork will be executed by the Department and returned to us and then to you by end of term. Best of luck with everything, and you know where I am. If not always wide open, the door is certainly ajar at all times.'

That was his best effort at humour. It was the type that leaves lots of room for ambiguity.

'Believe me, Olivia, we are all behind you.'

Not for the first time in the past few months, Olivia walked towards the staffroom in a daze. Her feet hurt.

Sometimes she felt as though there were two Olivias. The big pregnant one, whom people on the Dart stood up for and older women smiled at benevolently. Whose bump perfect strangers had an urge to touch.

Then there was the other Olivia, the teacher, the mortgage-holder, whose life hadn't stopped in the nine-month pregnancy bubble. This one still had to do corrections, plan for the future. This Olivia had to be a good mother and, God help her, a lover. Sometimes she thought Sean deserved a medal for persevering, telling her she was special, when the whole performance was the product of an absurd contortionist's imagination.

Olivia plonked down beside Barbara, putting her swollen ankles up on the wicker coffee table.

'Well, Vickers?'

'See you in December,' Olivia said.

'Brill'.' Barbara grinned. 'All sorted so?'

'Almost,' she said. 'Just a few things to get my head around.'

Barbara was well aware of Olivia's money problems. She herself wasn't far behind: the same negative equity, the same long commute and the same interminable quest for a permanent contract. Olivia knew things weren't the best at home for her. The seven-year itch had started scratching at three. Brendan had moved in and out twice already. Barbara was trying to hold it all together, but she'd been half thinking that if this was it, maybe it was better to get it over with so that she could move on before being past it.

Mike D'Arcy smiled warmly at her. He must know, Olivia thought; but maybe not.

'Hi, Olivia,' said Mike. 'When are you due?'

'Tomorrow, the way I feel at the minute.' She smiled back. 'No, seriously, not for another twelve weeks. But if you pricked me I'd burst.'

Immediately she realized this wasn't the right phrase, but it was out and gone. That horse was now cantering around the field while the stable door was well off its hinges, flapping around in the wind.

They both laughed.

'Do you have any idea if it's a boy or a girl?'

'No, but we are assured by the gynaecologist that it bears an uncanny resemblance to a blue whale, sex undetermined.'

'Jesus, would you stop?' giggled Barbara.

'By the way, Mike,' she asked, 'may I have Damien's number?'

There was a time when Damien D'Arcy didn't answer calls from numbers not in his address book. These days he answered anything that rang.

His phone hadn't rung often since the 'difficulties', as his ex-firm's press release referred to his fall from grace. But that was the rule in Ireland, as far as he could work out. Success was fêted, failure shunned. It was probably the same the world over, but Damien felt Ireland suffered from a particularly virulent strain.

Damien reckoned most people feared failure was contagious; certainly they all ran a mile from him once things went downhill. When you stripped everything back, status in the boom-time was more or less success by association. Just by being in the same circle as the movers and shakers, one could attain a state of elevated social grace. In the bust, there was a similar failure-by-association vibe going on, and Damien D'Arcy was infected.

The same lawyers, accountants and consultants who always used to be in the newspapers, falling over themselves to brag about their deals with large property owners and builders, had reappeared in different guises. These people, his former colleagues, didn't make things and sell them; they just made money from those who did. Damien now understood that not only was this behaviour a form of economic looting, pure and simple, but that looting was the objective. The better the looter, the more successful the firm.

As he read newspapers online, he began to see clearly that the economic looting at the top was totally indiscriminate. It knew no loyalty, no party lines. The same respectable firm of accountants that had audited Anglo and said nothing was amiss now audited NAMA. The estate agents who had overvalued property in the boom, those voluble cheerleaders of that disaster, had now re-emerged and were being paid by the state to act for NAMA. Law firms were being hired to give economic advice. The individuals who had been on the boards of banks and property companies were now working as government advisers. No one seemed to take the rap.

It was all about the fee.

Even their politics had changed. In the boom, Damien and his partners would take turns at dinner parties to criticize big government, like the good little libertarians they were. Now of course, his old friends couldn't get enough of the state's bounty. There was no point being on the inside unless you could use your pull. That was what it was all about. Who knew whom, whose network was the most fruitful, who could make the call, who could get the deal done. It was a club.

This isn't like America, he thought. There, glorious failure was celebrated – indeed Americans seemed to seek it out as a mark of character, and gave you another chance. Not here. God might like a trier, but nobody else did. When Damien fell, he fell alone.

At the school gates, his phone buzzed. He was early for William. He was always early on Wednesdays. He couldn't wait to see him. He stood aloof from the chatting mothers, a sea of blonde against the backdrop of black 4×4s parked lazily up on the kerbs outside the school.

He had William every Wednesday, and every Friday till early Sunday morning. It suited Sonya. She could be free on Friday and Saturday nights to get on with her new life. Damien dreaded Sunday morning when he had to drop William back before church.

Usually it was three days of nets in the back garden, with William doing his best Messi and Damien letting in goals as discreetly as he could. William lined up the ball and hit it with all the power his little left leg could muster; Damien feigned to save but usually managed to fumble, which led to wild celebrations by the five-year-old, Barcelona shirt pulled up over his head, running around in circles. This went on for hours and hours, and they both loved it.

'Damien, it's Olivia here. Olivia Vickers – from college.'

'Hi – I know,' he said. 'I recognize your voice.'

'As long as you didn't recognize my number –' She didn't mean to say that. It just came out. Jesus, he'd think she was a stalker.

'Why would I know that?' His voice was lawyer-cold – that emotionless distant monotone she remembered.

She tried a jaunty 'How's life?'

'OK, same old.'

'I saw your dad yesterday,' she said.

'I know.'

Of course he did, she thought. He wasn't doing anything else these days. It was hard to imagine him looking forward to chatting to his dad at 4 p.m. when the school day was over. It was tragic, but also funny to visualize him in an apron making his father's dinner, or listening to Joe Duffy after his walk on the strand. But that was his life.

'I was expecting your call,' he said.

He was so sure of himself. Perfect for what Olivia needed. Her Sean was so many things, but sometimes she wished he'd be a little bit more manly.

She took a deep breath. 'OK, Damien, remember you said if I ever needed a lawyer? Well that day has come. To cut a long story short, we're bust. Our mortgage is too big, the interest rate has just gone up, and our income keeps dropping. We can't pay it. I've been doing sums for the past few weeks, trying to find a way out, but there isn't any. But the thing is, I'm – we're – terrified of what's going to happen. Will they kick us out of the house? How do I tell everyone at school? The last thing the school wants is a bankrupt teaching their fee-paying children.'

'Don't worry about that school,' Damien said. 'At least you stayed here to face the music. Half the fathers of kids in that school have moved to England to declare themselves bankrupt so they can skip out on the twelve-year rule.'

This was good to hear, but it did not address her deepest worry. 'I was wondering, could you advise me on our legal options? We really have no idea. And, I should say, we could only pay you in little bits. It mightn't be worth your while, Damien.'

'Don't be silly, Olivia, this is more important than money. And, anyway, you're broke. You'd be broker still if you paid me.'

She heard him laughing. Its effect was immediate, and she was back on Sandymount Strand with him.

'The first thing is: don't panic. It will all be OK. We'll find a way.'

Just as she was about to giggle with relief, he switched into lawyer mode again. She didn't mind. 'What you should ask a lawyer about the course of action you're about to embark on, any course, is not "Can I do this?" You can do whatever you like. The question is "What are the legal ramifications if I do?" We first need to establish what we are trying to do. You need to give me all the information that you have, everything, every payment, every letter, every notification of any change to the mortgage.'

'Of course, no problem.'

'And before we even think about a more interesting path, what you have to do first is go into the bank and be honest. Tell them you need a break.'

'How do you mean?'

'Tell them you need a moratorium on payments until you can get your finances in order. Perhaps a six-month holiday from the payments, or that you need to move to interest-only payments, or some structure that allows you to avoid defaulting. It will be in their interests to accept a little bit less now to get more in the end.'

'OK, we'll do that,' she said. 'Thanks, Damien. You have no idea what this means to me.'

'Oh, yes, I do.'

This threw her.

'I know what it's like to feel under siege,' he said. 'I want to help you and other people like you. Let's just say it's God's work.'

17. The Mortgage Crisis – and What to Do about It

Gradually, then suddenly

Perhaps the best description of the journey from solvency to bankruptcy comes from Hemingway in his novel *The Sun Also Rises*. Two American characters have just met and are talking intently, each trying to figure out what the other is doing in rural Spain in the 1920s. One of them asks the other, 'How did you go bankrupt?' The other responds, 'Two ways. Gradually and then suddenly.'

When we look at how countries, firms and individuals go bankrupt, we see that Hemingway got this right. Initially, it is a gradual process, and the parties tend to be in denial. When dealing with a new reality – a difficulty in meeting a mortgage payment, or a drop in the value of our home – most of us tend to expect that things will return to normal. It takes a while to get our heads around a permanent fall in prices or incomes.

Over time, though, it becomes apparent that circumstances have changed, and that there is a monumental shift occurring under our feet. At the point when bankruptcy can no longer be avoided, things move rapidly. The run-up to bankruptcy is a panic situation: the creditor tries to get his hands on as much as possible and the debtor tries to preserve something for himself.

If we examine how the Irish state ended up in a position where no one would lend to it we see a similar evolution. For a year there was talk and jitters, but no real sense that we were close to being locked out of the markets. Then, in a matter of days, the state ran out of options. When the moment came, it came quickly: almost overnight, our economic sovereignty was gone.

At present, the Irish banks that have been bailed out using state capital have been exercising a moratorium on mortgage foreclosures:

this was the social price exacted in return for the state's financial infusion. But it can't go on forever. Mortgage arrears might yet break the banks again.

To emerge from this mess, against a background of still-falling house prices (and despite having been recapitalized by the state), the banks will need new capital. This will come only when investors are certain that there are no nasty surprises hidden on the banks' balance sheets. Who would invest in a bank knowing that the new capital invested would merely be filling the hole created by all the bad loans that haven't been written down yet?

As a result of this reluctance to inject fresh capital, Irish banks will have to finance themselves from their own resources for some time to come. To do this, they will need to get their loan-to-deposit ratios down to 100 per cent. The average figure for the big banks is now around 140 per cent. They must make fewer loans over the next few years, or raise more deposits, or both.

All of this implies that for the foreseeable future Irish banks will be little more than safe-deposit boxes, places where money is trapped, rather than engines for redistributing money around the economy. The velocity of money – the rate at which each euro changes hands in the economy – will continue to fall. In a thriving economy, the velocity of money is high. But if the velocity of money continues to fall – because the banks are not recycling cash by lending it out – it means we remain stuck in a liquidity trap. There is very little a central bank can do about that – other than to put money back into the people's pockets directly. This can be achieved only by engineering a dramatic one-off debt deal that reduces the monthly mortgage bill and frees up that money, so that it can be spent in the real economy on real things.

We don't have much time to spare.

At the time of writing, summer 2012, five years into this crisis – remember, with interest rates at an all-time low, we are still in the gradual phase, before the sudden bit – close to one in seven private residential mortgage accounts is over ninety days in arrears. The ratio of buy-to-let mortgages in arrears is twice that.

If these are the numbers when interest rates are at historic lows, it is not difficult to imagine what will happen when interest rates rise. The ongoing crisis in Europe may keep rates low for some time, but people with another twenty or twenty-five years on their adjustable-rate mortgages know they're going to get stung sooner or later.

So the endgame is that someone has to lose – either the debtor or the creditor. The best solution is co-responsibility, where both debtor and creditor take a hit and move on. In Ireland up to now, the debtors – the ordinary people with the huge mortgages – have been asked to shoulder everything, while the creditors – the banks that lent the money – are still behaving as if they expect to be paid in full. They won't be; nor should they be.

Doubtless, in some cases mortgage defaults are due to brazen financial recklessness. But these cases are the minority. For most, such as Olivia and Sean, the scale of the property and of the loan were perfectly normal for the time – the problem being that what was normal in the mid noughties in Ireland was completely insane. For many of those who borrowed at that time, there will come a moment when the numbers simply don't add up any more. Many people in Ireland, like Olivia and Sean, borrowed sums that were too big relative to their incomes even in the good times. The first driver for default is falling incomes; now that incomes are in decline, more and more of these people are getting into trouble. With incomes continuing to fall, the arrears statistics will get worse, and this factor alone could yet create a truly massive crisis.

The second possible driver of mortgage defaults, rising interest rates, has not yet reared its head. Olivia's situation is, in this respect, unusual: her interest rate has actually gone up a bit, but holders of mortgages like hers are in the minority. For the hundreds of thousands of households on super-cheap trackers, rates have never been lower. But there is only one direction in which their mortgage costs can go from here: up. It's impossible to say when European interest rates will rise, but we know that they won't stay at historic lows forever. And when they do go up, the debt problems in Trackerville will intensify, perhaps catastrophically.

According to the figures that the minister for finance cited in the Dáil in late 2011, household debt in Ireland is at a breathtaking 147 per cent of GNP. Any upward movement in interest rates will subsequently have a devastating impact on the average person's ability to repay mortgage debt.

Together with interest rates and income, a third major factor in the trajectory of debt dynamics and defaults is the attitude of the banks. As long as they don't insist on getting their money back immediately, there is a chance that a mass mortgage-default episode can be avoided for an extended period. This has come to be known as the 'delay-and-pray' strategy.

In general, the attitude of the banks will be decided by whether they can gain access to cheap money. If the central bank keeps financing them, banks can continue to exercise patience. But if a bank continues to overlook the bad debts on its books, it will remain a zombie bank, doing little new business and existing mainly to collect existing loans and to service its own debts. In order to linger in this state, the zombie bank will need a shareholder that doesn't care about the value of its investment. This may be possible under government ownership. However, this is not a plausible long-term prospect: a situation in which ordinary people indefinitely cover the losses of barely functioning banks is not tolerable. Banks must return to profitability at some stage, a necessity that may prove incompatible with the current moratorium on foreclosure.

Taken together, these three factors – income, interest rates and the attitude of the banks – will determine much about the next phase of the Irish mortgage crisis. But there is one more crucial ingredient to add to this toxic mix, and that is what happens in Europe.

If present policies are not changed, the eurozone could fall into a Japan-style 'lost decade' (or longer) of stagnation. In this scenario, Ireland's economy would continue to suffer in all the ways we are currently seeing. If, on the other hand, Europe finds some way of dealing with the debt crisis and resumes a growth path that is acceptable to financial markets, eases the debt burden and allows economies to expand, we will have some cause for happiness. For Trackerville, however, there will be a serious downside: interest rates will inevitably rise from their current historic lows, and Ireland, the eurozone economy with the highest level of household debt, will suffer mortgage default on a vast scale.

Counter-intuitively, a European recovery could make things worse for many, many people in Ireland. This is why we have to look for a solution to our mortgage-debt burden as soon as possible.

Here, the weight of mortgage debt falls overwhelmingly on relatively young people who bought houses in the past ten years. As a consequence, the extent and trajectory of defaults will largely depend on the attitudes of this generation. Up to now they have been stoical; most families are keeping their heads down and trying to keep up their payments. This will continue until it becomes impossible – or until it becomes socially acceptable to default.

In an environment where half of mortgages are in negative equity, the chance of mortgage defaults going viral intensifies. Each default will encourage the next guy to do likewise. As the nightmare scenario increasingly becomes the norm, default turns into a socially acceptable option. One of the many lessons of the Irish boom is that humans are herd animals.

The trajectory of bankruptcy – gradually, then suddenly – is likely to play out not only in individual households but on a macro level: there is a real danger that, quite swiftly, it will become apparent that vast numbers of distressed Irish borrowers have stopped repaying their mortgages.

An alternative to mass default

Is mass default desirable? If uncontrolled, no: it would trigger another Irish banking crisis (or a drastic intensification of the ongoing one), with potentially chaotic consequences. But the status quo – in which people can't afford to pay their mortgages, and the banks can't afford to write them down – is not sustainable, and conditions could get worse before they get better. Thus, a negotiated programme of mortgage-debt restructuring must be considered.

The question facing us, with regard to mortgage debt in Ireland, is: do we wait and watch the slow-motion crash, or do we do something about it?

In the corporate world, the answer is unambiguous: you do something about it. Ireland's corporate and personal bankruptcy regimes are antiquated and don't work, but other countries' bankruptcy regimes are built on the understanding that once personal or corporate debt becomes unsustainable, it's in everyone's interest to come to a new arrangement. In the US, Chapter 11 of the Bankruptcy Code is deployed regularly to save companies that have good underlying businesses but are carrying too much debt. Creditors accept that, while they will not be paid in full, they will get more through a negotiated restructuring of the debt than by forcing the borrower into failure. Such a mechanism is not unique to the United States: all over the world, highly indebted companies that are worth saving are rescued by debt deals that see old creditors accepting less in the short term in order to get more in the long term. Ordinary homeowners are different from companies, of course, but the principle is the same: if we want the people of Trackerville to be full participants in the economy – spending, investing, taking risks – the banks need to cut a deal with them.

To ignore the mortgage-debt problem today is as misguided and reckless as believing the conventional wisdom a few years ago about house prices only going up. We now know to our cost that letting the property bubble inflate brought about a national catastrophe. Similarly, allowing the debt burden to become heavier and heavier until it cannot be borne any longer, leading to chaotic viral mortgage default, would be similarly reckless.

At the height of the Great Depression, President Roosevelt, recognizing that the economy was being held back by debt and also understanding that a new wave of defaults would further destabilize the economy, stated it was his objective to 'relieve the small home owner of the burden of excessive interest and principal payments incurred during the period of higher values and higher earning power'. In the summer of 1933 he embarked on a comprehensive programme of debt relief by setting up the Home Owners' Loan Corporation (HOLC) to buy mortgages from banks in exchange for bonds. The government then restructured the mortgages, writing off significant amounts of principal. In all, one million mortgages were restructured.

Over time, as US conditions improved, and the mortgages started to perform profitably, it sold them back to the banks. Thus, a million Americans, who might otherwise have been kicked out of their homes, got back on track and paid off their loans.

How it could work

The first objective of an Irish mortgage-debt relief scheme would be to avoid a chaotic mass default. The second would be to give hope to hundreds of thousands of young Irish people who are drowning in mortgage debt and for whom the financial future offers little. A third and equally crucial objective would be to free the general domestic economy from the weight of too much debt.

Any initiative must not be an all-in amnesty. It ought to be targeted at those who bought during the bubble years and who are in genuine need of relief: people like Olivia. The scheme must be confined to owner-occupiers; some buy-to-let investors and owners of holiday homes have troubles of their own, but relief must be targeted at those, like Olivia and Sean, who bought their house or apartment for the purpose of living there.

The next two big questions are: who would administer the relief scheme, and who would pay for it? These questions, and their answers, go hand in hand.

There would be no need to create a new state agency to administer such a scheme: it could be run by the banks. Up to now, the banks have failed to do anything serious about writing down mortgages to realistic levels. This is not because they lack the capability to do so, but because they have had no clear incentive to do so, economically or politically. What is needed, from the Irish state, the Irish central bank and the ECB, is a new approach that makes it worth the banks' while to offer relief on unsustainable mortgages. The people who run this country must overcome their ruinous aversion to small risks, which has allowed much bigger long-term dangers, like a mortgage-arrears crisis, to build and build.

Given that house prices rose rapidly during the bubble years, the write-downs might be administered on a sliding scale, with those who bought at the peak getting the biggest break. Let's imagine an average loan write-down of one third. Picture a mortgage with €300,000 outstanding. The mortgage-holder applies for relief, and is accepted. Her mortgage is written down to €200,000, with repayments restructured accordingly.

This leaves a hole of €100,000 on the balance sheet of the bank that needs to be filled. One way of filling this hole – or a part of it – would be to give the bank an equity stake. When the house is sold, a percentage of the proceeds – perhaps matching that of the write-down – would go to the bank. This is a debt-for-equity swap: the bank takes equity and the borrower gets debt relief.

The equity stake would not wholly solve the bank's new balance-sheet problem, however, because a large proportion of the homes covered by the relief scheme would be in negative equity. The banks would need an infusion of capital from somewhere else in order to keep their balance sheets intact.

This is the point at which some readers might start to get nervous. Those who stayed on the sidelines during the boom might, understandably, assume that the losses crystallized in any mortgage-relief deal would inevitably be borne, directly or indirectly, by the Irish public – and they might see this as another instance of the prudent bailing out the imprudent. But the burden of mortgage relief need not inevitably fall on the Irish public. There is another way – but it involves negotiation, and it requires that our politicians and civil servants get out of the Good Room.

At the time of writing, late summer 2012, EU states are facing into high-stakes negotiations over a deal to diminish the burden of bank debt borne by the countries of the periphery, in keeping with the communiqué issued from the EU summit at the end of June. By the time this book has been published, it is possible that Ireland and other countries of the periphery will have been granted a useful degree of relief, with Germany and other countries of the core accepting a heavier burden. Equally, it is possible that negotiations will still be ongoing, or that talks will have broken down.

What we can say with some certainty is that this process will not produce a deal on relief for Irish mortgage-holders: the issue, as far as we know, is not even on the agenda, though it ought to be. A sensible reallocation of the burden of EU bank debt is something very much to be hoped for, but it will not make much difference to people like Olivia, who face unsustainable mortgage payments.

But if and when our leaders finally face up to the need to help mortgage-holders, they will be in a good position to secure ECB participation in a relief scheme, thus avoiding yet another big bill for the Irish taxpayer. The rationale for ECB involvement in the funding of the scheme would be the same as the rationale – accepted across the EU in June – for spreading the burden of bank debt: the Irish mortgage crisis would not have occurred had banks in Germany and other core countries not bankrolled the property bubble.

What if the Irish state secures money from the EU to fund the write-down process, but the banks simply sit on the capital and do nothing with it, just as they've done in the past few years?

This is where Draghi comes in. Write-down targets could be imposed on the banks' mortgage books, and the flow of ECB liquidity made contingent on their hitting these targets. Compliance could be monitored by the Irish central bank acting under licence from Frankfurt. If banks failed to meet their write-down targets, access to ECB liquidity could be limited or cut off.

The time is now

At the moment, the mortgage-debt crisis in Ireland mainly affects people like Olivia. But if it goes viral, it becomes a big problem for the banks, and hence for the ECB. The ECB is currently in fire-fighting mode and not doing much about fire prevention. The same can be said of the Irish state. But if and when mortgage defaults hit a critical mass in Ireland, a relief programme will be needed, so that the people and the banks alike can move on. And fairness and logic demand that the eurozone makes use of its stability funds to pay for this, so that the burden does not fall on the Irish taxpayer, already paying the price for the banks' madness. The principle of the EU sharing the burden of Ireland's bank debt has already been conceded. But a bank-debt deal without a mortgage-debt deal does nothing to help the hundreds of thousands of people like Olivia.

Despite all the evidence of a massive crisis in the making, there is still huge complacency about the real possibility that hundreds of thousands of people will decide they can no longer pay their mortgages. This is not surprising. During the boom, those running the show consistently ignored warnings that it would end in tears. First they ridiculed opposing views; then, when the truth became impossible to escape, they pretended that they had seen it coming all along.

It's not unreasonable to suggest that the same process will be repeated with respect to a mass mortgage default. When the combination of falling incomes, rises in interest rates and a moribund economy – impeded by the twin pressures of debt deflation and a liquidity trap – forces thousands into seeking mortgage deferrals or write-downs, events will sweep away conventional wisdom once more.

Surely, rather than waiting and hoping for a miracle, it would be wiser for our leaders to exploit the current power struggle in Europe, and the emerging indications of an evolving philosophy at the ECB, by pitching for a mortgage deal for Ireland? We know that Draghi is willing to deploy unorthodox methods to save the euro. We also know that the ECB and the Troika won't want to see Ireland – the best boy in the bailout class, the poster child for austerity – stumble into a fresh crisis. Ireland should now capitalize on these favourable conditions in Europe: the time is right to get out of the Good Room and to strike a mortgage-debt deal. We might not get a better chance.

18. Thirty Weeks

Olivia sat at the front of the class, scratching her bump. Up and down, nails digging in, until there were angry red streaks across her belly.

'You OK, Miss?'

She'd forgotten where she was. They were all staring, not even trying to hide their sniggering.

'I'm fine, Mr Kelly,' she said, still scratching the itch absent-mindedly.

At that moment, she realized her hand was not scratching her bump. It was halfway up her shirt, manically rubbing her left boob.

Oh, Jesus.

'Beats the Brest-Litovsk Treaty, Miss,' roared Evan O'Mahony from the back. The class erupted. Olivia laughed too, because when you're caught, you're caught.

'Mr O'Mahony, why is it you're not this quick when it comes to your classwork?'

'Dunno, Miss. I think it's a problem of motivation.'

Olivia grinned. 'Since you've mentioned it: before the Brest-Litovsk Treaty, the secret service of which European country facilitated Lenin's journey back to St Petersburg, and why?'

The bell rang, saving O'Mahony from the intricacies of early-twentieth-century politics.

As the class dispersed, three boys approached her. Kevin Gavigan spoke first.

'Miss, how long will you be here for?' He had a very serious face on – it was hard not to laugh. 'When are you leaving? It can't be long now.'

Olivia kept a straight face. 'Do I look like I'm about to pop, Mr Gavigan?'

'Well,' he stammered, 'something like that. It doesn't look comfortable.'

'It's not, to be completely fair,' she said, 'but you won't ever have to worry about being in this position.'

The boys laughed.

'Don't worry, gentlemen. We've done the whole course. We have two more weeks before we break up on the 1st of June, and I won't be abandoning you. We'll tie up the Cold War and go back over some of the terrain on Gladstone and then we are set. The exam, as I'm sure you're aware, isn't till the 13th.'

The boys, reassured, headed off to lunch. She would miss them.

Olivia sat in the empty classroom, rehearsing what she would say to the bank that afternoon. She thought about texting Sean again, but what was the point? He assumed nothing good could come out of a meeting. His sense of futility was starting to infect everything. He, Sean Doyle, the most dynamic student in the Arts Block ten years ago, was beginning to hate himself and the world.

'What's the point of going to the bank?' he'd said. 'We've no money, there's nothing we can do, bar humiliate ourselves in front of some prick in a suit who has already made up his mind.'

'Damien's email said we should be calm and listen; they are doing deals with lots of people. If we don't fly off the handle, he says we'll get a good hearing.'

'Damien, Damien, fucking Damien, our new saviour. Why don't you just go with your new best friend? Who is he, anyway? Some corporate reject clinging to the wreckage of our family's fucked finances, so he can feel better about himself. All very well for him to dispense advice; he's not involved. He doesn't have to live like a pauper and look people in the eye every weekend and know he's screwed.'

Yes, he does, Olivia thought; that's why he's listening to me. But she decided to let it go. Sean's rages were common now, triggered by the smallest things; but they usually blew themselves out. She loved him. It was horrible to see him so angry and frustrated.

★

In the end, Sean came round: there was nothing to be lost by hearing what the bank had to say. They'd arranged to meet outside the bank. He got there first; as Olivia approached, she saw that he was wearing a suit and tie, a sign of how little he understood why they were there.

'You dress up when you want money, dress down when you have none, duh,' she said, once she was in earshot. And then: 'C'mere and give us a hug, ye big gobshite.'

'Have you ever thought about selling the car, first off? It's not absolutely essential, is it? . . . Those mobile bills look quite hefty . . . Sean, your work is not bringing in much. If you feel that you won't get more hours, why not jack it in altogether? You do the day care, for free, and you save on outgoings. Sell the car since you won't need it – Olivia, you could take the bus to the Dart station.'

Listening to this, Olivia could feel Sean's pain; he was wounded rather than angry. This bank guy – Liam Henderson, ACA – didn't see them. He saw numbers, costs that could be cut, targets that might be met. He had no idea – and didn't care – about how his suggestions would affect their lives.

Olivia felt like a mammy called in by the principal to hear about her son's failings. There was little point in arguing with Henderson, she knew, but she couldn't help herself.

'Mr Henderson, there's no bus service between our estate and the Dart station. There's very little public transport of any kind out where we are. The amount of money we could save if we did what you suggest is pretty small, compared to the gap between what's coming in and what's going out. And we are expecting a baby, which will put a new strain on us financially. Is there not something the bank can do, like suspending payments until we get over this? Interest only or something?'

'We considered this, Mrs Doyle, but your case doesn't merit it. You can live within your means with some small tweaking, a bit of good housekeeping. It doesn't look to us, from the numbers, to be "a no bread on the table" case, if you know what I mean.'

*

'Daddy, what happens at night on the moon – is it daytime there?'

Damien felt the little hand come out from beneath the covers and search for his in the half-darkness.

'Yes, Willy, that's why it's so bright and that's why the man on the moon looks to be smiling at us.'

'Is it hot there? Like summer? Is he hot, the man?'

'Yes, and then when it's day here, it's night there, and he goes to sleep.'

'Would you like to go to the moon, Daddy?'

'Not really, darling.'

'When I'm big I'm going to go to the moon, right to the moon.'

He turned over, his little head shoved into the pillow, breathing it in.

'Daddy, do the sleepy, sleepy thing.'

Damien sat on the side of the little bed, stroking his son's head.

'Think about your toes, Willy, the little piggy first, then the next one and the next one. How do they feel? They're going fast asleep, sleepy, sleepy fast asleep, aren't they?'

'Yes, Daddy,' the boy groaned.

'They are so tired now, heavy, sleepy. Now move slowly up the soles of your feet, and think of your ankle. It is fast asleep, sleepy, sleepy, so heavy and tired. You can hardly feel it, it's so asleep. Now think about your shin. It's so sleepy. Now move gently to your knee, oh, it's so heavy, it can hardly move, sleepy.'

He half whispered, barely audible, hypnotic. When he knew the boy was gone, he crept out of the room and across the hall to his own, keeping the door open and the landing light on.

He woke his computer and scrolled through his inbox: an email from Olivia Vickers, explaining that the meeting with the bank had not gone well. She had also somehow got her hands on the bank's file for her mortgage, which she attached.

That was interesting, but the file seemed to be bog standard, nothing special. When they'd applied for the loan, Olivia and Sean had a combined income of €58,000. They bought a house for €350,000 – a ridiculous price-to-income ratio, but nothing unusual for the time.

According to the file, they paid a deposit of €35,000. The bank lent them €315,000, with the interest rate fixed for six years.

There were notes about Olivia's extra grinds, which were counted as permanent income – €5,000 a year.

It was getting late. He could hear William's tiny breaths next door.

As he flicked through the scanned pages of the file again, something caught his eye, just at the bottom of a page noting the details of Olivia's grinds, scrawled in pen. He tried to make it out.

Scribbled in blue pen was 'OK. Client known to the bank.'

Olivia slipped into the pub, dodging yet another hail shower, which was announcing the beginning of Dublin's tourist season. It had been Damien's choice to meet there. He didn't seem like the sort of lawyer to arrange a meeting in a pub, but at this stage Olivia would go wherever suited him.

She was a few minutes early. She leaned against one of the high stools facing the big window that framed the flower-sellers and gossiping taxi drivers outside the four-star hotel across the lane. She hardly dared get up on the stool in her condition.

'The thing is, love, the gas and air works a treat.'

A large, sweaty man, looking remarkably like an older, inflated version of Robbie Keane, eyed her up from the bar.

'Nearly ready to pop, love? From this angle anyway,' he leered.

He slicked back his hair and hitched up his trousers, but the push of his Ned Kelly and gravity were winning that battle hands down.

Olivia smiled weakly and turned back to the window. If someone else gives me their opinion of pain relief, she thought, I'll willingly do time for whatever pain I inflict on them.

The Dublin Don Juan was the fifth pregnancy pundit today. First Sean, then her mother, then Avril O'Connor pitched in, followed by the skinny wan in Starbucks who talked at her about acupuncture-induced deliveries, and, finally, this half-cut pub savant.

She signalled her unavailability for banter with headphones and a magazine, and then by texting furiously. But Dr Spock was a persistent type and having none of it.

'Ye see, love, the epidural is all grand if ye have a strong back. Stand up for a sec and give us a look at ye. It's all in the back.'

She pretended not to hear.

'You know they stick a huge yoke right in the back there, between the spine and – what d'you call them things? Vertebrates. Yeah, that's it. Right into your vertebrates.'

Trouser tug again.

'An' they squeeze all the drugs right down the tubey yoke, right inside ye.' He grinned. 'Works great.'

'Harry, would you leave the poor lady alone.' The barman was one of those unionized lads in a white shirt and black trousers. *Proper barmen,* her father used to call them. *Professionals. Men who know their trade.*

'I'm just saying is all, Rory,' responded the savant. 'So, unless you are making a complete disgrace of yourself, the gas an' air is your only man. Is all I'm saying.'

Miraculously, on this note he headed off to the jacks, a bit unsteady.

Freed from the effort of ignoring him, Olivia returned to her newfound fascination with the zodiac. Una was going to be a Leo. Normally she never gave a toss about things like this, but in the past few days she had devoured horoscopes, zodiac maps and all sorts from online cranks, astrologers and charlatans, looking for anything she could find on Leos. She had initially liked the idea, though now she was getting a bit lukewarm after extensive research in *OK* magazine.

Dominant, generous, independent, creative but jealous and possessive and needs to be the centre of attention. Can be bossy and egocentric. Vanity and pomposity can lead to Leo's downfall.

Olivia wasn't liking this that much.

Narcissistic and manipulative.

Jesus, was she about to give birth to Lady Macbeth?

They make excellent political leaders or heads of state.

Not quite within Olivia's parental ambitions, but she liked the idea of herself front seat at a future presidential inauguration.

Leos are very charming and charismatic, which attracts many admirers and followers throughout their life. And, like the lion, Leo has a certain air of dignity and grace. Leos are also very passionate, full of self-confidence, and very active individuals.

That's better, she thought.

They are good talkers and love novel things and new challenges. Famous Leos include Barack Obama.

OK, that seals it.

Olivia looked out of the window at the statue of Phil Lynott – another Leo – and waited. Her phone beeped.

Running 10 mins late, sorry. dd.

He gave her a warm hug, apologized profusely and ordered two cups of tea in one movement. 'How've the last few days been?' he asked.

'OK, you know how it is – all a bit crazy.' She rubbed the bump. 'Can't wait to get this out at this stage. But I really want to find an answer on the bank thing.'

'Are you sure?' Damien's tone was serious. 'You'll be up to your eyes in the months ahead.'

'I don't care. I have to do something.'

He smiled. 'Great stuff. OK, here's the deal. Do you want a pen to take notes?'

'Can I just listen and take it all in? Leaning over to write is difficult right now.'

'No sweat,' he said. 'I'll send you everything by email anyway.'

She felt a little rush inside. She didn't quite know what it was. He was much more handsome than she remembered. He'd always been cute, in a clean-cut way, but today he looked more dangerous, more powerful. She hadn't noticed his green eyes.

'OK, Olivia, I think we might have just had our first bit of luck.'

He produced a printout of the document with the 'OK. Client known to the bank' scribble.

'Do you know what they meant by this?' he asked.

'Well, my sister worked at the bank. It came up when we met to discuss the mortgage. It was all palsy-walsy, sister of Vivienne sort of thing.'

'Yes. I think this is our first piece of evidence that the bank were reckless. The reason the bank gave you much more of a loan than they should have was because your sister worked there.'

'But Damien, they were just trying to be nice to us. They said they'd "stretch it" for us.'

'Yes, I know, but it doesn't seem very nice any more, does it? Legally, Olivia, this could be our ace. By stretching it, as they called it, they were overlending. You qualified on the basis of something non-commercial, like the fact that your sister worked in the bank. You were one of the lads, so to speak. Now, we know that banks gave oversized loans to other people who weren't "known to the bank", but this note could put them in a tricky position. They may have to concede either that they were reckless in lending to you, because you were "known to the bank", or that they were reckless across the board. Either way, this could really help us.'

Olivia burst out laughing.

'So we can use their apparent generosity to our advantage. We can say they applied a non-commercial criterion and, in so doing, over-lent. Are you with me?'

'Yes, go on.' For the first time in ages, she felt she might have a chance.

'Now, armed with this little scribble, you might be able to go back to the bank and negotiate more manageable terms for the loan. But I want to propose something more ambitious – a confrontation with the bank, which could lead to a test case.'

He pulled his three-legged stool closer to her and planted his elbows on the table. Olivia leaned forward conspiratorially. She wasn't sure she liked the sound of 'test case', but she didn't relish another chat with Henderson either.

'There is absolutely no encouraging precedent for the sort of arguments I have in mind. The courts in Ireland have pretty much always taken the view that a contract is a contract, involving two informed and responsible parties, and that a loan contract between a bank and a borrower does not create a duty of care on the part of the bank. But I'm optimistic that the courts might start taking a broader view of these things. The law always eventually evolves to reflect what is going on in the greater society. The relevant statutes might not change, but judges don't judge in isolation. They're swayed by public opinion and the facts on the ground. Mind you, these are conservative people, and their natural stance is to uphold the status quo, but if they feel that the country is changing, their interpretation of the law will eventually change to reflect that.'

All she could do was nod. She was tired, and knew she wasn't taking it all in, but she sensed that all he needed was a nudge of encouragement.

'Oh, and just so you know, if we do end up in litigation, they're going to throw the book at us, using the best solicitors and the fanciest barristers. They'll try to figure out how you got a copy of the file, and accuse you and your sister of all kinds of things. But don't worry,' he said, not looking the least bit concerned, 'I'll take the flak for you. That's my job and something I'll relish. They'll fight, but not as hard as us, because they don't actually believe in what they're doing.'

She found his confidence strange, but she wasn't arguing.

He spread a few notes on the table.

'So here's the drill. First, we need to prove that they have a responsibility to behave prudently. We can draw on Article 45 of the Constitution, which states explicitly – and I am quoting here – "That in what pertains to the control of credit the constant and predominant aim shall be the welfare of the people as a whole." In other words, credit providers are part of the social fabric. We can also talk about the original Central Bank Act, which also explicitly refers to how the control of credit must be exercised in the interest of the welfare of the people as a whole, and about the Maastricht Treaty, which superseded the Central Bank Act and which put price stability at the heart of the control of credit. Encouraging massive house-price inflation through reckless bank lending is hardly consistent with price stability.

'These are our building blocks, if you see what I mean.'

She did.

'The purpose of our case, if it comes to pass, will be to try to create what lawyers would call a new tort – we might call it "reckless lending" – that has not yet been accepted by the courts.

'We want to convince a judge that a bank has a duty of care to a borrower, just as a doctor has a duty of care to a patient, and that in your case the bank failed in this duty by taking into account matters in the underwriting process that it ought not to have taken into account or that no reasonable banker would have taken into account. We will argue that they endangered you by lending you too much money for a bad reason. The bank will argue that no duty of care exists, and they'll be confident that the courts will agree. But the judges have one eye on public sentiment and the changing facts in the real world.'

Olivia had the strange feeling of being in the company of someone who would protect her.

Damien checked the time on his phone.

'We're not trying to write off your debt completely. We just want a fair settlement, which in my view would be to get the amount you owe reduced to the amount they should have prudently lent to you, based on the central bank's guideline that banks shouldn't lend more than three and a half times income. We all know that the guideline was completely ignored across the board, but it gives us a solid basis for claiming that the bank overlent and for seeking to get part of the loan written off.'

The drunken savant watched them suspiciously from the safe distance of the bar. At one point he tried to interject, but a single glance from Damien had him back behind his *Herald*.

'Now, the judges know that if they go against the banks, the whole system will come crashing down around them. If we were to win a case, there would be a queue of people like you from the Four Courts to Kildare. This would not only mean mayhem for the courts but it would also put the banks on the hook, as they should be, for all the greedy, despicable behaviour of the past ten years. No judge will relish this prospect. But I've been talking to people who follow these things closely, and they see changes ahead. Sometimes Irish judges wait for a development in the UK to give them the permission to change things here. It's the usual Irish way,' he said. 'Wait for someone else to make the running. So here is what is happening.'

Olivia was beginning to come under a sort of spell. It wasn't her style. But she found Damien's straight-backed integrity and his aura of calm extraordinarily attractive.

'In England there is a growing body of case law to the effect that the banks have a duty of care to the client. Just a few weeks ago one of our senior judges referred to this body of UK case law. It's a straw in the wind. It might mean we'd have a chance to convince a judge that the bank had a duty of care to you and Sean. The judiciary are afraid of bringing down the banking system, but they are also afraid that the law will be behind the times, and become less relevant.'

Three men, well heeled and a little portly, barged into the pub. One of them, glassy-eyed, moved to put down his briefcase but missed the table and shoved into Olivia.

Damien stood up.

'Watch what you are doing, please,' he said. 'Can't you see?'

The glassy-eyed man looked at Damien and laughed.

'If it isn't John the fucking Baptist.'

'Characteristically unoriginal, Theo,' replied Damien, controlled. 'I wouldn't have expected anything more from you, but then again I never expected anything from you in the first place.'

Ouch, thought Olivia.

'Now, let's leave it there, shall we?'

The glassy-eyed man evidently decided that he'd better leave it there. Olivia was shocked by Damien's unnerving calm and his unmistakable aggression.

'John the Baptist? What was that about?'

'Nothing,' he said. 'Just people I used to know. In a different life.'

'OK, Damien,' she said. 'What are our real chances?'

He shrugged. 'In truth, Olivia, slim-ish, but it would be morally wrong not to try.' She didn't see the grand moral dimension that he did. She just wanted to do the best thing for her children, including the one who was now kicking up a fuss below.

'Are you sure you don't mind doing all this?' Olivia asked. 'It will take you ages, and, as you know, Sean and I haven't a bean.'

'I haven't been more sure about anything in a long, long time.'

19.   What Next?

Where we're at

Not so very long ago, Irish people were reasonably confident about the future. Survey after survey reported how satisfied we were. We viewed our homes as repositories of wealth. We thought our banks were reasonably well managed. The currency in our pocket was stable, and here to stay.

Whatever we might have thought of our own politicians, we generally took the view that the European Union was efficiently run, if a bit boring. We were in safe hands.

Things haven't worked out that way.

On a daily basis – and this list is far from exhaustive – we are bombarded with headlines about the impending break-up of the euro, company closures, the continuing rise in mortgage arrears in Ireland and a heavy flow of emigration.

The EU has proved to have a serious design fault. It is built for slow movement in a single political direction. Faced with a crisis, it has shown itself to have the flexibility of a cargo train. This is a recipe for continuing drama and insecurity, because, whereas our institutions operate at a glacial pace, capital flows freely and instantaneously.

As each European financial intervention is superseded by yet another crisis, the bigwigs tell us that we need more European political and fiscal integration. Statements like this trigger wars in the commentariat. Those on the right spot a conspiracy by unelected federal elites, determined to circumvent democracy and the will of the people. Meanwhile, on the left, pundits berate our masters for kowtowing to unelected financial market traders, determined to circumvent democracy and the will of the people.

Is it any wonder people are confused?

Each eurozone bailout has involved passing the burden of ever more private debt into public hands. Ordinary citizens are being asked, all over Europe, to shoulder the debt not just of banks but also of bondholders who made the error of lending to governments and banks in countries such as Greece, Spain and Ireland.

The powers in Europe have moved to protect banks and creditors at all costs: this has turned out to be the defining aim of the European project over the past few years. Historically, this stems from an awareness that letting banks go bust in a disorderly fashion was a factor in creating the Great Depression of the 1930s and intensifying the Asian crisis of the 1990s. But foisting the costs resulting from bankers' stupidity on to ordinary citizens involves a vast unfairness, and the political consequences of this have yet to be seen. Why should the little guy pay for the sins of the rich guy? If this question is not answered properly, political tensions will only intensify.

Sado-fiscalism: If it doesn't hurt, you're not doing it right

Europe has lately succumbed to something that might be called 'sado-fiscalism', now formally enshrined in the Fiscal Compact. The practice is rooted in the false notion that a crisis caused by rampant greed and stupidity in the private sector is the fault of government spending. This falsehood carries the equally false implication that the crisis can be resolved by forcing governments to cut their deficits. The reality is that, in countries like Ireland and Spain, the budget deficits are the *consequence*, not the *cause*, of the slump. We are four years into this orgy of sado-fiscalism, and it is still not working on any level. Not only does the eurozone remain mired in a slump – its GDP contracted by 0.2 per cent in the second quarter of 2012 – but Europe's debt-to-GDP ratio is actually rising.

For Ireland – stuck, as we have seen, in an old-fashioned liquidity trap – sado-fiscalism is as useful as whipping a dead horse. But, trapped as our leaders are in a mental Good Room, there is no evidence that an alternative approach is being contemplated. The purveyors of austerity seem never to have encountered Keynes's concept of the paradox of thrift, or Richard Koo's analysis of the balance-sheet recession. Or, perhaps more to the point, they are not even asking the sort of questions that Keynes and Koo, or Minsky and Kindleberger, asked, because their agenda is far narrower. They're not interested in economic growth. They pay lip-service to it every now and then, but austerity is not a misconceived recipe for growth; it is a recipe for controlling inflation, even though the threat today is deflation, not inflation. Austerity also keeps financiers and creditor countries happy, and – they pray – for allowing the ECB to continue to operate in a manner unlike that of any other major central bank in the world.

The architects of sado-fiscalism hope that their policy will give the euro more credibility in the eyes of the financial markets. But even in this limited aim they are misguided. By hampering growth and fuelling unemployment and political instability, they are only creating fresh reasons for frightened capital to flow from the periphery to the core.

Against this background of massively indebted eurozone countries, no growth, unprecedentedly powerful and globalized financial markets, and a weak and misguided European leadership, it is impossible to be confident about predicting the future course of the common currency, or of the Irish economy. A dizzying number of variables will influence events. But there are, broadly, three possible paths for the eurozone.

Scenario 1: The Irish divorce, aka muddling through

When I was a kid in the 1970s and 1980s in Ireland, divorce was illegal and even separation was taboo. Unhappy couples in dysfunctional marriages stayed under the one roof like the shopkeeper couple in *Father Ted*, murdering each other. I know a fair few products of these unions, most of whom – with the safe distance of a few decades – tell tales of sheer madness and quite a bit of sadness too.

In the Ireland of the time, the opponents of divorce warned of social chaos if divorce were to be introduced. Better, they argued, to uphold the institution of marriage, no matter how dreadful the relationship. The eurozone is like a dysfunctional marriage in a country where divorce is illegal; and the prospect of a euro break-up is generally presented as impossibly destabilizing. At times, fear of the alternatives seems to be the main reason our leaders, and Europe's, have pinned their hopes on muddling through. We got married in haste, the whiff of the shotgun of German unification still fresh in our nostrils, and we had a few good honeymoon years getting to know each other, peppered with the excitement of financial dissipation. But soon the thrills wore off, and we realized we hadn't much in common after all.

The eurozone now has a choice. One option is to linger in a state you might call the 'Irish divorce'. This is the loveless marriage, both sides staying under the same roof for the sake of the children, seething all the while. The second option is to go to counselling, promise to mend our ways and reaffirm our vows, pushing on towards a closer union. The third option is genuine divorce: accept that the match wasn't right, divide up our possessions and head our separate ways.

Our leaders show no sign of trying to get out of the loveless marriage: they have gritted their teeth and resolved to muddle through. But they will have to muddle through differently, because the status quo has no chance of enduring. Fortunately for Ireland, in early autumn 2012 Mario Draghi pushed further ahead with his revolution at the ECB, moving to buy the short-term debt of peripheral countries. This is monetizing debt by another name. But even this dramatic shift in ECB policy can't guarantee success, because the economies of the periphery are still enfeebled and face ongoing fiscal contractions, which are the quid pro quo for the ECB's support.

When an economy is weak, imposing budgetary cuts as a path for growth – an idea known as the 'expansionary fiscal contraction' – is like putting an anorexic on a diet and hoping that she will eventually gain weight. The ECB buying bonds is like putting that same anorexic on a drip. It stabilizes a desperate situation, but it's a far cry from recovery.

The ECB's buying of bonds is necessary, particularly when you consider that Italy faces debt refinancing in 2013 to the tune of 29 per cent of GDP. There will now almost certainly be an EU bailout programme in Spain, and where Spain goes Italy is likely to follow. These bailouts might yet save the euro; but the insistence on austerity ensures that economic misery on the periphery will continue.

For Ireland, our neighbours' difficulty is our opportunity. The opening of the ECB balance sheet would greatly improve the chances of a deal on mortgage debt. If we don't get such a deal, the Irish economy is likely to suffer grievously in the years ahead from mortgage defaults in Trackerville. Our negotiators could take the position that if Draghi is buying up Spanish or Italian sovereign debt directly and in huge amounts, he could get a much cheaper win in Ireland by supporting a mortgage deal and have one less problem to cope with.

The Euro is a deeply dysfunctional currency union, in which differing countries face totally different interest rates, capital flight from the periphery is ongoing and Great Depression levels of unemployment are already being experienced in certain countries. It might stay together in its present form, but only if Germany tolerates a massive monetary defeat. And Germany will tolerate a massive monetary defeat only if it paves the way for the bigger political victory of political union.

The risk for Germany and the other creditor countries is that they face ongoing transfers of their cash to the periphery with no guarantee of political union. Once the ECB starts buying bonds, it will be very difficult for it to stop, unless the European Union makes the leap to full fiscal federalism.

This leads us to the second scenario.

Scenario 2: Ever closer union

The second scenario – one favoured by the more extreme EU enthusiasts – entails a muscular political response to the crisis and a giant leap to full political and fiscal union. The logic of such a move is clear. Currency union has failed because, in the absence of fiscal union, there are dramatic imbalances between the economic needs and policies of the eurozone countries, imbalances that are at the heart of the present crisis. Fiscal and political union – the centralization of political and economic decision-making, and the standardization of policy – would not change the fact that some parts of the eurozone are much wealthier, or more competitive, than others; but it would eliminate the incoherence created by the existence of seventeen different fiscal policies for a single currency.

For the countries involved, a move to political and fiscal union would mean the end of the nation state and national sovereignty as we have known it. It would mean full fiscal federalism, where national governments no longer control the purse strings. This is the dream of many Europhiles – though they rarely admit it – and has significant support amongst the eurozone elites.

For Ireland, which has already sacrificed much of its economic sovereignty as a condition of the Troika bailout, one of the most notable consequences of such a move would be the end of our ability to set our own tax rates – including, most prominently, the low corporation-tax rate that has helped to make Ireland attractive to foreign firms. It is impossible to know what effect the loss of Ireland's competitive advantage in this area might have, but over time the impact could be immense.

How would we react to the formal and theoretically permanent surrender of Irish national sovereignty, just as we're about to begin commemorating the centenaries of the various events that created that sovereignty? This is not a question that any of our leading political parties will relish answering. And Ireland is just one of seventeen eurozone members; all around Europe, a move to political and fiscal union would require a huge and complex leap of faith, at a time when the prestige of the EU and its institutions, and the patience of the European people, is at a low ebb. European countries, formed on the basis of national boundaries defined by ethnicity, are unlikely to vote to render their nations obsolete any time soon, no matter how big the economic crisis. In reality, electorates are likely to become more, not less, nationalistic as their economic security is threatened.

Given that full political union is unlikely, the creditor countries look set to be on the hook for the debts of the periphery: the ECB will continue to buy up the debt of Spain and Italy, even if these countries miss their budget adjustment targets.

And missing their budget adjustment targets is all the more likely precisely because these countries remain in the single currency. Without their own currencies, it will be very difficult for Spain and Italy to become competitive. Thus it is probable that their growth will remain anaemic, and the eurozone – with the rest of the world also slowing down rapidly – risks remaining stuck in the cycle of lurching from one crisis to another. The longer these crises roll on, the greater the risk that the creditor nations will get fed up with bailouts and the peripheral countries will get fed up with austerity – leading, ultimately, to the third scenario.

Scenario 3: Breaking up

The third scenario is that the eurozone breaks apart. Until very recently, this was all but unthinkable, but now it is a very real prospect.

A break-up could be triggered by Greece or some other peripheral country deciding to go it alone; or Germany might seek to escape from the financial and political burdens that come with keeping the weaker members in the club.

The rationale for Greece leaving the euro is very strong: it is the only clear way out of what otherwise looks like being an endless cycle of unsustainable borrowing, broken promises and ongoing economic contraction.

What if Greece remains within the euro but defaults again – and then needs more and more infusions of core taxpayers' money? What if crises recur in Spain and Italy, and the ECB can't keep a lid on things? In such a scenario, the banks of Spain and Italy might suffer a massive flight of capital, which could turn into a full-scale bank run. The ECB would probably not have the firepower to manage this.

What if the bond markets then abandon France because the French economy is weakening? France has been running both budget and current-account deficits, its banks are heavily exposed to the periphery, and it has proved to be a country where even modest changes to the economic order prompt massive reactions from the trade unions. In such a scenario, the German taxpayers might simply refuse to bail out everyone else, or to countenance the ECB constantly printing money to buy other countries' debt. After all, their savings are in euros, and when they reluctantly swapped their Deutschmarks for euros they sure as hell didn't bargain on getting lira. Germany may weigh things up and conclude that it can save France, or it can save Italy and Spain, but it certainly can't save all three and maintain the value of the euro.

Germany could leave and take France with it, pulling up the drawbridge behind them. This new, hard-euro zone would also include Finland, the Netherlands, Luxembourg, Austria and possibly Belgium. (In this scenario, Belgium would be included for geographical and political, rather than economic, reasons: its national debt is the highest in Europe after that of Greece.) Despite talk of firewalls and the like, few people have much faith in Europe's ability to limit such a crisis to Greece. For Germany, a big-bang solution – creating a 'hard' euro once and for all – would be better than allowing Greece to exit, only to be followed by massive capital flight and chaos in Spain, Ireland, Portugal and, ultimately, Italy.

In a recent survey 56 per cent of Germans indicated that they wanted the Deutschmark back, and this figure is rising steadily. A hard euro would offer most of the advantages of a renewed Deutschmark and less upheaval. Such a move would protect German taxpayers from the nightmare of years and years of transfers to the eurozone periphery, as each crisis gives way to yet another one. But it would also come with costs for Germany. As the major European creditor, Germany would stand to lose billions initially. Much of the money that Germany has already ploughed into the periphery would never be paid back, or would be paid back in a much weaker currency. And, perhaps most importantly, Germany would forfeit its happy position as a fiscally strong exporting nation operating within a relatively weak currency. The move to a stronger currency would make German exports less competitive. Yet Germany might calculate that the long-term cost of doing nothing would be even higher. It might conclude that it is better to define the terms of reality now, do something about it, front-load the costs, draw a line under European integration for a generation, and think of Greece, Spain and Italy only when contemplating sun holidays.

An examination of the rough cost of a Greek exit on its own can help us to see why the Germans might go for the big bang in order to get all this over with. If Greece reverts to the drachma, the Greek bonds held by the ECB – worth €40 billion-odd – would be marked down, as would the last bailout loan of €130 billion, not to mention the €100 billion-odd that the Greek central bank borrowed from the ECB. That's the guts of €270 billion for Greece alone.

Now consider the fallout in store for the rest of the periphery from this Greek shock. Billions would flee overnight, and the EU would simply not have the means to stop this. The recessions in these countries would quickly begin to look like depressions. The political implications would be enormous, because there is little doubt that pro-EU governments in each afflicted country would be forced from office.

Faced with this vista, the Germans and the rest of the eurozone core would need to come up with a massive public recapitalization of their own banks, to cover their losses from the defaulting periphery. Given the strong fiscal track record of the core, it would probably be possible to fund this by raising the money from financial markets and their own savers, in the same way that it was possible to finance German unification.

Breaking the euro in two would be expensive and messy – but don't think it's not possible.

What would happen in Ireland in the event of a eurozone break-up?

In a break-up scenario where Germany moves to create a new currency around itself, Ireland would face a choice: not between Boston and Berlin, but rather between Rome and London. We could go with the other peripheral countries into some sort of new, soft-euro currency union; or we might consider it more appropriate to institute a currency of our own – a punt nua.

Ireland is an outlier amongst the countries of the European periphery. Over half of our European imports come from Britain (excluding Northern Ireland), as opposed to 2.9 per cent from Italy and 2.4 per cent from Spain. Import prices are therefore largely determined by the exchange rate with the UK, which makes the relationship with Britain key for controlling future imported inflation. Tying ourselves to a Rome–Madrid axis – along with countries with which we do very little trade – would hardly make sense. In the event of a euro break-up, a move to a new Irish currency would be much more sensible.

The currency of a small country doesn't have to shadow another currency, but the dominance of Britain in our economic affairs would cause financial markets to regard the punt nua as being part of an unofficial sterling zone. Very quickly, Irish interest rates would track British interest rates.

The costs and benefits of such a move would not be spread evenly. The new currency would have to be announced over a weekend, and this would probably be followed by a bank holiday of two or three days, during which time people's savings would be trapped. The punt nua might initially be valued at one punt to one euro, but its value would quickly fall. In other words, your savings would be converted into punt nua on a one-to-one basis, but by the time you got your hands on the money the punt might be worth only 50 cents against the old euro you thought you had. Therefore, the first shock to be borne would be a dramatic fall in the value of savings. There is no way around this – it is an unavoidable consequence of the move from a strong currency to a weak one.

Wages in euro terms would fall rapidly, because they would be paid in the new currency. In order not to encourage a wage spiral, the state would link all future pay increases to productivity, not inflation. Thus, the public-sector wage bill would be cut by stealth, via inflation. Obviously, the trade unions and the government would be set for a significant collision, but it is difficult to see an alternative.

The debts of most ordinary individuals are overwhelmingly owed to Irish banks, so the move to the new currency would cause the debts to be redenominated in punt nua and subsequent inflation would reduce the real cost of debt.

The question of what would happen to the various categories of euro-denominated foreign debt owed by the Irish state, banks and companies is impossible to answer with total confidence; there would undoubtedly be legal disputes on various fronts. But there are a few things that can be said with assurance. The Irish state and banks would seek to get their foreign euro debt redenominated in punt nua. There would undoubtedly be resistance to this, but it would be largely academic. Freed from the constraints of the eurozone's Good Room, the Irish state, if faced with resistance over debt-redenomination, would have no reason not to do what debt-crushed countries have always done: default.

Leaving the euro would rebalance the cost structures in the Irish economy. Ireland would become very cheap very quickly, and this would spur new investment. Default is the quickest way to correct a broken balance sheet. Iceland is the most recent success in a long list of those who have adopted the 'devalue-and-default' approach. If a country looks to be on a growth path after default, the markets will come in to support it. Owners of Irish assets would lose out significantly; so too would savers. On the other hand, exporters would benefit from being able to price their goods in a weaker currency. As there has never been a case of American multinational investment retrenching because the dollar price of local costs fell, it is likely that a devaluation would cause a surge in foreign investment. Multinationals would see their Irish operations become dramatically more profitable overnight.

Leaving the euro would involve massive upheaval for Ireland, but it's important to bear in mind that many countries have survived such upheavals. In the past hundred years, about a hundred countries have left currency unions. Some of these moves were associated with the end of empires, when newly independent colonies broke away from their imperial rulers. Others came when a great ideology was swept aside – for example, the break-up of the Soviet Union brought about the end of the rouble zone and the great democratization of Eastern Europe and Central Europe.

Currency-zone break-ups can have unpleasant outcomes. If a country uses the break-up as an opportunity to print new money in reckless quantities, hyper-inflation can result – as it did, for example, in Austria and Hungary after the break-up of the Habsburg Empire's monetary union in 1918. And, as we've seen, even if a break-up is handled wisely, there will always be a degree of upheaval, and entire categories of people who lose out. But for a country like Ireland – which is suffering badly as a result of its adherence to policies dictated by the needs and priorities of countries with which it has little in common – there would also be real gains. At the moment there is no evidence that Ireland's rulers, or the wise men of Europe, are properly contemplating a break-up scenario – which could come to pass whether they like it or not. And the failure to take this prospect seriously is considerably more reckless than planning for it, however remote the possibility may be.

The march of events

We would all be wise to keep an open mind as to what might happen next. The range of possible outcomes is vast, and the stakes are extremely high. We will have to consider options that we would rather not contemplate.

The very solvency of a number of European countries is open to question. The big-picture theories of Minsky, Kindleberger, Fisher and Keynes are more relevant now than at any stage since the Great Depression, yet they are being ignored, while the narrow-gauge concerns of financiers are pandered to. In Ireland, the domestic economy has shrunk by a quarter in five years.

But it's worth returning to J. K. Galbraith's observation that the most effective enemy of conventional wisdom is not a more powerful idea that convinces people to change course, but rather the great march of events. And the great march of events is nothing more than the aggregation of millions of little incidents in the lives of people, including Irish people, every day, every week, in every town up and down the country.

People like Olivia Vickers.

20. Forty Weeks

Olivia squeezed Sean's hand and, for the second time, opened the door to the small office of Mr Liam Henderson, ACA.

She felt in control. Damien D'Arcy's composure was rubbing off. She would have preferred to have him there with them, but he thought it better that they went themselves, not lawyered up. 'Olivia,' he'd said, 'as you know by now, lawyers in the room, any room, profoundly affect the atmosphere – for the worse. It's not the time for gloves off just yet. Just be firm and make sure he realizes the significance of the note in your file.'

Her due date was two days away, and she was too distracted by the reality of the impending birth to be even a little bit scared of anything, let alone a bank official.

'Client known to the bank.' Liam Henderson's mouth curled around the expression as though he'd just swallowed sour milk.

Olivia fixed him with an insolently sweet smile – the kind she'd picked up from her cheekiest students. 'It means you gave us more money than you would otherwise have done,' she said, 'on the rather flimsy basis that my sister worked in your credit department.'

She folded her arms, resting them on Una. She resisted the temptation to wave two fingers at him, blow a raspberry and yell nahnahnahnahnah.

'There are many factors that go into lending decisions,' Henderson replied. 'And may I remind you that we lent you the amount of money that you sought?'

'Well, yes,' she said. Sean was watching her nervously; they'd agreed it was better if she did all the talking. 'But there are two parties to a loan agreement, and clearly this note raises a question about the rationale for the loan. We haven't missed a payment yet, but we are struggling, and we came to you seeking a restructuring of the mortgage so that we wouldn't have to default. You haven't indicated any willingness to go down that path so far. We hope you'll change your mind, but, if you don't, we need to consider other options. Obviously we'd hate to go legal.'

Henderson looked as though he'd been slapped in the face. 'I really think you're operating under a misunderstanding, Mrs Doyle.' He tried to regain his composure, clamping his hands together and sitting up straight, puffing out his chest.

Olivia leaned over about as far as she could go, with the bump acting as an airbag, and handed Henderson a copy of the document with the 'Client known to the bank' annotation.

'Well,' said Olivia, 'shall we leave it with you? Have your lawyers give you an opinion and get back to us.'

Later that morning, Barry and Shane were hurtling northwards on the M50 towards IKEA in Ballymun. The paint was barely dry on the back of their yellow-and-blue, fourth-hand Fiat Ducato. Emblazoned on the side, in huge blue letters: FLAT PACK SAM'S YOUR ONLY MAN. Barry knew he was on to something: punters couldn't put furniture together. More marriages were threatened by stacks of flat packs than by infidelity.

People weren't moving house: too many were stuck in negative equity, or just unable to raise the finance to trade up. But, like Olivia and Viv, and all their mates, they were still getting married and dropping sprogs. Nests were being built all over the country. People were settling down and they wanted kitchens, living rooms, shelving units, wall cabinets, slimline shoe tidies, drawer chests, bed frames, and those tricky sliding-door wardrobes that only NASA engineers could put together. Over the past few years Barry had watched as furniture shops all over Dublin closed; IKEA had crushed the competition. It hadn't capitalized on the housing boom, but it had on the recession: punters were being drawn in who might once have kitted out their places with high-end Italian or Scandinavian designer gear.

Barry's business plan was simple. He was going to make it easy for people. He'd go to IKEA on their behalf, pick up the flat packs, deliver them to their gaffs in his van and then assemble everything. He figured there were two distinct markets. Punters like Olivia and Seán were his bread and butter. To scoop them up, he placed ads with all the wedding websites, daft.ie and some of the smaller estate agents that were trying to boost business by offering add-on services. The second market was the landlords.

Barry's phone never stopped. The work had poured in. Pretty quickly he realized he needed more lads, so he placed an ad: 'Good job, simple work. If you liked Rubik's Cubes, you'll love this. *Only dyslexics need apply.*'

He'd enjoyed writing that ad. He was offering the only job in Ireland where the bar was set so high that only those who'd been laughed at and who'd struggled with reading in school could get in. He reckoned it was no coincidence that the man who'd founded IKEA was dyslexic. Barry didn't really mean it, of course – and he'd hired Shane and Vivienne, neither of whom met the criterion. Vivienne needed the gig, and he needed an accountant and someone to run the office. Shane needed the gig too, and was great craic in the van – as long as you never let him near a map.

Shane was a bit out of sorts with the court case hanging over him. He'd hoped for a result one way or the other, but the judge had kicked it out again for six months, suggesting that he and the bank should sit down again and get things sorted out. But there was no sorting it out. Since the court case, the bank had sold its business in Ireland and he now had to deal with some other crowd, who'd sent him a snotty letter.

'Mad to think they had a toll gate here,' he said, as their number plate was noted by a scanner mounted on a gantry.

Shane was miles away, looking for his smokes underneath the seat.

'Really? When?'

'Ah, not that long ago. Punters used to be backed up for miles at rush hour, waiting to chuck their few yoyos in the basket. Then the government asked some heads to build this thing above us. Then they gave them a piece of the action from the electronic tolling. Here, open the window if you're lighting up.'

'Now,' he continued, when Shane had rolled it down enough for the smoke to be sucked outside, 'cop this, Einstein: we're driving on government-built roads, right?'

'Yeah,' agreed Shane.

'And these roads – and only these roads – funnel punters on to the bridge. Right?'

'Yeah, Baz. But what's your fucking point?'

'You bring the punters to the bridge, then give the dude who builds the bridge a slice of the action; but you're bringing all the customers. Are you with me?'

Shane nodded.

'And without the customers there's no business, right?'

'Right,' said Shane. 'So what's the problem?'

'Well,' Barry said slowly, because Shane obviously spent too much time thinking at book-reading speed and couldn't keep up with the speed of actual thought, 'they shouldn't have given the dudes who built the bridge a slice of the action. Flat fee, man: that's the only way. Screams a fuckin' stroke to me. Typical Ireland.'

Olivia's list was getting longer as her time got shorter – nappies, cots, car seats, PJs, birth notice for the paper, mascara, phone charger.

'Don't forget the charger, Sean. I don't want the same fiasco as last time.'

Sam's birth had been announced to the world by a text from the midwife's phone, because both of theirs were out of battery. No one recognized the midwife's number, and so even Patsy Vickers thought the announcement of the arrival of her first grandchild was a hoax. There was a period of about four hours – before Sean managed to reach his parents on a landline – when Barry was in danger of being disowned by the entire family, because everyone figured he was the sort of messer to pull that kind of gag.

★

Bubbles Fagan sat in her kitchen, waiting for the tea to draw.

'Hard to believe, Sinbad, isn't it? Would you credit it – after sixty-two years? Nineteen hundred and fifty it was, early June.' The memory was as bright as that morning's sunrise. 'My Joe, strong as an ox, lifting beds and painting walls; me pregnant with the twins, and my mother, God rest her, bringing a flask and two bottles of milk, cheese and the biggest turnover you ever saw.' She could still taste that meal. 'And we sat right over there, on three paint cans, and scoffed the lot.'

The cat blinked back at her, nonplussed.

Bubbles looked up at the Sacred Heart. Jesus looked back down, as he had done for every day of those sixty-two years – well, not every day, because this particular Sacred Heart dated from that early-1970s trip to Lourdes with the parish. The one she'd got on her wedding day had given out by then, and everyone knew there was no point in having a Sacred Heart that didn't shine. It'd be like having tea without a drop of milk.

Bubbles scooped the last of the cat food out of the tin. Sinbad finally showed some interest in her, making a sound halfway between a purr and a yelp.

'There was no cat food back then, girl – only auld scraps for the likes of you.' Bubbles's face darkened. 'And now we – you and me both – are moving on. Like bloody itinerants, only worse.'

But better than that poor Winnie Clancy, she told herself. Winnie, the poor cratur, ended up in one of them homes, brutalized– she'd seen the pictures on the telly. Worse than Grangegorman, so it was, and her three young wans swannying around like nobbers and their auld lad, hard Tommy Clancy, spending half his time in the pawn shop and the other in Foley's, swallying pints. Bubbles gritted her teeth at the thought of him.

'My Joe, Lord have mercy on him, wouldn't darken that place. More a few bottles of porter at home type, so he was. All the sing-songs were right here in this kitchen, half the night. Hard to believe, but we're moving, Sinbad. Leaving it all behind.'

Bubbles caught herself. 'But not for good. When this auld leg of mine gets better, we'll be back, the pair of us. 48 St Patrick's Crescent won't be without a Fagan for long. Mark my words, girl.'

The cat, having cleaned the bowl, stared back.

Bubbles got up to fill her cup and took it into the good room. Sinbad followed her, tail curled, sneaking around the good couch. The cat knew better than to use anything in there to sharpen its claws, let alone sit on any furniture.

Bubbles sat, looking at all the photos on the wall. They were Bubbles's shrine to her own brood, the Fagan family archive.

In the middle was the oldest photo, one Olivia had always loved. It was a black-and-white portrait of Bubbles and Joe as newlyweds. It was in its own little frame, which bore the name of the photographer's shop on Talbot Street. They'd married in August 1949. At the time, they had been living with her mam and dad in Crumlin, waiting for the Corpo to finish the house. Pretty and jet-black-haired, nineteen-year-old Bubbles Lockhard had smiled into the camera, looking forward to her big adventure, her new life. Joe Fagan had stood beside her, looking like a man who couldn't believe his luck.

'Hard to believe we'll all be in the same house,' she told the cat. 'You, me, Patsy, Dermot, Barry and God knows who else. Me with not one but two great-grandchildren. Never thought I'd see the day, Sinbad, old girl. Did you?'

The cat crawled into her lap, nestling its little head against her, as Bubbles tickled her absent-mindedly.

'Better get ready, girl, they'll be here any minute now.' Through the window of the good room, the sun was streaming in.

The tide was well out, the sky dishwater dirty, and the rain pelting down on the corrugated sand of Sandymount Strand. There wasn't a sinner there, bar Damien D'Arcy. Every day, with the regularity and dedication of a daily communicant, he walked the beach and plotted.

Damien had expected the bank to cut a deal for Olivia and Sean at their first meeting. Now he'd sent them back to the bank, bearing the evidence that Vivienne had secured. Surely the bank would see a way to restructure the mortgage?

A part of him was hoping that the bank wouldn't see sense. If it did, there would be no test case. Was this the old, ambitious Damien D'Arcy back, the vain, unchristian one? Was he leading an unprepared woman into battle? He knew he could not be confident of winning. From his side, this case was the living embodiment of Leviticus, Deuteronomy and Amos; it was the word of Matthew, Mark, Luke and Ezekiel. But he couldn't count on a judge to see it that way.

His phone rang, and he hunkered down in the middle of the strand, facing the Pigeon House, so he could hear over the wind howling from the south-west.

'Olivia?'

'Hi, Damien,' she said, almost nonchalantly – as if absolutely nothing was coming down the track that she might have to be worried about. 'Let's go for it. You should have heard the little prick.'

'He's only doing his job,' Damien said. 'He's just a yes man – probably hoping he won't be culled next. We'll face much tougher enemies before this is over.'

'Damien, I can hardly hear a word – where are you?'

'On Sandymount Strand.'

'Do you ever leave that bloody place?'

'It does me good.'

'You're not getting cold feet, are you?'

'No, I'm just trying to prepare you.'

Olivia was surprised. 'But you said this was all about morality and doing the right thing. Surely if it's the right thing to do, it's the right thing irrespective of who we're facing?'

'Well, yes. But are you sure, Olivia? This will be a big fight. There could be lots of publicity – and lots of dirty tricks.'

Her laughter was loud down the phone. 'Don't get all soft on me now, Damien D'Arcy.'

'Olivia. We can win this case. I'll try my best for you, and if there's any justice, we'll be unassailable.'

'Great,' she said. 'Now get off that beach, padre, before I get worried about the sanity of my comrade-in-arms.'

He laughed. 'What about the baby? Are you sure now that you can deal with everything all at once?'

'Damien. I'm doing this *for the baby*.'

'Oh. Shit. Sean, it's coming.'

'You sure?'

'No, actually. April Fool's. Of course it's fucking coming. I don't usually wet the bed, do I?'

'Sorry. OK, babe, hang on.' He launched himself out of bed.

'You got the bag, hon?'

'Yep.'

'OK, then. Let's go.'

Becs, the midwife, showed them to their little cubicle on the left-hand side of the ward. Olivia was nervous but excited: she couldn't wait to see Una. But what if it was a boy? The contractions weren't that frequent yet; she could handle them so far.

She felt about as serene as anyone could who was about to give birth. She ought to arrange a meeting with the bank every time they have a child, she thought.

'We'll call him Ultan,' Sean blurted out. He was trying to look serious and helpful, but he was completely irrelevant in the maternity ward right now.

'No bloody way.'

'Tea?'

'Oh, shut up.'

Becs came in as if playing peekaboo through the curtains. She held Olivia's hand, giving it a little squeeze.

'Nearly time now, love, eight centimetres, you're doing just fine. Just a few things to check.' Another midwife, one Olivia hadn't seen before, came in. She smiled reassuringly.

'You again? We thought you'd never be back, Missus. You don't remember me, do you? I was around for your last one. He couldn't wait to get out and say hello – we nearly missed him. How is he?'

'He's at his nan's. Fast asleep, I hope.'

Olivia knew what the midwives were doing. They were trying to keep her mind off things. These women really were saints. Delivering hundreds of babies every week, operating in antiquated hospitals.

'I'm Annie. I'll be with you all the time. Right now we're just doing a few routine checks.'

She pushed a trolley with all sorts of wires attached to it up to the bed, then expertly strapped a few of them to Olivia's tummy. She had done thousands of these. It was a monitor designed to measure the baby's heartbeat, which should be around 150 beats per minute. There was a little chart on the monitor, blipping along. It was like being on *ER*. It'd be nice if there was a Clooney knocking around the place too, Olivia thought.

Suddenly the monitor sounded different. The graph dropped off the scale; the heart rate plummeted.

'Jesus – what's happening?' Sean sounded frantic.

'Don't worry,' the midwife said.

The heartbeat kept falling: 140 – 120 – 110 – 100 – 95 – 90 . . .

Annie picked up the phone. 'I need the obstetrician up here right now.'

'Annie, what's going on? Is the baby all right?' She could feel her own heart in her throat. 'Sean, where are you? I'm scared.'

'Here, Liv, I'm here.' He held her hand in his. 'It's probably nothing. Probably normal.' He was trying not to sound terrified. But Sean wasn't much of an actor.

'It's not fucking normal. Don't bullshit me.'

Then the obstetrician was at the bed. He whispered to Annie.

'Olivia,' he said, his voice soft and calm, 'the baby's heart rate has changed. I think we need to help it out.'

He sat on the bed beside her and held her hand. She only caught snippets: 'Change in heart rate'; 'Distressed'; 'Caesarean section'.

Her trolley was whisked down the corridor, veering left into a harshly lit operating theatre. Olivia could see faces lit up, strangers in matching green caps, trousers and tunics. The anaesthetist smiled as only people with large syringes and rubber gloves can.

'This won't hurt, Olivia.'

'Like hell it won't,' she managed.

The entire theatre laughed.

Sean was standing at the back, in the corner of her vision. He looked dishy in the green scrubs, she thought. Maybe not quite McDreamy, but *Grey's Anatomy* was a rubbish show anyway. He moved forward and held Olivia's hand as they shielded her tummy with a screen. Everything was shiny and surgical. She was falling in and out of consciousness. A crowd of green behind the screen meant they were probably opening her up. She was so glad to be in their hands. They were in control.

After all the palaver she and Sean had been through, she could barely believe she was thinking: thank God I live in Ireland with these people on the frontline, here when you need them. She didn't know what was going to happen with the bank, whether or not she and Sean would be trooping into court with Damien D'Arcy for a test case over the mortgage on 228 Hilton Park, but all that uncertainty wasn't important now. She was in good hands for the only thing that really mattered.

'Coming now, Olivia,' the obstetrician said. 'Your baby is coming.'

'It's a pretty strange-looking Una,' Sean said.

'It's no Una,' said the midwife. 'That's a boy. And a great pair of lungs on him. He's perfect. Everything there and in all the right places.'

Olivia snuggled the tiny slippery thing into her, breathing him in. He appeared to crawl up her chest as if trying to get to the nape of her neck. She loved him with everything she had. Their whole lives were ahead of them.

Sean kissed her on the top of her sweaty head. Olivia cried a little for him, for her, for them and for life, beautiful life.

'He looks just like you, Olivia.'

'What? Bald and wrinkly? Thanks a lot!'

Notes

p. 5 (migration figures) CSO population and migration estimates, April 2011, published September 2011.

p. 5 (*Irish Times*/Ipsos MRBI poll) Kathy Sheridan, 'The New Diaspora Speaks', *Irish Times*, 17 March 2012.

p. 5 (unemployment levels) CSO seasonally adjusted Standardized Unemployment Rates (SUR).

p. 6 (73,000 babies) CSO, 'This is Ireland: Highlights from Census 2011. Part 1', April 2011, published March 2012.

p. 7 (youth unemployment) CSO, 'Census 2011. Profile 3: At Work', published 26 July 2012.

p. 9 (number of tracker products) Central Bank Quarterly Bulletin, Q4 2009.

p. 9 (400,000 tracker mortgages) 'Two More Mortgage Rate Cuts Expected', www.rte.ie, 4 November 2011.

p. 9 (banks' mortgage books) Simon Carswell, 'Tracker Issue Must be Sorted for Banks to Have Future', *Irish Times*, 14 March 2012.

p. 9 (85 per cent of mortgages) Gerard Kennedy and Tara McIndoe Calder, 'The Irish Mortgage Market: Stylised Facts, Negative Equity and Arrears', Central Bank of Ireland Research Technical Papers 12/RT/11, November 2011.

p.9 (mortgages originating) Reamonn Lydon and Yvonne McCarthy, 'What Lies Beneath? Understanding Recent Trends in Irish Mortgage Arrears', Central Bank of Ireland Research Technical Papers 14/RT/11, November 2011.

p. 10 (2 per cent of clients) Oireachtas Library and Research Service, 'Debt. Part 2: Personal Debt and Consequences', April 2009, published 2010.

p. 10 (three years later) Ibid.

p. 11 (Paddy Power) Quants Department, www.paddypower.com, June 2012.

p. 25 (David Beers quote) Thomas Molloy, Michael Brennan and Fionnan Sheehan, 'Economy has "Turned Corner" Says Top Rating Agency Boss', *Irish Independent*, 13 October 2010.

p. 25 (Olivier Blanchard quote) 'IMF Economist Optimistic on Ireland', RTÉ News, www.rte.ie, 27 October 2011.

p. 26 (J. P. Morgan quote) Stijn Claessens, M. Ayhan Kose and Marco E. Terrones, 'What Happens during Recessions, Crunches and Busts?', IMF Working Paper WP/08/274, 1 December 2008.

p. 26 (recessions lasted less than ten months) Ibid.

pp. 26–7 (Wynne Godley quote) L. Randall Wray, 'Godley Got It Right', Wynne Godley Memorial Conference: Contributions in Stock-flow Modeling, Levy Economics Institute of Bard College, May 2011.

p. 27 ('balance-sheet recession') Richard Koo, 'The World in Balance-Sheet Recession: Causes, Cure, and Politics', *Real-World Economics Review*, No. 58, 12 December 2011, pp. 19–37.

p. 28 ('When I have it I spend it') 'The Tiger Tamed: A Tight Squeeze, as the Good Years End', *Economist*, 12 December 2002.

p. 29 (German unemployment) Floyd Norris, 'Germany's Jobless Numbers Buck Euro Zone Trend', *New York Times*, 3 August 2012.

p. 29 (German house prices) Renuka Rayasam, 'German Property Market Soars Amid Euro Crisis', www.spiegel.de, 22 June 2012.

p. 30 ('Panics do not destroy capital') John Stuart Mill, article read before the Manchester Statistical Society, 'Credit Cycles and the Origin of Commercial Panics', 11 December 1867, quoted in T. E. Burton, *Financial Crises and Periods of Industrial and Commercial Depression* (1931; first published 1902).

p. 31 ('push on a string', Keynes quote) Hal Varian, 'Dealing with Deflation', *New York Times*, 5 June 2003.

p. 31 (debt deflation) Irving Fisher, *The Debt-Deflation Theory of Great Depressions* (1933).

p. 32 ('Each of the participants') Charles Kindleberger, *Manias, Panics and Crashes: A History of Financial Crises* (fifth edition 2005; first published 1978), p. 41.

p. 32 ('In a world with capitalist') John Carney, 'Was "Post-Keynesian" Hyman Minsky an Austrian in Disguise?', www.cnbc.com, 29 March 2012.

p. 33 ('We'd stay up all night') Richard D. McKinzie, 'Oral History Interview with Charles P. Kindleberger', Harry S. Truman Library and Museum, 16 July 1973.

p. 33 ('Positive feedback develops') Charles Kindleberger, *Comparative Political Economy: A Retrospective* (2000), p. 321.

p. 35 ('Success breeds a disregard') Hyman Minsky, quoted in Stephen Mihm, 'Why Capitalism Fails – The Man Who Saw the Meltdown Coming Had Another Troubling Insight: It Will Happen Again', www.levyinstitute.org.

p. 38 (Michael Noonan) Dáil Éireann Debate, Vol. 740, No. 1, 14 September 2011.

p. 38 (McKinsey study) Charles Roxburgh, Susan Lund, Toos Daruvala, James Manyika, Richard Dobbs, Ramon Forn, Karen Croxson, 'Debt and Deleveraging: Uneven Progress on the Path to Growth', www.mckinsey.com, January 2012.

p. 39 (€127 billion) Stefan Avdjiev, Christian Upper, Karsten von Kleist, 'Highlights of International Banking and Financial Market Activity', www.bis.org, June 2010.

p. 40 (savings ratio) Richard Koo, 'The World in Balance-Sheet Recession: Causes, Cure, and Politics', *Real-World Economics Review*, No. 58, 12 December 2011.

p. 40 (16 per cent of income) Ibid.

p. 41 ('greatest economist') Milton Friedman, *Money Mischief: Episodes in Monetary History* (1994), p. 37.

p. 56 (capital inflows into Thailand) Steven Radlete and Jeffrey Sachs, 'The Onset of the East Asia Financial Crisis', NBER Working Papers 6680, August 1998.

p. 57 (export growth) Ibid.

p. 57 (Malaysia current-account deficit, Thailand, Korea) Ibid.

p. 77 (James Carville) Quoted in Liz Phillips, 'Forex Focus: Who's Afraid of the Bond Market?', www.telegraph.co.uk, 29 November 2011.

p. 78 ('Ireland's fundamental backdrop') Donal O'Mahony, 'Bond Market is Starved of Irish Paper', *Irish Times*, 17 February 2012.

p. 78 (home loans 2011 and 1972) Charlie Weston, 'Mortgage Lending Drops to Lowest Level since 1971', *Irish Independent*, 22 June 2011.

p. 78 (house prices) Ciara O'Brien, 'Property Prices Fall 16.4% in Year', *Irish Times*, 24 May 2012.

p. 78 (tax revenue) Carmel Crimmins and Conor Humphries, 'Irish Tax Revenues Fall Further behind Target in November', uk.reuters.com, 2 December 2011.

pp. 78–9 (national income figures) CSO Quarterly National Accounts, Q1 2012, published 12 July 2012.

p. 80 (Troika loans) Luke Baker and Jan Strupczewski, 'Greece Secures Provisional Approval for New Bailout', uk.reuters.com, 1 March 2012.

p. 80 (Greek economy contraction) Ambrose Evans-Pritchard, 'Just as Greece Complies at Last, Europe Pulls the Plug', *Telegraph*, 16 February 2012.

p. 80 (over 100,000 companies) Prokopis Hatzinikolaou, 'Dramatic Drop in Budget Revenues', www.ekathimerini.com, 7 February 2012.

p. 80 (outstanding debt) Helena Smith, 'IMF Official Admits Austerity is Harming Greece', *Guardian*, 1 February 2012.

p. 81 (Finland) Lars Jonung, Jaako Kiander and Pentti Vartia, 'The Great Financial Crisis in Finland and Sweden: The Dynamics of Boom, Bust and Recovery 1985–2000', European Commission, Economic and Financial Affairs, Economic Papers 350, December 2008.

p. 81 (40 per cent devaluation) Ibid.

p. 81 (160 per cent of GDP) Robert Holmes, 'With Greek Impasse, Europe's Debt Mess is Just Beginning', www.forbes.com, 10 February 2012.

p. 82 (Greek agreement EU) 'Greece's Debt Swap Offer to Private Creditors', RTÉ News, www.rte.ie, 24 February 2012.

p. 84 (Italy's debt ratio) Buttonwood's Notebook, 'The Italian Job', www.economist.com, 11 July 2011.

p. 86 (Bank of England gilt stock) David Miliband, 'Speech on "Economy and Living Standards"', House of Commons, 1 December 2011.

p. 86 (Fed US Treasury stock) Thomas Mucha, 'Who Owns America? Hint: It's Not China', www.globalpost.com, 21 July 2011.

p. 86 (Bank of Japan) Takeo Hoshi and Takatoshi Ito, 'Defying Gravity: How Long Will Japanese Government Bond Prices Remain High?', www.indiana.edu, 30 March 2012.

p. 87 (€400 billion) 'Leaders Look to IMF Again, as Euro Crisis Lingers', *New York Times*, 3 December 2011.

p. 88 (Italian bond yields) Mary Watkins and Miles Johnson, 'Spanish Bond Yields Hover Near 7%', www.ft.com, 6 July 2012.

p. 90 (€1 trillion) Mike Dolan, 'Hair of the Dog? Citi Says More LTROs in Store', blogs.reuters.com, 19 April 2012.

p. 91 (ownership of domestic government debt) Yalman Onaran, 'Spanish Banks Gorging on Sovereign Bonds Shifts Risk', www.businessweek.com, 17 April 2012.

p. 104 ('a hedge fund') Michael Lewis, 'When Irish Eyes are Crying', *Vanity Fair*, March 2011.

p. 104 ('plus an agreement') Martin Ziegler, 'West Ham Sage Ends in Takeover', *Guardian*, 21 November 2006.

p. 104 (George Lincoln Rockwell) Jamie Jackson, 'He's the Real Thing', *Guardian*, 2 September 2007.

p. 105 ('There was something worrying') Jason Burt, 'West Ham's Icelandic Connection Drawing to a Close', *Daily Telegraph*, 9 January 2010.

p. 105 (Straumer) Ibid.

p. 106 (15.8 per cent of GDP) Paul Maidment, 'Icelandic Meltdown', www.forbes.com, 26 June 2008.

p. 106 (banking-sector assets) Ibid.

p. 107 (90 to the euro) 'Euro Foreign Exchange Reference Rates', previous rates, www.ecb.int/stats.

p. 108 (documentary) *Addicted to Money*, ABC Australia, aired October 2009.

p. 108 (9 per cent) Statistics Iceland, www.statice.is.

p. 127 (€1.3 billion) 'Greek Debt Will be Paid on Time', www.rte.ie, 4 May 2010.

p. 127 (ECB bullied) Stephen Collins, 'Letters Show Extent of Pressure Put on Lenihan for Bailout', *Irish Times*, 1 September 2012.

p. 127 ('I do not want to see') Michael Brennan and Barry Duggan, 'No Vote Will Frighten Investors – Taoiseach', *Irish Times*, 28 April 2012.

p. 128 ('It is vital that we do') Opening remarks by Deputy Governor Matthew Elderfield, at the Central Bank of Ireland Stakeholder Conference, 27 April 2012.

p. 128 ('allowed to drink in the bar') 'Undecided Voters Hold Key to Treaty Outcome – Poll', www.rte.ie, 17 May 2012.

p. 129 (bond auction) 'Bonds Sale "Recovery Milestone"', *Irish Independent*, 5 July 2012.

p. 129 ('healthily oversubscribed') Dan O'Brien, 'Auction Paves Way for Further Bill Sales', *Irish Times*, 6 July 2012.

p. 142 ('The defenders are able') John Kenneth Galbraith, *The Affluent Society* (1998; originally published 1958), p. 9.

p. 143 ('Ireland's boom is') Daniel McConnell and Tom Lyons, 'Whistleblower's Dire Warnings Silenced by Senior Finance Chiefs', *Irish Independent*, 22 April 2012.

p. 147 (current-account gaps) Eurostat news release, 'Second Estimate for the First Quarter of 2012', 19 July 2012.

pp. 148–9 (IMF chief) Speaking at conference in Riga, 5 June 2012.

p. 149 (CEPR report) Mark Weisbrot and Rebecca Ray, 'Latvia's Internal Devaluation: A Success Story?', www.cepr.net, December 2011.

p. 149 ('They had promised') Mark Weisbrot, 'IMF Chief Praises Latvian "Success Story" – A Scary Speech for the Eurozone', www.cepr.net, 7 June 2012.

p. 150 (household-debt-to-income ratio) http://kitichai1.blogspot.ie/2012/05/greece-spain-ireland-by-lgt.html.

p. 162 (Interest rates were increased) John Kelly, 'The Irish Pound: From Origins to EMU', Central Bank of Ireland Quarterly Bulletin, Spring 2003.

p. 164 ('In March 2012') Fourth Global Financial Markets Forum, Abu Dhabi.

p. 166 ('In late July 2012') 'ECB "Ready to Do Whatever It Takes"', *Financial Times*, 26 July 2012.

p. 166 ('do whatever was necessary') David Milliken and Marius Zaharia, 'Draghi Sends Strong Signal that ECB Will Act', www.reuters.com, 26 July 2012.

p. 166 (The Germanic view) 'The Euro Debate Gets Philosophical', www.gavkal.com, 29 November 2011.

pp. 167–8 (Financially Bayern operates) 'The "German Model" Explained: Governance, Regulation and Financial Performance', www.supporters-direct.org, 17 May 2012.

p. 168 (Unemployment was less than 3 per cent) Eurostat Newsletter 104/2012, 4 July 2012.

p. 169 ('and property prices are inflating') Renuka Rayasam, 'German Property Market Soars amid Euro Crisis', www.spiegel.de, 22 June 2012.

p. 169 (No Bundesliga team has gone bust) 'The "German Model" Explained: Governance, Regulation and Financial Performance', www.supporters-direct.org, 17 May 2012.

p. 183 (loan-to-deposit ratios) Donal O'Mahony, 'Guest Post: Donal O'Mahony on NAMA', www.irisheconomy.ie, 22 September 2009.

p. 183 (ninety days in arrears) Central Bank of Ireland, Residential Mortgage Arrears and Repossessions Statistics, Q2 2012, published 23 August 2012.

p. 183 (buy-to-let mortgages in arrears) 'Davy Urges Banks to Take Series Action on Buy-to-let Mortgages', www.rte.ie, 17 August 2012.

p. 185 (household debt) Deputy Michael Noonan in response to Deputy Peter Matthews, 'Written Answers – Debt Levels', http://debates.oireachtas.ie/dail/2011/09/14/00105.asp, 14 September 2011.

p. 186 (half of mortgages are in negative equity) 'Over 50% of Irish Mortgages in Negative Equity – Davy', www.rte.ie, 17 August 2012.

p. 206 (GDP contracted by 0.2 per cent) Eurostat news release, 'Flash Estimate for the Second Quarter of 2012', 14 August 2012.

p. 206 (debt-to-GDP ratio is actually rising) Eurostat news release, 'Third Quarter 2011 Compared with Second Quarter 2011', 6 February 2012.

p. 209 (29 per cent of its GDP in 2013) Robert Lenzer, 'Why 2013 Could Be Another Version of 2008 unless the Germans Act', www.forbes.com, 23 June 2012.

p. 212 (current-account deficits) William Horbin, 'French Current Account Deficit Wider in June', www.euroinvestor.com, 13 August 2012.

p. 212 (recent survey) Carried out by ARD public television in June 2012.

p. 213 (Greek bonds) George Georgiopoulos and Marc Jones, 'ECB Mulls Losses on Greek Bonds Held by National Banks', uk.reuters.com, 17 February 2012.

p. 213 (€100 billion-odd) Stefan Kaiser, 'A Greek Default Would Hit the ECB Hard', www.spiegel.de, 13 January 2012.

p. 214 (European imports) CSO, External Trade, November and December 2011, published 15 February 2012.

p. 215 (left currency unions) Andrew K. Rose, 'Checking Out: Exits from Currency Unions', draft of Centre for Economic Policy Research (CEPR) Discussion Paper DP6254, published 15 December 2006.

p. 216 (by a quarter) Daniel McConnell, 'Our Economy Has "Fallen off a Cliff"', *Irish Independent*, 28 March 2010.

Acknowledgements

After hours of discussion, argument and more than a few laughs, I would like to thank the people who have helped me put this book together. The first of these is Eoin Cunningham, my right-hand man, who read everything, researched all classes of unusual stuff, ran up a few blind alleys and yet remained good-humoured throughout. Thanks as always, Eoin. Aoife O'Brien checked, dug and found hidden statistical gems with a wonderful sense of curiosity. I couldn't have a better pair of researchers.

Big thanks to Clare Ridge for her intimate knowledge of the Coombe maternity hospital and for her graphically hilarious notes on every month of pregnancy. And thanks to Nadine McDonagh Cunningham, mother and teacher, for parachuting me metaphorically into her classroom, and to Helen Cosgrove for her maternity insights.

For explaining the finer points of club GAA, I am indebted to Ger O'Callaghan and Joe Dean of Castlegregory.

On the economic front, I am very grateful to: Professor Kevin O'Rourke of All Souls College, Oxford, for the time he spent reading early drafts and for his judgement; Professor Morgan Kelly of UCD for long chats about the state of the place and the future of the euro; and Professor Karl Whelan, also of UCD, for setting me right on central banks, mortgage relief and the like. Thanks also to Peter Lunn of the ESRI for his knowledge of Irish demographics.

Thanks to my former colleague from years back, Paul McCulley, for reintroducing me to the wisdom of Hyman Minsky on a blisteringly hot afternoon in San Diego last May; to Martin Lousteau in Argentina for giving me the Latin perspective on the global crisis; and to Professor Jeffrey Sachs of Columbia for retracing the Asian crisis with me.

Huge thanks to Ross Maguire SC for his insights into the workings of the legal system and to Dearbhail McDonald of the *Irish Independent* for letting me tag along with her down at the Four Courts. One of the characters in the book could not have been created without the guidance and biblical knowledge of Pinchas Landau, Amos Rubin and Pastor Rob Jones, who leads the New Expressions congregation in Dublin. A special mention must go to the quants team at Paddy Power, in particular Simon Moore and Rob Reck, for trying to explain probability, Cheltenham, football statistics and the intricacies of the gambling world to me.

Thanks to my agent, Marianne Gunn O'Connor. This book would not have appeared without the diligence, creativity and skill of my editor at Penguin, Brendan Barrington, whose editorial craft, encouragement and determination were an inspiration to me throughout the last year. Thanks, Brendan. And thank you to Michael McLoughlin of Penguin for believing in this book and keeping me focused.

Finally, to my wonderful wife, Sian, who read every word and challenged every notion, and kept the house sane while I was holed up in the attic scribbling – thank you so much. A huge thanks and an even bigger hug to our children, Lucy and Cal, for putting up with a preoccupied and distracted dad for so long.

Dublin, September 2012

Index

Note: The index covers only the chapters of non-fiction.

AIB (Allied Irish Banks) 9, 46, 90
All-Ireland football 1–4
Allianz Arena 167
Allied Irish Banks (AIB) 9, 46, 90
Anglo Irish Bank 126
Argentina 83
Asian crisis (1997) 53, 54–66, 206
  and the IMF 54, 58, 62–4, 66
  and Russia 60–62
austerity 27–8, 80, 83, 128, 207
Austria 212, 216
Aviva Stadium 167

'balance-sheet recession' 27, 207
bank attitudes to debt 185
bank guarantee 126, 127
bank loans 8–10, 29, 30, 31, 35, 37, 41
  borrower types 36–7
  German 29, 38, 39
  loan-to-deposit ratios 183
  property lending and the Finnish
    banking crisis 81
  see also mortgages
Bank of England 85–6
Bank of Ireland 9
Bank of Japan 85–6
Bank of Scotland 8
Bank of Thailand 58–9
bank trading desks 60–61
bankruptcy 63, 81–2, 127, 182, 186, 187
Bayern München 167–8

Beers, David 25
Belgium 212
Bellamy, Craig 105
betting 12, 32
birth rate 6
Black Wednesday 65
Blanchard, Olivier 25
BNP 54, 60–61
bond markets 53, 76–9, 87, 89–92,
    166, 206, 212
  and the ECB 79–93, 127
  Greek bonds 82, 83
  Irish bonds 77–9, 85, 129
  Italian bonds 88
  oversubscription, in Irish bond
    auction 129
booms
  boom-time reporting 55
  credit booms/binges 4, 6, 30, 31–2,
    39, 112
  economic 25–6
  export 57
  and human nature 35
  inflationary 162
  property 30, 35, 57
  see also bubbles
borrower types 36–7
Brandt, Willy 111
bubbles 30, 32, 36, 91, 107, 114
  credit 162
  property 8, 57, 58, 187–8, 189, 190

Bundesbank 88, 160–61, 166
Bundesliga 167–8, 169–70
Burt, Jason 105

capitalism 82, 110
Carville, James 77
Castlegregory 3, 5
    GAA football club 1–4
Central Bank of Ireland 85, 128, 189
central banks
    and the Asian crisis 66
    in classical economics 29
    direct lending to government 86
    ECB *see* European Central Bank
    and inflation 160
    Irish central bank 85, 128, 189
    as lenders of last resort 84–5
    squabbles between European 34
Chelsea football club 167, 168
civil service 143
Clarke, Ken 65
Clinton, Bill 76–7
co-responsibility 184
Cold War 108
College of Europe, Bruges 161
competitiveness 8, 25, 56, 112, 113,
    148, 162
contagion, financial market 33–4,
    53–66
    and the Asian 1997 crisis 54–66
    Kindleberger on 33–4
    panics and 33–4, 54, 59–65
conventional wisdom 142–4, 146,
    165, 217
    of internal devaluation 147–50
crashes, financial *see* financial crashes
credit
    availability 29, 30, 35, 58 *see also*
        bank loans
    booms/binges 4, 6, 30, 31–2, 39, 112

bubble 162
creating liquidity in a credit crisis 91
crisis stages 35
crunch/withdrawal 35, 36, 61, 63
cycles 30, 32, 57
and debt-deflation 31, 191
demand 29, 30
in Germany 30
price of *see* interest rates
and tracker mortgages 7–11
Creditanstalt 33–4
Croke Park, Dublin 1, 2
current-account gaps, eurozone 147

Daily Telegraph 105
debt
    Asian 58 *see also* Asian crisis (1997)
    bank attitudes to 185
    build-up 35
    and classical economics 28–31
    and co-responsibility 184
    debt-deflation 31, 191
    debt-to-GDP ratio 38, 87, 150,
        185, 206
    debt-to-GNP ratio 38
    defaults on *see* default
    and Draghi's LTRO 89–93
    and economies 25–41
    eurozone crisis *see* euro-debt crisis
    eurozone current-account gaps 147
    to German banks 39
    Greek 79–80, 81–4
    Ireland's ability to pay its debt 38–9
    Irish household debt 185
    mortgage 6, 7–11, 37, 79,
        182–92, 209
    and the paradox of thrift 26–8, 31,
        40–41, 207
    and respectability of the Good
        Room mentality 125–30

socialization of private debt 40, 53
total Irish debt (2011) 38
and Troika bailouts *see* Troika (EU, ECB and IMF)
default 80, 82–4, 86–7, 215
and dealing with Ireland's mortgage-debt problem 186–8, 191
deflation 26, 66, 114–16, 162, 191, 207
'debt-deflation' 31
deleveraging 28, 37, 114
Department of Finance 25
deposit margins 61
depression, economic 6, 31, 34, 40, 41, 63, 115
Great Depression 31, 34–5, 36, 62–3, 187–8, 206
Deutschmark 161, 212
devaluation 66, 147, 161–2, 215
of the Finnish markka 81
internal 147–50
displacement 35
divorce 207
drachma 86, 213
Draghi, Mario 79, 86, 87–92, 93, 165, 166, 190, 191–2, 208, 209
Dyer, Kieron 105

Easter Rising 146
ECB *see* European Central Bank
economics 11–12
bubbles *see* bubbles
contagion *see* contagion, financial market
crashes *see* financial crashes
debt and classical economics 28–31
deflation *see* deflation
depression *see* depression, economic
and the euro crisis 38, 64
German thinking on 160–61, 165, 166
and the Gold Standard 112–16

Iceland v European orthodoxy 109–10
inflation *see* inflation
interest rates *see* interest rates
and Kindleberger 31–4
Minsky cycles 35–7, 58
panics *see* panics, financial
economy, German 29, 33, 169
economy, Icelandic 82, 104–11
economy, Irish
2012 contraction 79
and austerity 27–8, 207
birth rate as response to economic depression 6
and bondholder payments 127
booms 25–6
and conventional wisdom 142–4, 148
crash 35, 38–9, 125–30
and credit *see* credit
debt *see* debt
displacement event of joining the euro 35
and the ECB 127
economic recession *see* recession
and EU negotiations and relations 125–30, 190
and the eurozone 30, 37–40, 93, 207–17
forecasts 25
GDP *see* GDP (gross domestic product)
and generations 6–7
and Germany 130
Global Irish Economic Forum 76
and the Good Room mentality 125–30, 206
and Greece 126, 127
import prices 214
influence of collective mood on 25–6

economy, Irish – *cont.*
  Irish bonds 77–9
  leaving-the-euro scenario 213–16
  and the mortgage crisis 10–11,
    182–92
  and the paradox of thrift 26–8, 207
  sectoral financial balances 27
  sovereignty of 77, 182, 210
  'talking down' the economy 25
  Troika bailout 27, 39–40, 77,
    128, 210
  'turning the corner' 25–6
  velocity of money 183
education 5
  Leaving Cert 143
Elderfield, Matthew 128
emigration 4–6, 78
EU *see* European Union
euphoria 31, 35
euro (currency)
  genesis 111, 128
  Ireland's joining the euro 35, 111
  promise of the euro 80
  survival of the euro 144, 162–3,
    166–7
euro-debt crisis 34, 37–8, 53, 55, 76
  choices and scenarios 207–16
  and conventional wisdom 144,
    147–50
  and Germany 34, 37–8, 92, 149–50,
    162–7, 170, 211–13
  and Greece 79–80, 81–4, 86–7,
    211–12, 213
  as a long war 141–50
  and political sleepwalking 141–50
  and the wrong medicine of internal
    devaluation 146–50
European Central Bank (ECB) 34,
  39, 84
  and the bond market 79–93, 127

Draghi 79, 86, 87–92, 93, 165, 166,
  190, 191–2, 208, 209
  and Germany 85, 86, 88, 92–3
  and Greece 83, 84
  and holding together the eurozone
    165–6
  interest rate 8, 10
  and Ireland's mortgage-debt
    problem 189, 190–92
  LTRO 90–92
  and Weber 164–5
  see also Troika (EU, ECB and IMF)
European Fiscal Compact 27, 144,
  149–50, 206
European GDP 28
European Monetary Union 111
European unemployment 28, 161, 209
European Union (EU) 40, 205
  and Greece 82, 83
  Irish negotiations and relations with
    125–30, 190
  see also Troika (EU, ECB and IMF)
eurozone 30, 37–40, 66, 82
  borrowing between member states 147
  break-up option 211–16
  choices and scenarios 207–16
  closer union option 209–11
  crisis *see* euro-debt crisis
  current-account gaps 147
  and Draghi's LTRO 89–93
  genesis of the euro 111, 128
  'Irish Divorce' option 207–9
  and the Irish economy 30, 37–40, 93,
    207–17
  and the need for flexibility over
    rules 165–7
  trade imbalances 147
  Troika bailouts *see entries under*
    Troika (EU, ECB and IMF)
  unemployment 28, 161, 209

export
  boom, Asia 57
  growth 25

family pretence, and the Good Room
  122–5
Federal Reserve, US 84, 85–6, 114, 160
Finance, Department of 25
financial crashes 31–2, 33–5, 53–4
  Asian 1997 crisis 53, 54–66
  contagion of *see* contagion, financial
    market
  economic depression *see* depression,
    economic
  Icelandic 82, 104–11
  Irish crash 35, 38–9, 125–30
  and leadership 34
  panics and *see* panics, financial
  and Troika bailouts *see* Troika (EU,
    ECB and IMF)
financial globalization 60–62
Financial Regulator 7–8
Finland 81, 111–12, 212
First World War 145–6
  Marshall Plan 33
Fiscal Compact 27, 144, 149–50, 206
Fisher, Irving 31, 40, 41, 216
football
  Champions League final, Munich 167
  Chelsea 167, 168
  GAA 1–4
  German 167–8, 169–70
  Real Madrid 168
  West Ham 104–5
France 38, 111, 212
  franc fort policy 161
  and Germany 111, 113, 161,
    163–4, 212
  and the Gold Standard 113, 114
Friedman, Milton 41

GAA (Gaelic Athletic Association) 1–4
Gaeltacht football club 2
Galbraith, John Kenneth: *The Affluent
    Society* 142, 216–17
gambling 12, 32
GATT agreements 56
GDP (gross domestic product)
  debt-to-GDP ratio 38, 87, 150,
    185, 206
  European 28
  Thailand 56
Generation Skype 4–6
Germany 160–70
  and America 33
  bank loans 29, 38, 39
  and credit 30
  current-account surplus 147
  and the Deutschmark 161, 212
  and the ECB 85, 86, 88, 92–3, 209
  economic thinking 160–61, 165, 166
  economy 29, 33, 169
  and the euro crisis 34, 37–8, 92,
    149–50, 162–7, 170, 211–14
  exit from the Gold Standard 34
  financial culture 160–61
  and the Fiscal Compact 149–50
  football 167–8, 169–70
  and France 111, 113, 161, 163–4, 212
  and the genesis of the euro 111
  and the Gold Standard 113–15
  house prices 29
  hyper-inflation of the 1920s 85,
    93, 165
  interest rates 29
  and Ireland 130, 165
  Marshall Plan 33
  Nazism 85, 115, 160
  panic and contagion in 33–4
  post-war culture 160
  savings 92

Germany 160–70 – *cont.*
    and Spain 169
    unemployment 29, 168, 169
Global Irish Economic Forum 76
globalization, financial 60–62
Godley, Wynne 26–7
Gold Standard 34, 112–16
Goldman Sachs 89, 165
Good Room of the Irish
        home 122–5
    mortgage debt and getting out of
        the Good Room 190–92
    respectability and the Good Room
        mentality 125–30
Gorbachev, Mikhail 108, 110
Government of Ireland Act 145
Great Depression 31, 34–5, 36, 62–3,
        187–8, 206
Greece 34, 37, 38, 39, 55, 57, 79–80,
        81–4, 86–7, 206, 211
    drachma 86, 213
    and the genesis of the euro 111–12
    and the possible breaking up of the
        euro 86, 211–13
Greek bonds 82, 83
gross domestic product *see* GDP
Guardian 104
Guðmundsson, Björgólfur 104
Guðmundsson, Mrs 104

'hedge borrowers' 36, 37
Hemingway, Ernest: *The Sun Also
        Rises* 182
Heseltine, Michael 65
HOLC (Home Owners' Loan
        Corporation) 188
Hollister 142
Home Owners' Loan Corporation
        (HOLC) 188

Hong Kong 60–62, 65
    dollar 60
Hope's Children generation 7
horse racing betting 12, 32
Houghton, Ray 4
house prices 9, 30, 35, 78,
        142, 183, 189
    German 29
    and negative equity 10
Hungary 216

Iceland 55, 82, 104–11, 215
    and European orthodoxy 109–10
IMF (International Monetary Fund)
    and the Asian crisis 54, 58,
        62–4, 66
    and Greece 83
    and internal devaluation 148–9
    see also Troika (EU, ECB and IMF)
incomes
    balance between expenditure and
        income 27
    falling 7, 26, 31, 36
    rising 33
    and types of borrower 36–7
Indonesia 63
inflation 32, 85, 160, 162, 207, 214
    German hyper-inflation of the 1920s
        85, 165
    inflationary policies 66
Institute for New Economic
        Thinking 141
interest rates
    in the 1992/93 currency crisis 162
    Asian 59, 64
    and borrowing 35
    causing panic 59, 106
    in classical economics 29, 31
    ECB 8, 10

effect of high rates on the
economy 64
and the eurozone 30
German 29
and house prices 35
of Icelandic banks 106, 107
Iceland's rates to foreign lenders 105
and the liquidity trap 31
and mortgages 184–5, 186
internal devaluation 147–50
International Monetary Fund *see* IMF
Irish bonds 77–9, 85, 129
Irish currency 161
joining the euro 35, 111
leaving-the-euro scenario 213–16
Irish economy *see* economy, Irish
Irish home rule 145
Irish Parliamentary Party 145–6
Irish referendum (May 2012) 127
Irish Times 30, 78, 129
irrationality 11–12
Italian bonds 88
Italy 55, 57, 87, 88, 89, 90, 91, 92,
113–14, 125, 209, 211, 212
deficit 147

Kaupthing Bank 110
Kenny, Enda 76, 77–8, 127–8
Keynes, John Maynard 26, 28, 31,
41, 59, 207, 216
Killarney 1
Kiltimagh football club 3
Kindleberger, Charles 31–4, 41, 216
Koo, Richard 27, 207
Korea 58, 59, 60, 63
Krugman, Paul 33, 41, 59

labour market 25
Lagarde, Christine 148–9

Lahm, Philipp 167
Lamont, Norman 65
Latin America 85
Latvia 148–9
Leaving Cert 143
lending market, Irish 8–9
see also bank loans
leverage 57, 61
deleveraging 28, 37, 114
liquidity
and compliance 190
creation of 89–92
traps 31, 41, 64, 86, 183, 191
Ljungberg, Freddie 105
Long-Term Capital Management 62
Long-Term Refinancing Operation
(LTRO) 90–92
Luxembourg 212

Maastricht Treaty 128
McCreevy, Charlie 4, 28
McCulley, Paul 34
Magnússon, Eggert 104
Mahathir Mohamad 60
Major, John 65
Malaysia 58, 60, 63
margins, deposit 61
market, financial
contagion *see* contagion, financial
market
economics of *see* economics
market confidence 64
Marley, Bob 53
Marshall Plan 33
Merkel, Angela 92
Mill, John Stuart 30
Minsky, Hyman 31–2, 34–7, 41, 216
Minsky cycles 35–7, 58
Mitterrand, François 161

momentum investors 32
monarchy 124–5
Money Advice and Budgeting
    Service 10
money multiplier 56
Monti, Mario 165
Morgan, John Pierpont 26, 84
mortgages 6, 9, 10, 37, 78
    and bank attitudes 185
    and the ECB 189, 190–92
    and income 184
    and interest rates 184–5, 186
    Ireland's mortgage crisis 10–11,
        182–92, 209
    need for debt relief scheme 188–92
    tracker 7–11, 35, 79
    US 187–8
Müller, Thomas 167

National Lottery 11
Nazism 85, 115, 160
negative-feedback loops 63
negative equity 10
Netherlands 38, 111–12, 212
Newton, Isaac 33
Noonan, Michael 38, 128, 129

O'Callaghan, Ger 1–4
O'Donnell, Gene 2
O'Driscoll, Brian 4

Paddy Power 11
panics, financial 31, 33–5, 38
    and contagion 33–4, 54, 59–65
    in Germany 33–4
    Kindleberger on 33–4
    over housing prices 30
    from raising interest rates 59, 106
Papademos, Lucas 165
paradox of thrift 26–8, 31, 40–41, 207

Parker, Scott 105
Permanent TSB 9
Philippines 63
PIMCO 34
'Ponzi borrowers' 36, 37
Pope's Children generation 6–7
Portugal 39, 57, 90, 91, 212
    deficit 147
    and the genesis of the euro 111
professional classes, Irish 143
profit-taking 35
property market/industry 9
    booms 30, 35, 57
    bubbles 8, 57, 58, 187–8, 189, 190
    and conventional wisdom 142, 144
    general property prices 35, 169
    house prices *see* house prices
    property lending and the Finnish
        banking crisis 81
    'soft landing' idea about 142–3
    and tracker mortgages 7–11

Queen's Speech 124

rating agencies 57, 58
Ray, Rebecca 149
Reagan, Ronald 108, 110, 111
Real Madrid 168
recession 5, 12, 26, 28–31, 41, 207
    'balance-sheet recession' 27, 207
    debt, classical economics and 28–31
    thrift, austerity and 26–8, 206–7
Redmond, John 145–6
redundancies 148
Rehn, Ollie 80–81
'rent-seekers' 143
respectability 125–6, 142
Reykjavik 107–9, 110–11
Rockwell, George Lincoln 104
Roosevelt, Franklin D. 115, 187–8

Rugby World Cup, Auckland 4–5
ruling class, Irish 144
Russia 83, 104
   and the Asian crisis 60–62

Sachs, Jeffrey 54
sado-fiscalism 206–7
savings 26, 27, 29, 37, 214
   American solution to 1990s Savings
     and Loans bank crisis 126
   German 92
   ratio 40
Schopenhauer, Arthur 144
Schweinsteiger, Bastian 167
Sinn Féin 146
social ranking, and the Good Room
   122–5
social reward system 143–4
'soft landing' idea 142–3
Somprasong Land 58
Soros, George 60
Soviet Union 108
   collapse of 81, 111
Spain 38, 39, 57, 87, 88, 90, 92, 113–14,
   125, 147, 206, 209, 211, 212
   deficit 147
   and the genesis of the euro 111
   and Germany 169
   Spanish banks 55, 91, 211
'speculative borrowers' 36, 37
spending–savings ratio 40
Standard & Poor's 25
Stark, Jürgen 166
sterling 65, 115, 162
stockbrokers 78
Straumur 105

Thailand 55, 56, 57–9, 63
thrift, paradox of 26–8, 31, 40–41, 207
tracker mortgages 7–11, 35, 79

trade unions 147, 215
Treaty on Stability, Coordination and
   Governance in the Economic and
   Monetary Union (Fiscal
   Compact) 27, 144, 149–50, 206
Troika (EU, ECB and IMF) 27,
   28, 192
   European bailouts 39, 80, 127, 206
   Irish bailout 27, 39–40, 77, 128, 210

UBS 165
unemployment
   Asian 63
   in classical economics 28–9
   eurozone 28, 161, 210
   German 29, 168, 169
   Icelandic 108
   Irish 5–6, 10, 78, 127, 148, 161
   and wages 148
   youth 7
United Kingdom
   exchange rate with the euro 213
   and the Gold Standard 34, 113,
     114, 115
   sterling 65, 115, 162
United States of America
   Bankruptcy Code 187
   debt-deflation 31
   Federal Reserve 84, 85–6, 114, 160
   and Germany 33
   and the Gold Standard 113, 114,
     115–16
   mortgages 187–8
   New Deal 116
   Savings and Loans bank crisis of the
     early 1990s 126
   and the Soviet Union 108

velocity of money 183
Venizelos, Evangelos 80, 81

Index

wages
    effect of possible euro break-up on
      Irish wages 214
    and unemployment 148
    wage-slashing, internal devaluation
      147–50
Weber, Axel 164–5, 166

Weisbrot, Mark 149
West Ham Football
    Club 104–5
West Kerry league 1
World Bank 58

youth unemployment 7